100 GREAT DISHES MADE EASY

Philippa Davenport

Marshall Cavendish

Picture Credits
Brice Atwell   40
Rex Bamber   71
British Poultry Assoc.   82
Barry Bullough   23
Camera Press   113
John Cook   12
Alan Duns   20, 27, 35, 47, 59, 65, 101, 104, 114, 117,
   149, 153, 159, 178, 185, 203, 208
DELU/PAF International   134
Melvin Grey   8
Christine Hanscombe   24
Jerry Harpur   56
Anthony Kay   124, 126, 128
Paul Kemp   43, 171, 176, 204
Don Last   11
Michael Leale   160
David Levin   36, 80, 119, 123, 156
David Meldrum   38, 195
Key Nilsson   137
Roger Phillips   15, 16, 32, 48, 50, 52, 55, 60, 63, 66,
   72, 78, 85, 89, 93, 95, 97, 98, 102, 109, 131, 136, 146,
   166, 172, 180, 187, 192, 196, 198, 206
Iain Reid   155, 175
Paul Williams   188, 191
George Wright   2, 28, 44, 89, 90, 140, 173

Editor: Pepita Aris
Designer: Anita Ruddell

Published by Marshall Cavendish Books Ltd
58 Old Compton Street
London W1V 5PA

© Marshall Cavendish Ltd 1980, 1982

First printed 1980
Second printing 1982
Printed in Hong Kong
ISBN 0 85685 838 2

Contents

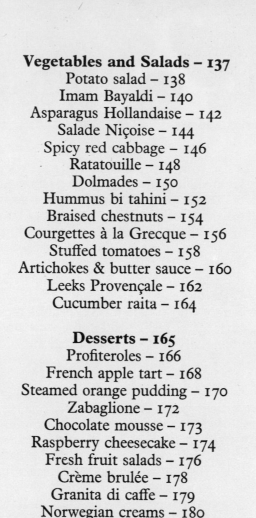

Author's introduction

This book contains recipes for some of the dishes I most enjoy cooking and eating – a selection of good things from many countries. The recipes are not intended to be a definitive list of the 100 greatest dishes in the world (I certainly would not dare to undertake such a contentious compilation!). Nor are they my personal 100 top favourite dishes – that list would have to include such things as juicily grilled calf's liver and creamy rice pudding; and foods like raw oysters with fresh lemon juice, radis au beurre, and lightly boiled eggs with bread-and-butter 'soldiers', which are perhaps too simple to justify inclusion in a recipe book. These recipes are simply a cross-section of some of my favourite dishes, and they have been deliberately chosen to illustrate different cooking techniques and to offer a variety of textures and flavours. Some of the dishes are light and fresh-tasting, others are luxuriously rich. Some are marvellously quick to prepare, others demand considerable time on the part of the cook. Some are very inexpensive, others are decidedly costly. All of them are, I think, delicious and worthy to be called great.

Such a selection may come as a surprise to those for whom the phrase 'great dishes' conjures up a feast of rich and ritzy recipes culled exclusively from the repertoire of haute cuisine, dishes that invariably require a plethora of ingredients (and mostly expensive ones) as well as hours of hard labour in the kitchen. But man cannot live by lobster Thermidor alone! More seriously, I do not believe that the phrase great dishes is a synonym for rich and elaborate dishes. Of course such dishes can be great, but so too can very simple dishes be great. For a great dish is, I believe, nothing more and nothing less than a dish which makes outstandingly good eating. And, if you accept this definition, I am sure you will agree that whether the dish is plain or elaborate is really rather irrelevant. What matters – and these are the hallmarks of all great dishes – is that the ingredients are the finest of their kind available, that they are beautifully cooked and appetizingly presented.

It may be obvious that a dish can never be better than the ingredients that go into it. But this is a truism worth thinking about in an age when the importance of careful shopping is often neglected and we succumb to the convenient lure of the supermarket. I am convinced that it pays dividends to seek out specialist shops. A really good butcher, fishmonger and greengrocer are the cook's greatest allies. Enlist their help and you will not only get better quality produce, but you can also pick up more basic information and practical tips than you will find in a whole

shelf full of recipe books. It goes without saying that it pays to be as choosy about quality when shopping for 'ordinary' ingredients, such as butter and cabbage, as when selecting expensive items like salmon or pheasant.

Cooking is sometimes described as Art with a capital A, and the subject is treated with awe and deference, as though mere mortals can not and should not aspire to producing great dishes. This is nonsense. The chef who *creates* a magnificent new dish may well be an artist in the true sense of the word. But the cook who seeks to *reproduce* that recipe in his or her home kitchen requires more of what might better be described as craftsmanship than Art. And this is something we can all aspire to and acquire, for it is fundamentally a matter of paying thoughtful and practical attention to detail – in such things as accurately measuring ingredients, selecting the right equipment for the job, impeccable timing, and perfect temperature control.

For example, if just a little fat is placed in a heavy-based pan, and it is allowed to become very hot indeed before a small quantity of perfectly dry cubes of meat are added, the meat surfaces will be seared and become beautifully crusted. This happens automatically, through no Art of the cook. On the other hand, if the fat is merely hottish, or if the meat is damp or too much of it is added to the pan at one time, the meat surfaces can only take colour quite slowly, and much of the flavoursome meat juices will inevitably leak out during the process. This is bad crafts-manship.

Given fine ingredients, it is I am sure (in at least nine cases out of ten) the observance or ignor-ance of such seemingly small points of detail as these which makes the difference between poor and fine cooking. To say 'sauté the meat' may be accurate, but it is inadequate if the cooking of great dishes is to be a pleasure we can all share in and enjoy. This is why I have avoided the cookery shorthand usually employed in recipe books, and have given instead fairly detailed descriptions of cooking techniques throughout this book. I think and hope that this will help to make the craft of cooking great dishes a pleasure that everyone can enjoy.

But however fine the ingredients, and however beautifully they are cooked, they must also be appetizingly presented in order to draw an eager family and friends to the dining table. The way food is presented plays a surprisingly large part in the pleasure of eating, and I think there is sometimes a dangerous tendency – particularly when entertaining – to gild the lily. Let discretion win, remembering that fancy garnishes tend to distract and to detract from, rather than to enhance, fine foods. Equally, never forget that no meal, however grand the occasion, should ever include more than one creamy rich dish – because a variety of textures is vital if each dish is to be fully appreciated in its own right and the menu is to add up to a delicious and well-balanced whole.

Dedication: for Michael

Author's note:
The number of servings given at the end of each recipe
should be treated as a guideline. Appetites vary
considerably and much depends on what other dishes
are served at the same meal. Some recipes are
particularly suitable for serving at dinner, where they
will be preceeded by a first course. Others are more
appropriate for a two course Sunday lunch, when
larger helpings of each course are more usual. Account
has been taken of this when writing the recipes.

Recipes have been tested both in metric and imperial
and are also given in American measures. Please follow
one set of instructions throughout a recipe.

SOUPS

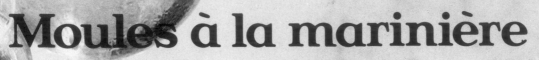

Moules à la marinière

Mussels are lovely to look at – brilliant orange flesh, blue-black shells – their flavour is excellent, and they are, thank goodness, the one shellfish cheap enough to eat frequently. This superb French soup can be served in small quantities as a first course, but I like to make a meal of it in the fisherman's fashion – tucking a napkin round my neck, tipping the mussels from shell to mouth with my fingers, then spooning up the delectable broth.

Metric/Imperial	American
3kg(3qt) fresh mussels	6lb mussels
1 large onion	1 large onion
1 small garlic clove	1 small clove garlic
a bunch of parsley	a bunch of parsley
1 bay leaf	1 bay leaf
1 sprig of lemon thyme	1 sprig of thyme
a few celery leaves	a few celery leaves
25g(1 oz) butter	2 tablespoons butter
200ml(7fl oz) dry white wine	1 cup dry white wine
150ml(¼pt) double cream	⅝ cup heavy cream
salt and freshly-ground black pepper	salt and freshly-ground black pepper

1. Like all shellfish, mussels must be as fresh as possible to be really good. Buy from a reputable fishmonger (fish dealer), checking that the mussels smell sweet and do not include more than one or two with broken shells or gaping mouths. As soon as you get them home, put the mussels into the sink and rinse them with cold water to wash away seaweed and any other loose debris. Put them into a large bucket or plastic bowl with plenty of cold, heavily-salted water and set aside in a cool place until ready to prepare them. Add a handful of oatmeal if you wish: the mussels will feed on it and this is said to plump and whiten the flesh.

2. Put the mussels back into the sink, letting the soaking water drain away. Wash out the bucket and refill it with cold water, unsalted this time. Fill the sink with cold water, again unsalted. Examine each mussel. Throw away any with broken shells, also any with open shells that refuse to close when sharply tapped with a scrubbing brush. Be ruthless about this. Clean all the good mussels, tugging away any little pieces of seaweed clamped between the shells (called beards) and scrubbing away seaweed, dirt and barnacles. Put the cleaned mussels into the bucket. When all the mussels have been dealt with, empty the bucket again, swirl the mussels in the sink under cold running water, then return them to the bucket with a final dose of fresh cold water.

3. Chop the onion and garlic very finely. Put them into a pan with the butter and cook over low heat for 5-10 minutes until slightly softened but not coloured. Crush a few parsley stalks, reserving the leaves, and tie them with string together with the bay leaf, celery leaves and thyme. Add the bunch of herbs to the pan, cover it with a lid and set aside. Snip up a good quantity of parsley leaves in a cup with the scissor tips. Cover with plastic film to prevent drying out and set aside.

4. When almost ready to serve, measure the wine into a pan large enough to hold all the mussels. Bring the wine to a rapid boil. Put the mussels into the pan, cover with a lid and cook for 4-5 minutes until the mussels are opened: the steam will force their shells open. Shake the pan quite vigorously several times during cooking to ensure that the steam circulates and reaches all the mussels. Then reduce heat to low and cook the mussels for 2 minutes more. Turn the contents of the pan into a strainer placed over a bowl to separate mussels and liquid. Then strain the liquid through a cheesecloth-lined strainer into the pan containing the onions. Using a cloth is essential in order to extract the tiny particles of mud and sand released when the mussel shells opened up during cooking. Let the onion and mussel-flavoured wine mixture simmer uncovered for 5 minutes to concentrate its flavour. Meanwhile boil the cream until reduced by half. Also transfer the mussels to a large, warmed soup tureen. Check the mussels as you transfer them, throwing away any that are closed (the rules are reversed at this stage). If you wish, you can also remove the empty half shells from the opened mussels. It is not worth doing this if the mussels are tiny – it would take so long that the mussels would be almost cold by the time you had finished.

5. Discard the bundle of herbs. Stir the chopped parsley, a good grind of pepper (and salt if needed) into the deliciously-flavoured broth. Swirl in the cream. As soon as it is hot and well-blended, pour the liquor over the mussels and serve. *Serves 3-6*

Iced Vichyssoise

Louis Diat, the French chef who spent many years delighting New Yorkers with his cooking at the Ritz-Carlton Hotel, created this popular iced soup and named it after the spa town near his birth place. It is one of my favourite soups and a good example of how humble ingredients, cleverly used, can be made into an elegant dish. Diat advocated using the white parts of leeks only, and he sweated the vegetables in butter before adding the liquid. I like to include the tender green parts as well: it seems wasteful not to and they add delicate colour to the soup. But I omit the sweating as I find the creams provide enough richness.

Metric/Imperial	American
900g(2lb) tender young leeks	2lb tender young leeks
350g(¾lb) potatoes	¾lb potatoes
700ml(1¼pt) light chicken stock	3 cups light chicken stock
10ml(2 teaspoons) fresh tarragon	2 teaspoons fresh tarragon
salt and freshly-ground white pepper	salt and white pepper
275ml(½pt) milk	1¼ cups milk
575ml(1pt) double cream	2½ cups heavy cream
150ml(¼pt) single cream	⅔ cup light cream
150ml(¼pt) sour cream	⅔ cup sour cream
a large bunch of chives	a large bunch of chives

1. Trim the leeks and slice them thickly – the net weight should be 450g (1lb). Wash them thoroughly in several changes of cold water. Peel and dice the potatoes.

2. Bring the stock to boiling, add the vegetables, tarragon and some salt and pepper. Bring back to boiling, cover and simmer gently for about 10 minutes, until the vegetables are just tender – no longer or the fresh flavours will be spoiled. Turn the contents of the pan into a blender and reduce to a very smooth, very thick purée.

3. Scald the milk. Stir it into the purée and blend again to ensure a really smooth textured soup. Pour the soup into a large bowl. Scald the double (heavy) and single (light) creams together and blend them into the soup, using a balloon whisk. Adjust seasoning and set aside until cold.

4. Finely chop most of the chives and stir them into the soup. Cover and refrigerate until icy cold.

5. Just before serving, chop the remaining chives and beat the sour cream until smooth and creamy. Swirl the sour cream into the soup to create a marbled effect and sprinkle the chives over the surface. *Serves 10*

French onion soup

S ubstantial, inexpensive and very warming, this French peasant soup is sensibly bolstered with a dash of brandy to keep cold weather at bay. It makes an excellent choice for a simple lunch in winter; and an omelette or soufflé makes an admirable light main course to follow the soup.

Metric/Imperial	American
1kg(2¼lb) onions	*2¼lb onions*
7ml(1 slightly heaped teaspoon) caster sugar	*1 heaped teaspoon superfine sugar*
30ml(2 tablespoons) oil	*2 tablespoons oil*
75g(3oz) butter	*6 tablespoons butter*
60ml(4 tablespoons) brandy	*4 tablespoons brandy*
12 slices French bread	*12 slices French bread*
75-90g(3-3½oz) Gruyère cheese	*3-4oz Gruyère cheese*
salt and freshly-ground black pepper	*salt and freshly-ground black pepper*

For the beef stock:	**For the beef stock:**
2-3kg(5lb) shin of beef bones with meat, chopped	*5lb beef shin, chopped in pieces*
2 pig's trotters	*2 pig's feet*
3 large carrots, thickly sliced	*3 large carrots, thickly sliced*
2 Spanish onions, each studded with 2 cloves	*2 yellow onions, studded with 2 cloves each*
1 bay leaf	*1 bay leaf*
a bunch of crushed parsley stalks	*a bunch of parsley stalks, crushed*
2-3 sprigs of thyme, preferably lemon thyme	*2-3 sprigs thyme (if possible lemon thyme)*
5ml(1 teaspoon) black peppercorns	*1 teaspoon black peppercorns*
5ml(1 teaspoon) coriander seeds	*1 teaspoon coriander seeds*
5ml(1 teaspoon) salt	*1 teaspoon salt*

1. Make a good beef stock as described on *page 17, steps 2-4*. Remove the grease from the top when it is cold, then reduce by fast boiling to 1.7L (3pt) or about 7½ cups and adjust seasoning to taste.

2. Start making the soup about 1½ hours before the meal. Choose fairly small onions if possible. Slice them thinly. Warm the butter and oil over medium-low heat in a heavy-bottomed pan. Add the onions to the pan. Stir them until well coated all over with fat: the onions will separate into rings as you do this. Then cook for 15-20 minutes until golden brown. Shake or stir the pan occasionally during this time to prevent sticking. Stir in the sugar, add a seasoning of salt and pepper and pour on the stock. Bring the liquid quickly to boiling point. Then reduce heat to a gentle simmer, cover the pan with a lid and leave to cook gently for 30 minutes.

3. Meanwhile pre-heat the oven to 200°C (400°F) gas mark 6. Put the thin slices of French bread in a single layer directly onto an oven shelf (rack) and bake for 10 minutes, turning the slices over halfway through this time. Select 6 ovenproof soup bowls or plates, individual casserole dishes or an ovenproof soup tureen with a large surface area. Grate the cheese.

4. When the soup has been cooking for 30 minutes, is richly coloured and the beef stock is well flavoured with the onions, add the brandy to the saucepan and continue simmering – uncovered this time – for 5 minutes more. Divide the soup between the individual soup bowls, or pour it into the tureen. Heap the grated cheese onto the toasted slices of French bread and float them on the surface of the soup.

5. Put the soup into the oven for 10 minutes so that the bread begins to soak up the delicious onion and beef flavoured liquid and the cheese melts. Serve immediately.

Serves 6

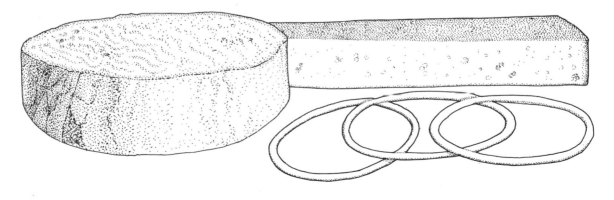

Jellied bortsch

eetroots (beets) are always the main ingredient of this famous Russian soup. The choice of other ingredients is considerable. Bortsch (or borsch) served piping hot and thick with shredded cabbage, potatoes and other vegetables makes a hearty dish, comforting during a bitter Russian winter. But I like bortsch best as a jellied consommé. Its sparkling colour and sweet and sour taste are refreshing on a summer's evening. When luxuriously garnished with caviar, sour cream and fresh dill, it makes a lovely dinner party dish.

Metric/Imperial	American
350-450g(¾-1lb) raw beetroot	¾-1lb fresh beets
2 large carrots	2 large carrots
2 large dill-pickled cucumbers	2 large dill pickles
1 Spanish onion	1 yellow onion
5cm(2in) cinnamon stick	2in stick of cinnamon
2 cloves	2 cloves
1 bay leaf	1 bay leaf
a few parsley stalks	a few parsley stalks
a few sprigs of dill	a few sprigs of fresh dill
2 lemons	2 lemons
a little caster sugar	a little fine sugar
salt and freshly-ground black pepper	salt and freshly-ground black pepper

For the garnish:	**For the garnish:**
275ml(½pt) soured cream	1¼ cups sour cream
a small pot of caviar or Danish lumpfish roe	a small jar of caviar or Danish lumpfish roe
15ml(1 tablespoon) fresh chopped dill	1 tablespoon fresh chopped dill
wedges of lemon	lemon wedges

For the beef stock:	**For the beef stock:**
1.8kg(4lb) beef shin bones with meat, chopped	4lb beef shin, chopped in pieces
2 pig's trotters	2 pig's feet
2 carrots, thickly sliced	2 carrots, thickly sliced
2 Spanish onions, each studded with 2 cloves	2 onions, studded with 2 cloves each
1 bay leaf	1 bay leaf
a bunch of crushed parsley stalks	a bunch of crushed parsley stalks
2 sprigs of thyme	2 sprigs of fresh thyme
5ml(1 teaspoon) black peppercorns	1 teaspoon black peppercorns
5ml(1 teaspoon) salt	1 teaspoon salt

1. Make the beef stock as described on *page 17, steps 2-4*. Chill it, remove the solidified fat, then reduce by fast boiling to 1.7L (3pt) or 7½ cups.

2. Starting a day ahead of eating, peel and grate the beetroot (beets) and carrots coarsely. Finely chop the dill-pickled cucumbers and onion. Put all four vegetables into a very large saucepan or stockpot. Add cinnamon, cloves, bay leaf, parsley stalks and dill, and pour on the stock. Bring to boiling point, cover with a lid and simmer gently for 45 minutes.

3. Remove the pan from the heat and set aside, still covered, for 30 minutes to allow the vegetables to continue giving up their flavours to the liquid. Strain the soup through a sieve lined with a double thickness of cheesecloth to extract the vegetables and all the spicy sediment. Season the clear red liquid with a pinch of sugar, a generous grind of pepper, some salt and about 45ml (3 tablespoons) freshly-squeezed lemon juice. Allow the soup to become cold, then taste it and adjust seasoning if necessary. Cover the soup and refrigerate it for several hours until icy cold and set to a light jelly.

4. Just before serving, chop the jellied soup with a knife and turn it into a chilled soup tureen. Turn the sour cream into a small bowl and garnish with chopped dill. Serve the caviar in a separate bowl, and the lemon wedges in a third bowl – pass these at the table so that everyone can help themselves.

Serves 6-8

Augolemono soup

Egg and lemon – avgolemono in Greek – is a favourite combination in Greek cookery. These ingredients gently whisked into a well-flavoured stock make a lovely light and creamy soup that is quick to make and marvellously versatile. Use chicken broth or veal stock in place of fish stock if you prefer. Serve the soup either hot or cold. The lemony flavour is more pronounced when cold, and is deliciously refreshing on a warm day.

Metric/Imperial	American
For the fish stock:	**For the fish stock:**
1kg(2¼lb) fish heads, trimmings and bones	*2¼lb fish heads, trimmings and bones*
1 large leek	*1 large leek*
1 medium-sized carrot	*1 medium-sized carrot*
2 celery stalks	*2 celery stalks*
the zest of a lemon	*the rind of 1 lemon*
a bouquet garni of fresh herbs	*a bouquet garni of fresh herbs*
6 black peppercorns	*6 black peppercorns*
6 coriander seeds	*6 coriander seeds*
salt	*salt*
1 small glass dry white wine	*1 small glass dry white wine*
To finish the soup:	**To finish the soup:**
50g(2oz) long grain rice	*¼ cup long grain rice*
4 medium-sized eggs	*4 medium-sized eggs*
1-2 lemons	*1-2 lemons*

1. Fish stock, unlike meat stock, is extremely quick to make, and it does not need degreasing after cooking. Moreover, most fish sellers will freely give you the heads and trimmings from fish which have been filleted for other customers. Turbot and sole give stock best flavour and texture, so ask for these if possible. If the fishmonger does not have a sufficient weight of bones and trimmings, make up the difference in weight by buying some cheap fish to bolster the flavour of the stock. It does not matter what sort of fish you buy so long as it is white fish; oily fish such as mackerel and herring are unsuitable for making stock.

2. To make fish stock, first wash the fish heads, bones and trimmings under cold running water to rinse off dirt and specks. If you do not do this, the stock will be unnecessarily cloudy. Put the fish trimmings into a large saucepan and pour on the wine. Wash trim and chop the vegetables and add them to the pan. It is important to chop the vegetables very finely: the more cut surfaces there are the quicker the vegetables will yield up their flavour – and the vegetables *must* flavour the liquid quickly when making fish stock because cooking time is 20 minutes only. Pour on enough water to cover the ingredients generously and bring to the boil.

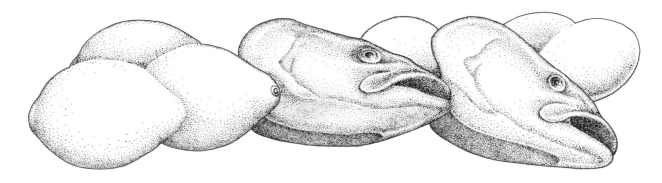

3. Using a perforated spoon, skim away scum as it forms. Then add the remaining stock ingredients to the pan. (They are not added earlier because they float to the top and might be skimmed away with the scum, instead of giving flavour to the soup.) When the liquid comes back to a fast simmer, reduce heat as low as possible, three-quarters cover the pan with a lid, and leave it to simmer gently for precisely 20 minutes. The reason for this careful timing is that fish bones yield all their goodness very quickly and if cooking is prolonged the bones will give off a rather unpleasant bitter and gluey flavour.

4. Strain the liquid through a cheesecloth-lined sieve, pressing the solid ingredients to extract all the juices. Then return the liquid to the washed-out saucepan and boil, uncovered, until the stock is reduced to a well-flavoured 1.25L (2¼pt) or 5½ cups. Check seasoning and adjust to taste. If the stock is not for immediate use, cool it as quickly as possible, then cover and refrigerate it or freeze it. Use within 24 hours if refrigerating or within 28 days if freezing.

5. To make the soup, reheat the stock. Sprinkle on the rice, stir once and bring to a fast simmer. Then reduce heat, cover the pan with a lid and let the soup simmer very gently for 15 minutes or until the rice is quite tender. Beat the eggs lightly in a small bowl. Add 45ml (3 tablespoons) lemon juice, a little salt and some freshly-ground black pepper. Beat again. Gradually beat in a few spoonfuls of the hot broth. Then slowly pour the contents of the bowl into the soup pan, stirring all the while. Continue stirring – I use a balloon whisk for this – until the soup is thoroughly heated through and slightly thickened: about 5 minutes. Do not allow it to boil or the eggs will scramble and the soup will curdle. Then cover the pan and let it stand for 5 minutes by the side of the stove. Add extra lemon juice to taste and serve. *Serves 6*

†Boiled rice, left over from a previous meal, could be used to make avgolemono soup. Allow 100g (¼lb) cooked weight of rice or 1½ cups. Let it simmer gently in the hot stock for 2 or 3 minutes until well heated through before adding the egg and lemon mixture.

Lobster bisque

E ven the name of this soup, bisque d'homard, rolls off the tongue with a velvety richness. It is indeed probably the most luxurious of all soups. Yet, as lobster dishes go, it is not all that extravagant; there is no other way that I know of for six people to share one lobster between them so handsomely.

Metric/Imperial	American
1 hen lobster weighing 700g(1½lb)	*1½lb female lobster*
75ml (5 tablespoons) brandy	*5 tablespoons brandy*
210ml(7½fl oz) dry white wine	*1 cup dry white wine*
1.25L(2½pt) fish stock	*6 cups fish stock*
1 onion	*1 onion*
2 small carrots	*2 small carrots*
2 celery stalks	*2 celery stalks*
2 or 3 sprigs of tarragon	*2-3 sprigs fresh tarragon*
a few parsley stalks	*a few parsley stalks*
a sprig of thyme	*a sprig of thyme*
40g(1½oz) long grain rice	*⅛-¼ cup long grain rice*
75g(3oz) unsalted butter	*6 tablespoons unsalted butter*
5ml(1 teaspoon) tomato purée	*1 teaspoon tomato purée or paste*
30ml(2 tablespoons) oil	*2 tablespoons oil*
175ml(6fl oz) double cream	*¾ cup heavy cream*
salt and freshly-ground black pepper	*salt and freshly-ground black pepper*

1. This soup can be prepared ahead and reheated. Choose a fine fresh lobster and kill it as described on *page 125, steps 2-3*, or request your fishmonger to do this. Completely sever the lobster body from the tail. Split the body lengthways. Remove and discard the stomach sac, the black intestinal vein and the feathery gills which lie close to the leg joints. Scrape out and reserve in a mortar the creamy green-black liver and the roe (coral). Reserve the lobster juices separately. Remove legs and claws. Crack the claws with a hammer or with nutcrackers. Cut the tail into slices, cutting across the tail joints in the shell.

2. Scrub the celery and carrots. Dice them and the peeled onion. Cook them in a large heavy-bottomed pan for 10 minutes in 30ml (2 table-spoons) butter until slightly softened. Remove the vegetables with a slotted spoon and add the oil to the pan. When it is very hot add the pieces of lobster complete with shell. Sauté, turning as necessary, for about 5 minutes until the shell colour magically changes from blue-black to scarlet. Add the brandy to the pan, set it alight and turn the lobster in it.

3. When the flames die down, pour in the wine. Let it bubble up and cook until reduced by half – about 5 minutes. Then pour on the lobster juices and enough fish stock to cover the lobster. Tie the fresh herbs together to make a bouquet and add to the pan; bring quickly back to boiling point. Reduce heat, cover the pan and simmer gently for 5 minutes more to tenderize the lobster meat completely.

4. Remove the pan from the heat. Lift out the lobster pieces with a slotted spoon. As soon as cool enough to handle, detach a few large pieces of shell from the lobster and return the shell to the pan. Add the softened vegetables, rice and remaining fish stock. Bring to boiling point, stirring continuously. Reduce heat, cover the pan and cook very gently for 20-25 minutes until rice and vegetables are quite tender.

5. Meanwhile prepare the lobster butter with which to enrich the soup just before serving: but first set aside a small spoonful of the roe (or coral) to use for garnish. Pound the rest of the roe and liver with a pestle, then beat in the remaining butter to make a smooth paste. Reserve in a cool place. Remove the cooling lobster meat from the pieces of shell and chop it into small pieces.

6. When the rice and vegetables are tender, remove the herbs from the pan. Reduce the soup to a purée together with the diced lobster meat. Blend the ingredients together at least twice to make a really smooth-textured soup.

7. When you are ready to serve the soup, warm a tureen and soup plates, then reheat the soup gently. Stir in the cream as you warm the soup and heat it to barely simmering – but on no account let it boil. Check seasonings and adjust to taste. Turn off the heat but leave the pan where it is. Using a balloon or sauce whisk, beat the roe butter into the soup, a knob at a time. When the butter is absorbed and the roe (coral) and liver are cooked – this takes only a second or so – pour the soup into the warmed tureen. Swirl the spoonful of reserved coral into the soup, letting the specks float to the surface as they colour. Sprinkle with fresh chopped tarragon and serve immediately. *Serves 6*

Gazpacho

This best known of all Spanish soups makes a fine dish for a summer's day. It is almost a meal in itself. I am very fond of it and inclined to make it quite often – particularly when I am counting the calories. As it consists almost entirely of salad vegetables, it is a dish of which one can partake lavishly without fear of putting on weight! The garnishes are traditionally very plentiful: each diner helps him or herself, stirring them into the thin puréed soup until it is so stiff that a spoon can almost stand up in the bowl. Gazpacho is sometimes served with ice cubes floating in it. I think this is the least sensible way to chill this soup: the melting ice cubes dilute the flavour and spoil the texture and appearance of the soup. It is far better to chill both soup and soup tureen thoroughly well in advance of serving.

Metric/Imperial	American
575g(1¼lb) large, firm tomatoes	1¼lb firm, ripe tomatoes
1 slice of brown bread	1 slice wholewheat bread
3 spring onions	3 scallions
2 garlic cloves	2 cloves garlic
half a large red pepper	half a medium-sized red bell pepper
quarter of a large cucumber	half a cucumber
15ml(1 tablespoon) tarragon or red wine vinegar	1 tablespoon tarragon or red wine vinegar
5ml(1 teaspoon) fresh chopped basil	1 teaspoon fresh chopped basil
45ml(3 tablespoons) olive oil	3 tablespoons olive oil
575ml(1 pt) canned tomato juice	2½ cups tomato juice
salt	salt
freshly-ground black pepper	freshly-ground black pepper
For the garnishes:	**For the garnishes:**
half a large red pepper	½ medium-sized red bell pepper
1 green pepper	1 green pepper
1 Spanish onion	1 mild or Bermuda onion
three-quarters of a large cucumber	1 large cucumber
50-75g(2-3oz) black olives	½ cup black olives
3 hard-boiled eggs	3 hard-cooked eggs
a few slices of slightly stale bread	a few slices of day-old bread

1. Start making the soup well ahead; 24 hours chilling is not too much. Skin, seed and roughly chop the tomato flesh. Trim and chop the spring onions. Crush the garlic with some salt. Seed the red pepper and chop roughly. Peel the cucumber, remove seeds and dice the flesh.

2. Break the slice of bread into pieces, put it into the goblet of an electric blender and reduce to crumbs. Add the garlic, spring onions (scallions), chopped basil, olive oil and vinegar and reduce to a smooth purée. (Add a little of the tomato juice to prevent the blades sticking if necessary.) Gradually add the soup vegetables and the tomato juice to the blender and reduce them all to a perfectly smooth purée. The most satisfactory results are usually achieved by

blending the ingredients in batches, and I think everything should be blended at least twice. The purée should be absolutely smooth – nothing is more unattractive looking than gazpacho that has a curdled lumpy appearance.

3. When the soup is beautifully smooth, thin it to the consistency of cream by stirring in some icy cold water. Season to taste with salt, pepper and a little more vinegar if you wish. Blend the soup once more, then cover and refrigerate it for several hours.

4. Prepare the garnishes far enough in advance to be able to chill them too, putting each type in an individual container. Peel, seed and finely chop the cucumber. Wipe the peppers clean, remove stalks, pith (membranes) and seeds and cut the flesh into small dice. Chop the hard-boiled eggs. Pit and chop the olives. Skin and quarter the Spanish onion; cut each quarter into paper thin slices and push into rings. Rub the bread with garlic, cut into croûtons, fry in olive oil, blot well on paper towels and chill.

5. Serve the soup in a well-chilled tureen. Pass the garnishes separately, each type in a separate bowl with a small spoon so that everyone can help themselves. *Serves 4-6*

Petite marmite

There is something very satisfying about making your own translucent beef consommé enriched with chicken. Petite marmite is sometimes heavily laced with meat and vegetables to make a substantial dish which can be served as a nutritious meal in its own right. I think it is more in keeping with the fine qualities of the consommé to garnish it delicately. With just a few curls of leek, julienne strips of other vegetables and a few slivers of steak and chicken breast floating in it, petite marmite makes a superb and elegant start to a dinner party.

Metric/Imperial	American
For the consommé:	**For the consommé:**
1kg(2¼lb) beef marrow bones	*2½lb beef knuckle bones with marrow*
1kg(2¼lb) shin of beef bones with meat attached	*2lb beef shin with meat*
450g(1lb) minced beef	*1lb ground beef*
2 pig's trotters	*2 pig's hocks*
1.35kg(3lb) roasting chicken	*4lb roasting chicken*
3 large carrots, thickly sliced	*3 large carrots, thickly sliced*
2 Spanish onions	*2 Bermuda or sweet onions*
6 celery stalks, cut into chunks	*6 stalks celery, thickly sliced*
crushed parsley stalks	*crushed parsley stalks*
a few sprigs of thyme (preferably lemon thyme)	*a few sprigs of thyme (if possible lemon thyme)*
2 bay leaves	*2 bay leaves*
4 cloves	*4 cloves*
5ml(1 teaspoon) black peppercorns	*1 teaspoon black peppercorns*
5ml(1 teaspoon) coriander seeds	*1 teaspoon coriander seeds*
5ml(1 teaspoon) salt	*1 teaspoon salt*
extra salt and freshly-ground black pepper	*extra salt and freshly ground black pepper*
the whites and shells of 2 large eggs	*the whites and shells of 2 large eggs*
For the garnish:	**For the garnish:**
the breast of the chicken used for the consommé	*the breast of the chicken used for the consommé*
3×1.2cm(½in) thich slices of crustless white bread	*3×½in thick slices of crustless white bread*
225g(½lb) rump steak	*½lb rump steak*
115g(¼lb) carrots, trimmed weight	*¼lb cleaned carrots*
115g(¼lb) white part of leek, trimmed weight	*¼lb cleaned leeks*
115g(¼lb) celery, trimmed weight	*¼lb cleaned celery*
freshly-grated Parmesan or Gruyère cheese	*freshly-grated Parmesan or Gruyère cheese*

1. When buying the trotters (hocks) and bones, ask the butcher to saw them into 5cm (2in) lengths: this will enable them to fit your pan easily and also speed the yielding up of their flavour. Start making the soup up to 2 days ahead. Preheat the oven to 230°C (450°F) gas mark 8. Make a cut down the length of the chicken's breast. Peel back the skin, carefully work the breast meat free from the bone, easing it gradually with a small knife. Wrap the raw breast meat and refrigerate it to use for the garnish.

2. To brown the ingredients to give colour to the beef stock, chop the rest of the chicken roughly and put it into a large roasting pan, together with the giblets. Add the beef bones and pig's trotters (hocks). Halve the onions without peeling them (the skin will add colour to the consommé), and stud each half with a clove. Tuck the onions, celery and carrot pieces among the bones and roast for 45 minutes. The fat will begin to run from the meats and all the ingredients will brown nicely at the edges. This method of browning the ingredients is far simpler than the traditional method of cooking on top of the stove.

3. When the oven is cool make the croûtons. Dice the bread and dry out the cubes in the oven until they are pale gold.

4. Transfer the meats and vegetables to a stockpot (if necessary, divide them between two large heavy-bottomed saucepans). Add the minced (ground) beef. Pour water into the roasting pan, swirl it around and add to the stockpot. This makes sure all the flavourful pan juices go into the stock – and also simplifies washing up! Pour more water into the stockpot to cover all the ingredients generously and bring to boiling point. Skim off any surface scum as it forms. Add the bouquet of herbs, peppercorns, coriander seeds and salt. Three-quarters cover the stockpot with a lid and let it simmer for 5 hours, by the end of which time you will have a good brown beef stock enriched with chicken. Strain off the liquid, discarding all the meat, bones, vegetables and herbs. (If this seems wasteful, try eating a little of the meat: you will find it dreary and tasteless, for all its sweetness and flavour have passed to the liquid.) Set the bowl of stock in a cold place and leave overnight so that the fat solidifies on top.

5. Next day, scrape the fat from the stock with a spoon, removing every scrap of grease. Turn the stock into a saucepan and boil, uncovered, until the liquid is reduced to 2L (3½pt) or 2 US qt stock. Taste and season generously with salt, freshly-ground black pepper – and a little lemon juice if you like. Stand the bowl of stock in a pan filled with ice cubes or ice-cold water to cool it quickly.

6. Meanwhile prepare the meat garnishes. Trim away all fat and sinew from the steak and chicken breasts, then cut the meat into thin slivers about 6mm × 3cm (¼ × 1¼in). Blanch both meats. Bring a pan of water to boiling point, add the strips of beef, bring quickly back to boiling, then reduce heat and simmer for 2 minutes. Remove the beef with a slotted spoon. Then blanch the chicken in the same way, but cook it for 1 minute only. Rinse both meats under cold running water to cool them and to wash away scum, and pat dry with paper towels. Reserve. Thoroughly wash the vegetables and cut them into julienne strips – delicate slivers no larger than the pieces of meat. Reserve each type in a separate covered container, to prevent drying out or mixing of the flavours.

7. When the stock is tepid it should be clarified – that is it should have all specks and impurities removed to transform it into a translucent clear consommé. Put the stock into a pan over low heat. Add the raw egg whites and crushed shells. Whisk continuously with a rotary beater until the stock is approaching simmering point and a foam begins to form on the surface of the stock. Stop whisking, let the stock reach boiling point and then simmer for 5 minutes. Turn off the heat and leave the pan where it is for 10 minutes before gently sliding the contents of the pan into a sieve lined with a double thickness of damp cheesecloth placed over a pan. The egg whites, shell and all the specks will be trapped in the cloth, leaving a golden, clear liquid in the pan below.

8. Just before serving, reheat the consommé gently. When it reaches simmering point, add the julienne strips of vegetable and simmer for 3 minutes. Add the chicken and steak to the pan and simmer for 3 minutes more. Transfer the delicious and handsomely-garnished soup to a hot soup tureen and serve immediately, passing the toasted croûtons and a bowl of grated cheese separately. *Serves 8*

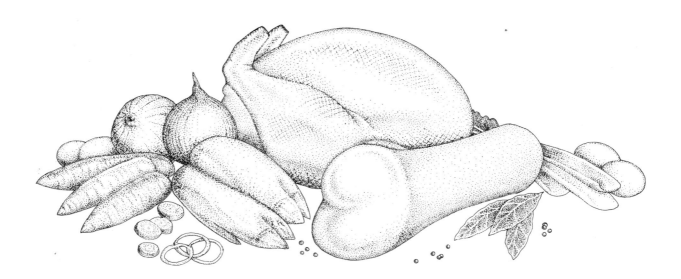

CHEESE
EGGS
&
PASTA

Soufflé en surprise

Whenever I am keen to impress but my finances are low and my time is short, I choose this recipe. Magnificently risen, crusted with gold and creamy in the centre, a perfect soufflé never fails to thrill. Few other dishes, irrespective of cost, are accorded such acclaim. I love the sense of drama, the moment of hush with which a soufflé is greeted at the table. Cheese is the classic choice of flavouring, and this version prolongs the drama – because, by some seemingly magical process, boiled eggs with soft yolks are found nestling in the soufflé mixture when it is cut open for serving.

Metric/Imperial	American
7 large (no. 2) eggs	7 large eggs
40g(1½oz) Parmesan cheese	⅓ cup Parmesan cheese, grated
50g(2oz) Gruyère cheese	⅓ cup Gruyère cheese, grated
30ml(2 tablespoons) butter	2 tablespoons butter
30ml(2 tablespoons) plain flour	2 tablespoons all-purpose flour
200ml(7fl oz) milk	⅞ cup milk
5ml(1 teaspoon) fresh chopped chives	1 teaspoon fresh chopped chives
AND 5ml(1 teaspoon) fresh chopped parsley	AND 1 teaspoon fresh chopped parsley
OR 30ml(2 tablespoons) Danish lumpfish 'caviar'	OR 2 tablespoons red caviar
15ml(1 tablespoon) toasted breadcrumbs	1 tablespoon toasted breadcrumbs
salt, black pepper and cayenne	salt, black pepper and cayenne pepper

1. Preheat the oven to 200°C (400°F) gas mark 6, placing a baking sheet on a shelf just above the centre. Boil 4 of the eggs for precisely 4½ minutes. As soon as cooked, cool them under cold running water to arrest cooking. Transfer the eggs, still in their shells, to a bowl of cold water and set aside. Use a fluted white china soufflé dish about 15cm (6in) in diameter and 7.5cm (3in) high. Butter the base and sides of the dish, coat all the surfaces with toasted breadcrumbs. Tap gently and tip out the excess.

2. Heat the milk in a large saucepan. When hot, pour into a jug. Add the butter to the pan and melt it over low heat. Away from the heat stir in the flour. When smooth, return the pan to low heat and cook for 1 minute, stirring continuously. Away from the heat, add the hot milk, stirring to blend it in smoothly. Return the pan to the heat and cook, still stirring, until the sauce is perfectly smooth, thick and bubbling hot.

3. Remove the pan from the heat. Grate the cheeses and stir into the pan. The heat of the sauce is enough to melt the cheeses, yet their addition will cool the sauce sufficiently to enable you to add the egg yolks immediately. Separate the three raw eggs, placing the whites in a large mixing bowl and adding the yolks, one at a time, to the saucepan. Beat each yolk as you add it, until broken up and absorbed by the sauce. By the time all three yolks are incorporated, the sauce will be beautifully glossy. Season with salt, freshly-ground black pepper and cayenne – bearing in mind that the addition of egg whites will slightly mute the flavour of the mixture.

4. Drain the soft-boiled eggs and shell them carefully. Check that the oven has reached the required temperature, then whisk the egg whites until they are stiff but not dry. Use a manual rotary beater, not an electric one, to get really good volume, and move it all around the bowl so that all the egg whites are whisked to the same degree. Using a plastic spatula, scrape all the whisked egg whites out of the bowl into the saucepan. Fold the egg whites into the mixture gently but thoroughly. Use figure-of-eight movements, cutting down through the mixture and lifting it over and up in a rather exaggerated way to keep everything really light and airy – the bubbles in the egg white must not be deflated. Turn half the soufflé mixture into the prepared dish. Make four hollows in it. Sprinkle them with the fresh herbs or 'caviar' and lay the cold, soft-boiled eggs in them. Spoon the rest of the soufflé mixture over the eggs and top with a sprinkling of cayenne pepper.

5. Place the soufflé dish on the hot baking sheet. Close the oven door gently, and reduce temperature to 190°C (375°F) gas mark 5. After 30 minutes the soufflé will be perfectly cooked – magnificently-risen above the rim of the dish with a golden crusted top – while the centre is still delectably creamy. Amazingly, the yolks of the boiled eggs will still be soft. Serve instantly! *Serves 4*

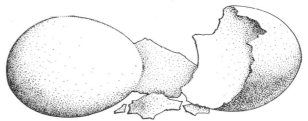

Spaghetti alla carbonara

Spaghetti alla carbonara is a delicately flavoured dish and a very great treat if made with exquisite raw Parma ham (prosciutto crudo). I find it one of the most useful dishes in the world. If bacon is used, the ingredients are all items most people keep in permanent stock, which makes it an ideal dish to turn to on occasions when unexpected guests arrive near mealtime. Since spaghetti alla carbonara takes less than 20 minutes from start to serving, it is an admirable choice when you are in a hurry. Moreover it can just as easily be made in half or even quarter quantities – very appealing when you want a quick, simple nourishing meal for one.

Metric/Imperial	American
400-450g(14-16oz) spaghetti	up to 1lb spaghetti
175g(6oz) prosciutto crudo or streaky bacon	6oz raw Italian ham or bacon slices
4 medium-sized eggs	4 medium-sized eggs
125ml(4fl oz) double cream	½ cup heavy cream
60ml(4 tablespoons) grated Parmesan cheese	4 tablespoons freshly grated Parmesan
salt	salt
freshly-ground black pepper	freshly-ground black pepper
extra grated Parmesan cheese to serve	extra Parmesan cheese to serve

1. Bring a large pan of water to the boil – pasta should always be cooked in plenty of water, allow about 1L (2pt) or 5 cups for every 100g (¼lb) of pasta. Add a generous quantity of salt and a spoonful or so of oil; this will prevent the strands of pasta from sticking together during cooking. Add the spaghetti, pushing it down into the pan: it will bend as it softens, curling to fit the pan. Stir once and cook, uncovered, at a fast simmer until tender – this is unlikely to take longer than 10 minutes. Do not overcook or the pasta will become mushy and lose its flavour.

2. While the spaghetti is cooking, prepare the bacon or prosciutto. Cut the meat into matchstick strips and remove bacon rinds. Put the strips into a large flameproof casserole and place it over low heat. Cook very gently until the fat begins to melt. Then increase the heat a little and cook for a few minutes

longer, stirring occasionally to prevent burning.

3. Break the eggs into a bowl. Season generously with salt and pepper. Stir in 60ml (4 tablespoons) freshly-grated Parmesan cheese and the cream. Grate more cheese to serve with the dish.

4. When the spaghetti is cooked, turn it into a colander and drain very thoroughly. Remove the pot from the heat. Add the drained spaghetti and pour the egg mixture over it. Turn the pasta gently but thoroughly with wooden spoons until every strand is coated with the meat-flecked sauce – the heat of the pasta will cause the egg and cream mixture to scramble lightly.

5. Serve immediately, accompanied by a large bowl of freshly-grated Parmesan cheese so that everyone can help themselves. *Serves 4 as a main course*

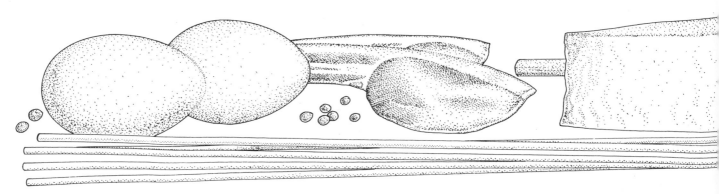

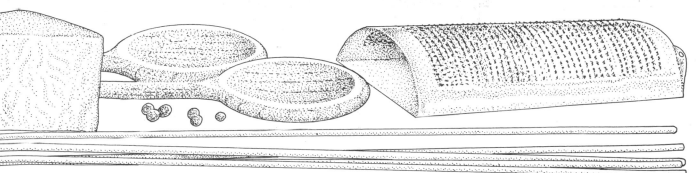

Trenette al pesto

B asil is perhaps my favourite herb – warm, spicy and pungent. It is worth growing just to make this distinctive and exquisite Genoese sauce. I love pesto so much that I serve it not only with pasta, as described here, but also with new potatoes boiled in their skins and with grilled steaks and chops (top each piece of meat with a nugget of pesto just before serving).

Metric/Imperial	American
500g(18oz) trenette, or linguine or tagliatelle	*1⅛lb trenette, linguine or tagliarini*
a little olive oil	*a little olive oil*
For the pesto:	*For the pesto:*
75g(3oz) fresh basil leaves without stalks	*3 tablespoons fresh basil leaves*
40g(1½oz) pinenuts, or walnuts	*1½oz Indian nuts or walnuts*
3-4 garlic cloves	*3-4 cloves garlic*
90ml(6 tablespoons) olive oil	*6 tablespoons olive oil*
60g(2¼oz) freshly-grated Parmesan cheese	*¼ cup freshly-grated Parmesan or Romano cheese*
salt and freshly-ground black pepper	*salt and freshly-ground black pepper*

1. Pinenuts are usually available from Italian and Greek shops, good delicatessens and some health food shops. They give authentic flavour to pesto but walnuts make a good substitute. Start making the sauce about three-quarters of an hour before eating. Chop the nuts and garlic into pieces. Put them into a mortar. Roughly cut up the basil leaves (snip them in a cup with scissors) to reduce their bulk. Add them to the mortar, and pound the three ingredients with a pestle until reduced to a thick, smooth paste. It takes 10-15 minutes to reduce them to this consistency. Pounding these sweet-smelling ingredients is, for me, an essential part of the pleasure of pesto. The scent is heady, the pounding rhythm is soothing, and one feels like an ancient apothecary brewing magic potions! In an electric blender reduce all the ingredients, except the Parmesan, to a purée.

2. When the paste is quite smooth, stir in half the oil – just a little at a time, making sure each spoonful is properly absorbed by the paste before adding the next. Stir in the cheese, then blend in the remaining olive oil and season with a little salt and pepper.

3. Pesto is not cooked but it should be left to stand for 30 minutes between making and using so that flavours blend and develop to the full.

4. Trenette are the narrowest of all ribbon noodles – only about 2mm (1/10in) wide – and are tradi-

tional with pesto, but any type of thin noodle or spahetti can be used. Cook them in plenty of salted boiling water with a small spoonful of oil (as described on *page 22, step 1*). Drain well, toss in a little olive oil so that each strand glistens, and serve topped with spoonfuls of the sauce. The sauce can be diluted with a few spoonfuls of the pasta cooking water if wished – this encourages the sauce to coat the pasta evenly. Serve with an accompanying bowl of freshly-grated Parmesan cheese. *Serves 6-8*

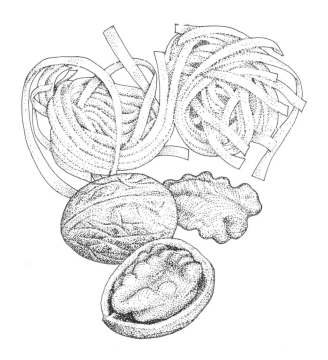

Quiche Lorraine

T his classic savoury custard baked in rich shortcrust pastry must be one of the best known of all French recipes – and one that is often wrongly made. The filling of a true quiche Lorraine is exquisitely delicate, containing no cheese or onions.

Metric/Imperial	American
For the rich shortcrust pastry:	**For the rich pastry base:**
110g(¼lb) plain flour	*1 cup all-purpose flour*
55g(2oz) butter	*4 tablespoons butter*
1 medium-sized egg	*1 medium-sized egg*
a good pinch of salt	*a generous pinch of salt*
For the filling:	**For the filling:**
150g(5oz) smoked streaky bacon	*7-8 strips smoked bacon*
225ml(8fl oz) double cream	*1 cup heavy cream*
2 medium-sized (no. 3) eggs	*2 medium-sized eggs*
freshly-grated nutmeg	*freshly-grated nutmeg*
salt and freshly-ground black pepper	*salt and freshly-ground black pepper*

1. To make the rich shortcrust pastry, sift the flour and salt into a mixing bowl. Add the butter and cut it into the flour with a palette knife (spatula) until each piece of fat is no larger than a pea. Then, quickly, lightly and thoroughly, rub in the fat with your fingertips. Shake the bowl occasionally so that any large lumps come to the surface. After 6 minutes or so, the ingredients will look like bread-crumbs or ground almonds. Make a hollow in the middle of the ingredients. Break the egg yolk into it (reserve the white in a cup). Add 5ml (1 teaspoon) cold water. Stir it into the yolk with the knife, then gradually draw in the 'crumbs' or dry ingredients. Press the mixture together with the blade of the knife to make a dough. If it seems very dry, add another spoonful of cold water. Scoop the mixture into a ball with your hands and turn it out onto a work surface. Knead it lightly until smooth – that is draw the outer edges of the mixture to the centre with your fingertips, repeatedly. Put the ball of dough back into the bowl, cover it with plastic film and refrigerate for at least 45 minutes.

2. Starting about 1¼ hours before you plan to eat, preheat the oven to 200°C (400°F) gas mark 6 with a baking tray on the shelf just above centre. Roll out the chilled pastry and use it to line a 20cm (8in) fluted flan tin (quiche pan) with removable base. Prick the pastry base all over with a fork, and refrigerate for another 10 minutes. Meanwhile cut out a circle of greaseproof or waxed paper about 28cm (11in) in diameter. Lay the paper in the chilled pastry case and weigh it down with dried beans or rice, enough to come two-thirds of the way up the pastry sides. This, like the pricking, is to ensure the pastry base remains flat and to prevent the pastry walls from caving in. Place the pastry case on the hot baking sheet and bake for 10 minutes.

3. Remove from the oven then carefully remove the paper and beans. Brush the pastry base and sides with the reserved egg white, and cook the pastry for 8 minutes more. The pastry will not be completely cooked at the end of this time, but enough to prevent the filling soaking into it; the egg white will set a seal on the pastry – an added precaution against the filling making it soggy.

4. While the pastry is in the oven, prepare the filling. Remove any bacon rind and cut the bacon into matchstick strips. Put it into a frying-pan over very low heat and cook just long enough to colour and let the fat run. Remove the bacon with a slotted spoon and eat a piece to check on its salt content. Break the eggs into a bowl, pour on the cream, add a good seasoning of black pepper, some nutmeg and as much salt as you consider necessary. Beat the custard mixture lightly and thoroughly.

5. When the pastry is ready, reduce oven temperature to 375°F (190°C) gas mark 5. Scatter the bacon over the pastry base, pour on the custard and return the quiche to the oven. Cook for about 25 minutes until puffed up and pale gold and just firm. Let the cooked quiche cool for a few minutes before serving: it is at its most delectable when warm. *Serves 4-6*

27

Tomato mozzarella salad

I always think that this should be the national dish of Italy: the colours are those of the Italian flag and the ingredients are three of the most delectable to be found in Italian cookery – mild Mozzarella cheese from Naples, sweet well-flavoured tomatoes and spicy fresh basil. The flavour is sunny, making this salad a perfect appetizer for a summer lunch party.

Metric/Imperial	American
8 firm, ripe tomatoes	*4 ripe large tomatoes*
1 Mozzarella cheese	*½lb Mozzarella cheese*
fresh basil	*fresh basil*
about 90ml(6 tablespoons) olive oil	*6 tablespoons olive oil*
coarse salt	*coarse salt*

1. Dip the tomatoes in boiling water to loosen their skins. Refresh under cold running water, dry and slip off the skins. Slice the tomatoes thickly and arrange the slices around the edge of a dish, over-lapping them slightly.

2. Cut the cheese into slices. (It must be the genuine Mozzarella made with buffalo milk which comes from southern Italy; the flavour and texture of Danish and other imitations are simply not good enough for a very simple dish of this sort, where each ingredient has a vital role to play.) Put the cheese in the centre of the dish.

3. Sprinkle salt and freshly-chopped basil over both the tomatoes and cheese – about 7ml (a heaped teaspoon) of coarse salt and a generous 90ml (6 tablespoons) of coarsely-chopped basil. Then drizzle the olive oil over the tomatoes only. Leave for 2 or 3 minutes before serving so that the salt begins to dissolve slightly and both salt and basil impregnate the oil with their flavours. *Serves 4*

Pizza Napolitana

Pizza is one of those foods which put me instantly into a holiday mood. Large round pizzas washed down with plenty of robust red wine, and followed by cheese and a salad, make a splendid informal meal for hungry people; while oblong pizzas cut into fingers make a savoury snack which is popular with all age groups at any time of day or night. My recipe uses an enriched pizza dough: this is so that the pizza really can be enjoyed at any time. A plain pizza dough made only with flour, salt and water is more traditional, but it must be eaten within minutes of cooking to be good. When kept warm for latecomers or second helpings a plain dough quickly changes from being delicious to unappetizingly tough.

Metric/Imperial	American
For the pizza dough:	**For the pizza dough:**
225g(½lb) strong plain flour	*½lb all-purpose flour*
7g(¼oz) dried yeast	*¼oz package active dry yeast*
a pinch of caster sugar	*a pinch of superfine sugar*
5ml(1 teaspoon) salt	*1 teaspoon salt*
30ml(2 tablespoons) olive oil	*2 tablespoons olive oil*
1 medium-sized egg	*1 medium-sized egg*
For the topping:	**For the topping:**
1 large onion	*1 large onion*
900g(2lb) tomatoes	*2lb tomatoes*
1 celery stalk	*1 celery stalk*
25ml(1½ tablespoons) olive oil	*1½ tablespoons olive oil*
5ml(1 teaspoon) caster sugar	*1 teaspoon superfine sugar*
5ml(1 teaspoon) lemon juice	*1 teaspoon lemon juice*
1-2 garlic cloves	*1-2 garlic cloves*
15ml(1 tablespoon) tomato purée	*1 tablespoon tomato purée*
10ml(2 teaspoons) oregano	*2 teaspoons oregano*
salt and freshly-ground black pepper	*salt and freshly-ground black pepper*
50g(1¾oz) can anchovy fillets	*2oz can anchovy fillets*
24 small black olives	*2doz small black olives*
1 Mozzarella cheese (optional)	*½lb Mozzarella cheese (optional)*

1. Put 15ml (1 tablespoon) of boiling water into a cup and add 30ml (2 tablespoons) cold water. Stir in a pinch of sugar and, as soon as this has dissolved, sprinkle on the yeast. Cover and set aside for 10-15 minutes until the yeast is reactivated and the mixture well frothed up. Meanwhile warm a large mixing bowl by filling it with boiling water. Lightly oil a sheet of plastic film large enough to cover the top of the bowl. Measure the flour and assemble the other dough ingredients.

2. Empty the water out of the mixing bowl. Dry it thoroughly. Sift the flour and salt into the bowl and make a well in the centre. Measure the oil into the well. Add the egg and mix it lightly into the oil with a fork. Immediately pour on the frothy yeast mixture. Mix it with the egg and oil, then draw the flour into the liquid with the fork. Continue mixing the ingredients until the dough begins to bind together, leaving the sides of the bowl to form one mass. (Add an extra spoonful or so of warm water to the dough if necessary – precisely how much is needed depends on the brand of flour used.)

3. Press the dough into a ball with your hands, and turn it out onto a work surface. Flour your hands lightly and knead the dough until it is smooth, plump and elastic. How you knead does not really matter. The most popular method involves pushing part of the dough away from you, folding the dough back on itself, giving it a quarter turn, then repeating these movements over and over again. The aim is simply to push and stretch the dough so that the gluten in the flour is strengthened, which will make

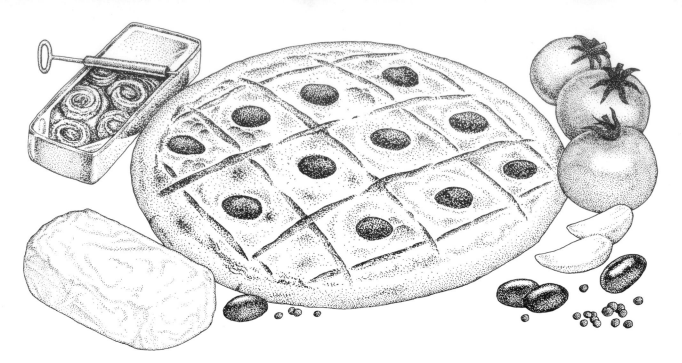

the dough rise. Put the kneaded dough back into the mixing bowl. Cover the bowl with the oiled film and set aside until the dough has doubled in bulk, has become spongy and light and is slightly sticky when touched. How long it will take to rise depends on the surrounding temperature – about 1½-2 hours in a warm place such as an airing cupboard (*do not* put it over a radiator: this would heat and toughen the bottom of the dough instead of surrounding the dough with even warmth). It will take about twice as long at room temperature 18-21 °C (65-70 °F), or about 8 hours in an unheated room or a traditional larder. Choose whichever is most convenient to your time schedule.

4. To make the topping, first make the tomato sauce. This, like the dough, can be prepared well in advance. Chop the onions, celery and garlic very finely. Skin and chop the tomatoes roughly. Heat the oil in a large, wide-based pan: this will speed up evaporation of the tomato liquid. Cook the onion, celery and garlic very gently for 5-7 minutes until slightly softened. Add the tomatoes, lemon juice, sugar and half the oregano to the pan. Stirring continuously, bring the mixture quickly to boiling point. Then reduce heat slightly and cook, uncovered, for approximately 50 minutes – until the sauce is reduced to about 275ml (½pt), 1¼ cups or less, is very well-flavoured and very thick. Stir the pan occasionally during this time, particularly towards the end, to prevent sticking and burning. Then stir in the tomato purée to give the sauce a rich colour and season it to taste with salt and pepper. Add a little extra sugar and/or lemon juice to taste.

5. When the dough has doubled in bulk, looks puffy and soft, turn it out onto a work surface. Punch it a few times with a clenched fist to flatten

it and get rid of any air pockets. Knead it again, just for a minute or two, then shape it. Shape it to fit two 20cm (8in) pizza pans or plates or flan tins with removable bases, or to fill one baking tray measuring approximately 23 × 30cm (9 × 12in). Whichever shape you choose, first brush the metal surface with a little olive oil. Put the ball of dough onto the oiled surface, flatten it with the palm of your hand, then gradually push it with your knuckles to fill the pan. Raise the edges of the dough slightly to make a rim to contain the filling during baking. Spoon the warm tomato sauce directly onto the dough, spreading it evenly with a palette knife or spatula. Top with the anchovy fillets – either snipping them into little pieces with kitchen scissors, or splitting each fillet in half then arranging the strips to make a lattice pattern. Sprinkle on the olives and the remaining oregano, then drizzle on the oil from the anchovy can.

6. Preheat the oven to 220 °C (425 °F) gas mark 7. Set the pizza(s) to one side while the oven heats up. During the 15-20 minutes it takes for the oven to reach the correct temperature, the dough will be able to recover from handling and will start to rise again. Bake the pizza(s) in the hot oven for 15 minutes. To include Mozzarella cheese on top, cut the cheese into thin slices while the pizza(s) start baking. When the 15 minutes are up reduce oven temperature to 190 °C (375 °F) gas mark 5. Now lay the slices of cheese on top of the pizza(s) and continue baking them for 10-15 minutes more, by the end of which time the dough will be perfectly cooked, the topping piping hot and aromatically scented and the cheese just melted. (If the cheese had been added at the beginning of baking, it would be stringy and tough by the time the dough is ready.)

Serves 4-8

Omelette aux fines herbes

We live in an age when quick food is in constant demand. Snack bars and 'take-aways' abound, usually offering foods which show clear signs of quality having been sacrificed for the sake of speed. Nothing is quicker or less trouble to cook than a classic French omelette, and nothing could be more delicious than an omelette made with the finest ingredients and cooked to creamy perfection.

Metric/Imperial
3 large fresh eggs
unsalted butter
fresh chives, tarragon and parsley or chervil
salt and freshly-ground black pepper

American
3 large fresh eggs
unsalted butter
fresh chives, tarragon and parsley or chervil
salt and freshly-ground black pepper

1. One of the most important things about making a really good omelette is to have top quality ingredients – really fresh eggs and best unsalted butter (salted butter burns too easily).

2. The second important point is to keep the filling simple (fancy ingredients such as lobster in a rich sauce are inappropriate) and quantities modest. A French omelette should never be stuffed or the delicate egg flavour will be overpowered; a discreet tablespoonful or two is plenty. A few sliced and sautéed fresh mushrooms, matchstick strips of fried bacon, or tiny croûtons of slightly stale (day-old) bread which have been fried in butter until golden, are all good. But perhaps best of all is an omelette lightly sprinkled with green herbs that have been picked and chopped only minutes before making the omelette. As soon as a herb is cut its aromatic oils are released: capture them at their finest by snipping herbs directly onto the eggs, preferably while raw or alternatively as they cook in the pan.

3. It is not necessary to reserve one pan exclusively for omelette-making, but it is important to use one that has a flat, heavy bottom and a shiny smooth interior with curved sides so that the omelette can slide freely about in it and be turned out easily. The pan must also be the right size – if too large the omelette will be thin and leathery, if too small the omelette will be stodgy, solid and thick. I think it is best, and looks prettiest, to give each person his or her own individual omelette. Serve the omelettes on warmed, not hot, plates – they will continue to cook even after you have turned them out of the pan – and eat the moment served.

4. Set an 18cm (7 in) omelette pan over low heat to warm up slowly. Meanwhile crack the eggs into a bowl. Add a little salt and a grinding of pepper. Snip some of each of the fresh herbs into the bowl – you will only need about 20-25ml (a heaped tablespoonful) in all. Use a fork to break up the egg yolks and stir them lightly into the other ingredients. Do not beat the egg vigorously and definitely do not use a whisk.

5. Add a good knob of butter to the pan and increase the heat. As soon as the butter is melted swirl the pan to just coat the entire base and the sides of the pan with fat. Pour in the eggs and almost immediately tip the pan away from you. Use the fork to draw the cooked egg upwards towards you; the raw egg will run down across the pan to take its place. Set the pan flat on the heat again – just for a moment or so until the whole base of the omelette is set but the surface is still deliciously soft and creamy, or *baveuse* as the French call it. (Chopped herbs can be added at this stage rather than mixing them into the raw eggs if you wish.) Using a palette knife, or small spatula, fold the half of the omelette nearest you over the other half, then slide the omelette out onto a warmed plate. Top with a flake of butter and serve immediately. *Serves 1*

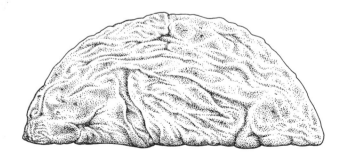

Potted Stilton

Stilton is said to be the king of English cheeses, and a whole Stilton is part of the traditional festive fare in many households at Christmas. I include this recipe because it is such a practical way to use up the remnants of a whole cheese which are invariably left over at the end of the Christmas holidays – too good to throw away yet too ragged to look handsome on the cheeseboard. The method can be used for other blue cheeses – not the same but still good. Serve potted Stilton with oatmeal biscuits (graham crackers) and plenty of celery, standing the celery in a pitcher of iced water to keep it cold and very crisp.

Metric/Imperial
350g(¾lb) Stilton cheese
75g(3oz) unsalted butter, at room temperature
20-25ml(4-5 teaspoons) brandy
a good pinch of celery salt
walnut halves
***OR** clarified butter (page 62, step 3)*

American
¾lb blue cheese, Stilton, Roquefort or Danish
6 tablespoons butter, at room temperature
4-5 teaspoons brandy
a generous pinch of celery salt
walnut halves
***OR** clarified butter (page 62, step 3)*

1. Remove the rind from the cheese and also any very hard or dark patches. Break the cheese into pieces, then mash with a fork until reduced to crumbs, moistening the cheese with brandy as necessary.

2. In a separate bowl, beat the butter until very soft and creamy. Add it to the cheese, a little at a time, mashing and beating the two ingredients together until well blended and the mixture is a smooth, thick paste. Season with celery salt.

3. Pack the mixture firmly into a pot and seal the top with clarified butter, then cover and refrigerate (stored this way it will keep for 15 days). Alternatively, if the cheese is to be eaten within 24 hours, shape the mixture into a disc using spoons dipped in brandy. Cover the entire surface of the top and sides with halved walnuts, pressing them gently into the cheese. Cover with an inverted bowl and store in the refrigerator. Whichever method you use, allow the cheese to 'breathe' at room temperature for 45 minutes before serving. *Serves 4*

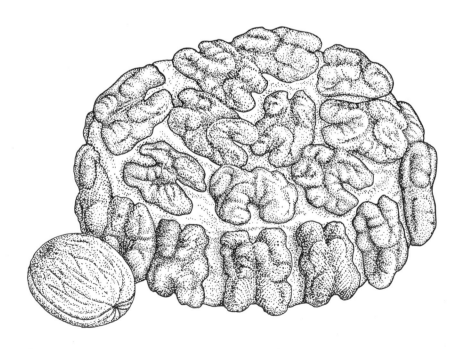

Oeufs en cocottes

This is my favourite egg dish – simple, elegant and very soothing. Success depends on high quality ingredients and impeccable timing. Err on the cautious side rather than risk overcooking the eggs, remembering that they will continue to cook slightly after they come out of the oven because of the heat of the dishes. Serve the dishes in prettily-folded napkins and accompany the eggs by melba toast.

Delicious variations can be made by the inclusion of extra ingredients. A few sliced and sautéed fresh mushrooms, or matchstick strips of cooked ham, or snippets of anchovy fillet can be placed on the base of each dish. The timing will not be altered. Or you can delicately flavour the cream by stirring into it a pinch of grated Parmesan cheese or a few chopped fresh herbs.

Metric/Imperial	American
4 large fresh eggs	*4 large fresh eggs*
7g(¼oz) unsalted butter	*½ tablespoon unsalted butter*
salt	*salt*
freshly-ground black pepper	*freshly-ground black pepper*
60ml(4 tablespoons) double cream	*4 tablespoons thick cream*

1. Preheat the oven to 180°C (350°F) gas mark 4, and bring a kettle of water to the boil. Use the butter to grease the base and sides of four ramekins, cocotte or individual soufflé dishes. Ridged white china dishes are traditional; heatproof earthenware is equally suitable but does not absorb and retain heat quite so efficiently.

2. Break an egg into each dish and season the white, but not the yolk, with salt and a good grinding of pepper. Stand the egg dishes in a baking or roasting pan, and pour enough boiling water into the pan to come halfway up the sides of the dishes. Cover the pan with a sheet of kitchen foil and place it on the centre shelf of the oven.

3. After 5 minutes, when the egg whites have begun to set, remove the pan from the oven. Dribble a spoonful of cream over the white of each egg, taking care to avoid the yolks. Cover the pan again with its foil lid and return to the oven to complete cooking. This will take about 10 minutes – exact timing depending on the idiosyncrasy of the

oven and on the heat-retaining quality of the dishes used.

4. Remove the pan from the oven as soon as the egg whites are set, the cream hot and the yolks still slightly runny. Dry the dishes and serve immediately, preferably accompanied with toast or melba toast. *Serves 4*

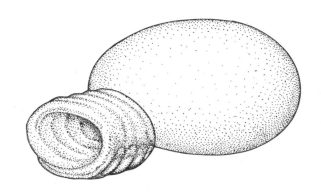

36

MEAT

Beef Wellington

Arthur Wellesley, 1st Duke of Wellington, must be the best known and loved of all English generals, and it seems appropriate that his London residence – Apsley House on the corner of Piccadilly and Hyde Park Corner – is still affectionately referred to as 'no. 1 London'. Variously nicknamed 'the grand duke' and 'the iron duke', Wellington waged long and bitter battles against Napoleon – and this richly-embellished variation of roast beef was probably created for a banquet to celebrate one of Wellington's victories over the armies of Napoleon. Beef Wellington is certainly a superb, albeit costly, dish – just right for celebrating a special occasion.

Metric/Imperial	American
900g(2lb) fillet of beef	2lb fillet of beef
10ml(2 teaspoons) brandy	2 teaspoons brandy
75g(3oz) paté de foie gras	3oz paté de foie gras
175g(6oz) small cap mushrooms, finely chopped	¼–½lb small mushrooms, finely chopped
1 medium-sized onion, finely chopped	1 medium-sized onion, finely diced
1 small garlic clove, crushed	1 small clove garlic, crushed
25g(1 oz) clarified butter (page 91, step 4)	2 tablespoons clarified butter (page 91, step 4)
salt and freshly-ground black pepper	salt and freshly-ground black pepper
puff pastry made with 100g(¼lb) flour	puff pastry made with 1 cup flour
OR 200-225g(7-8oz) packet of puff pastry	OR 1 package refrigerated dinner roll dough
1 small egg, beaten	1 small egg beaten,

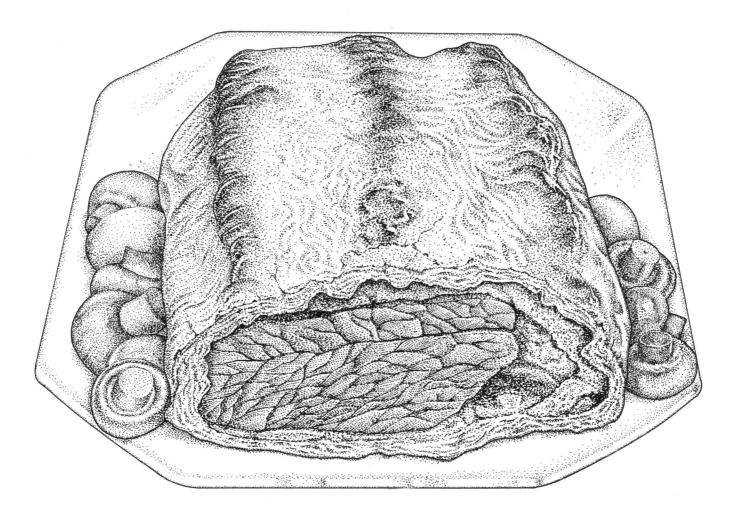

1. If you are using frozen puff pastry, remove it from the freezer about 3½ hours before you plan to eat. Allow it to defrost for 2 hours at room temperature.

2. Trim all fat and membrane from the beef, brush it with brandy, rub it with pepper and tie into a neat bolster shape. Heat a frying-pan over high heat. Add the butter. When foaming hot, brown and seal the beef all over. Then lower the heat and fry the beef more gently for 10-12 minutes, turning the meat to cook it evenly. Remove from the pan and cool. Sauté the mushrooms for 3-4 minutes, then remove with a slotted spoon. Then soften the onions and garlic in the fat remaining in the pan. Drain off fat, mix the vegetables, season generously and leave to cool completely.

3. About 1¼-1½ hours before serving, roll the pastry to a rectangle slightly wider than the beef and more than twice its length. Lay half the cold vegetables near one end of the pastry, in an oblong about the size of the meat.

4. Remove the string from the cold meat and lay it on top of the vegetables. Beat the pâté until soft, spread it over the beef and lay the rest of the vegetables on top. Brush the pastry borders with beaten egg. Fold the pastry over the meat to encase it completely, pinch the seams securely to seal and trim away the excess pastry. Use the pastry trimmings to make decorations, sticking them on the top with beaten egg. Carefully lift the parcel of beef onto a baking sheet, with the help of a fish slice (pancake turner). Chill it for 30 minutes so that the pastry recovers from handling. Meanwhile, preheat the oven to 220°C (425°F) gas mark 7.

5. Brush the pastry all over with beaten egg. Cook the beef for 20 minutes in the oven, then reduce oven temperature to 180°C (350°F) gas mark 4 and bake for a further 12-15 minutes. *Serves 6*

English roast beef

Roast beef is synonymous with the best of British cooking, and few meats are more delicious than high quality well hung beef, simply but beautifully roasted. Horseradish sauce makes an admirable and traditional accompaniment, as does Yorkshire pudding. This crisp, light savoury batter pudding used to be served with gravy, before the meat, to take the edge off appetites before the main dish was served.

Metric/Imperial	American
1.35kg(3lb) boned and rolled sirloin of beef	*3lb round of beef or rib roast, rolled and boned*
40g(1½oz) beef dripping or unsalted butter	*3 tablespoons beef dripping or unsalted butter*
half a garlic clove (optional)	*half a clove garlic (optional)*
120ml(scant 4fl oz) red wine	*½ cup red wine*
175ml(6fl oz) good beef stock	*¾ cup good beef stock*

For the horseradish sauce:	**For the horseradish sauce:**
45ml(3 tablespoons) freshly grated horseradish	*3 tablespoons freshly grated horseradish*
7.5ml(1½ teaspoons) fresh mustard	*1½ teaspoons French mustard*
210ml(7½fl oz) sour cream	*scant 1 cup sour cream*

For the Yorkshire pudding:	**For the Yorkshire pudding:**
125g(¼lb) plain flour	*1 good cup all-purpose flour*
125ml(4fl oz) cold milk	*½ cup cold milk*
150ml(¼pt) cold water	*⅔ cup cold water*
2 medium-sized eggs	*2 medium-sized eggs*
salt and freshly-ground black pepper	*salt and freshly-ground black pepper*

1. Preheat the oven to 220°C (425°F) gas mark 7. Weigh the meat and calculate the roasting time allowing 15-25 minutes per 450g (1lb) depending on whether you like beef very rare, medium or fairly well done. Then arrange your timetable so that the meat will complete cooking 30 minutes before you plan to serve it.

2. Rub the meat all over with pepper and the cut garlic clove. Heat a roasting pan on top of the stove, then melt the fat in it. Add the meat when the fat is very hot, brown and seal all over. Transfer the pan to the oven and roast the meat for 15 minutes. Reduce the temperature to 190°C (375°F) gas mark 5 and continue roasting, basting the beef occasionally.

3. Meanwhile make the horseradish sauce. Stir the mustard into the sour cream, beating to blend well. Add the horseradish and beat until smooth. Cover and chill.

4. To make the Yorkshire pudding, first sift the flour, a pinch of salt and some pepper into a bowl. Make a hollow in the middle and break the eggs into it. Pour in the liquids, whisking them into the eggs as you do so. Gradually draw the flour into the liquid mixture and continue whisking until the batter is a smooth cream.

5. Ten minutes before the end of roasting time, spoon 30ml (2 tablespoons) of fat (drippings) from the meat into a second roasting pan. Put this on the top shelf of the oven, move the meat to a lower shelf and increase the temperature to 230°C (450°F) gas mark 8.

6. When roasting time is up, remove the meat from the oven. Transfer the beef to a hot serving dish and put in a warm place to 'rest'. Give the batter a final stir and pour it into the hot pan on the top shelf. Cook for 15 minutes, then reduce the temperature to 220°C (425°F) gas mark 7 and cook for 15 minutes more – until puffed up and golden.

7. Meanwhile, add the wine and stock to the fat and juices remaining in the meat pan and stir to scrape the meaty sediment off the base. Cook over high heat, stirring occasionally, until the liquids are reduced by about half. Season, pour into a gravy boat and serve with the meat, sauce and pudding. *Serves 6*

Greek lamb kebabs

L amb grilled on skewers is popular throughout the world. I associate it in particular with Greece, where the grilling is usually done over charcoal outdoors, and I shall never forget arriving in a small village one night, very late and very tired. On the corner of the square, next to a cafe-néon where his friends were reading and discussing the newspapers, playing backgammon, sipping tiny cups of sweet black coffee or glasses of ouzo, and seemingly totally oblivious of time, an old man stood fanning the slow-burning embers of a charcoal brazier. The smell of that lamb aromatic with wild rigani (a mild Greek marjoram), bay and thyme, combined with the soft blue smoke of charcoal, was one of the most marvellous and welcoming of greetings I have ever received – and the taste of the kebabs was as good as the aroma. I prefer kebabs with just lamb, onion and bay leaves, but you can add tomatoes, slices of green pepper and even button mushrooms if you like.

Metric/Imperial	American
550g(1¼lb) lean boneless lamb	*1¼lb of lamb, boned*
the juice and zest of 1 large lemon	*juice and grated rind of 1 large lemon*
75ml(5 tablespoons) olive oil	*5 tablespoons olive oil*
20ml(1 heaped tablespoon) fresh marjoram	*1-2 tablespoons fresh chopped marjoram*
OR 10ml(2 teaspoons) dried marjoram	*OR 2 teaspoons dried marjoram*
20ml(1 heaped tablespoon) fresh lemon thyme	*1-2 tablespoons fresh chopped lemon thyme*
OR 10ml(2 teaspoons) dried lemon thyme	*OR 2 teaspoons dried thyme*
1 garlic clove	*1 garlic clove*
2 small onions	*2 small onions*
a few bay leaves	*a few bay leaves*
4 tomatoes, halved (optional)	*4 tomatoes, halved (optional)*
extra lemons, quartered for garnishing	*lemon wedges for garnish*
salt and freshly-ground black pepper	*salt and freshly-ground black pepper*

1. Prepare the marinade about 8½ hours ahead of serving. Chop the garlic finely then crush with the back of a knife and put into a large bowl. Add the finely-grated zest (rind) and juice of the lemon, the olive oil, chopped marjoram, thyme, a few bay leaves and a generous grind of black pepper – but no salt as this would toughen the meat and encourage juices to leak out. Mix together well.

2. Trim the meat of any fat and membranes and cut into 2.5cm (1in) cubes. Add the meat to the bowl, toss to coat all over, cover and leave to marinate in a cool place but preferably not the refrigerator, for 8 hours. The meat will become very tender and deliciously flavoured with the herbs.

3. Heat the grill or broiler as hot as possible. Drain the meat, reserving the marinade liquid. Cut the onions into chunks. To prevent the onions falling to pieces during grilling, cut them up as follows: peel an onion, stand it on its root end and cut a thick slice off one side. Turn the onion and cut off another thick slice. When you have cut four slices

from the outside you will be left with an oblong shaped centre of onion. Cut this in half lengthways. Put all the pieces of onion into the marinade liquid and turn to coat lightly. Dip four long metal skewers into the marinade too – this will make it easier to thread the ingredients onto them. Then thread the cubes of lamb, pieces of onion and bay leaves onto the skewers. Do not pack them too tightly, unless you specifically want medium-rare lamb, because the heat will not reach all the cut surfaces.

4. Lay the prepared skewers on the rack of a grill, or suspend them across a flameproof gratin dish and pour the marinade liquid over them. Grill or broil them for 8-10 minutes, turning the skewers quite frequently and basting with the marinade as necessary. If using tomatoes, add these to the end of each skewer a few minutes before the end of cooking time, as they are quicker to cook than the meat. Lay the cooked and aromatically-scented kebabs on a bed of freshly-boiled rice. Pour the pan juices over them, garnish with lemon wedges and serve immediately. *Serves 4*

Wienerschnitzel

Crumbly eggs, fresh-flavoured parsley, tangy lemon, capers and anchovies are all used in this classic Viennese dish to foil the flavour and texture of tender crisply-fried veal. The combination is delicious and looks very pretty.

Metric/Imperial	American
4 veal escallopes, each weighing 90-115g(3½-4oz)	*1lb thinly sliced veal cutlet*
90g(3½oz) unsalted butter	*6-7 tablespoons unsalted butter*
30ml(2 tablespoons) oil	*2 tablespoons oil*
1 lemon	*1 lemon*
2 large hard-boiled eggs	*2 large hard-cooked eggs*
1 medium-sized egg	*1 medium-sized egg*
50g(1¾oz) can anchovy fillets	*2oz can anchovy fillets*
a small bunch of parsley	*a small bunch of parsley*
30ml(2 tablespoons) capers	*2 tablespoons capers*
about 75g(3oz) dried white breadcrumbs	*2 cups dried white bread crumbs*
a little flour	*a little flour*
salt and freshly-ground black pepper	*salt and freshly-ground black pepper*

1. If not already done by the butcher, trim all fat, skin and membrane from the slices of veal. Lay the meat between two sheets of greaseproof or waxed paper or plasticfilm and beat with a rolling pin until the meat is flattened to 6mm (¼in) thick.

2. Season a little sifted flour with plenty of salt and pepper. Dust the meat with this and shake off excess. Break the raw egg into a soup plate, beat lightly with a spoonful of water. Spread the homemade, dried breadcrumbs out on a large baking tray. Dip the meat, a slice at a time, into the beaten egg to moisten it all over. Drain briefly, then coat with a fine even layer of crumbs: lay the slice of meat on the tray of crumbs, sprinkle more crumbs over the top of the meat and press lightly but firmly with a palette knife (spatula). Coat the remaining slices of meat with egg and crumbs in the same way. Lay the coated escallopes in a single layer on a large plate, cover lightly and leave in a cool place for about 1 hour.

3. Prepare all the garnishes, putting each one ready on a separate saucer. Drain the oil from the anchovy fillets and roll each one up. Drain the capers and chop them. Chop the whites of the hard-boiled eggs, and sieve the yolks. Reserve yolks and whites separately. Chop a good quantity of fresh parsley – snip it in a cup with scissors, Cover the cup and the egg dishes to prevent the ingredients drying out. Halve the lemon, cut 4 slices from one half, squeeze the juice from the other half into a cup.

4. When ready to cook, heat 25g (1 oz) or 2 tablespoons butter and 15ml (1 tablespoon) oil in a large heavy-bottomed frying-pan. When hot, put two of the escallopes (scallops) into the pan and fry over medium heat for 3-4 minutes on each side, until the meat is tender and well cooked and the coating is crisp and golden. Drain well on paper towels and keep hot. Add another quantity of butter and oil to the pan and cook the remaining escallopes in the same way.

5. Arrange the four escallopes on a large hot serving dish. Garnish prettily with the hard-boiled eggs, parsley, lemon slices, anchovies and capers, and keep warm. Wipe out any fat and crumbs remaining in the frying-pan using plenty of paper towels. Add 40g (1½oz) or 5 tablespoons butter to pan. Melt gently and continue cooking until it begins to smell nutty and starts to brown. Remove the pan from the heat immediately. Add 15ml (1 tablespoon) or more of lemon juice to the pan together with a little salt and pepper. Swirl the pan so the flavourings are well mixed into the melted butter. Drizzle the flavoured butter over the escallopes and serve immediately.

Serves 4

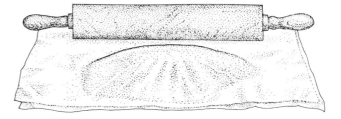

Jellied pork with truffles

I save up for months to buy a tin of truffles so that we can feast on this unforgettably good dish, surely the loveliest of all ways to eat cold meat. The succulent pork is studded with nuggets of truffle, encased in a layer of creamy fat and surrounded by an exquisitely-flavoured jelly. When truffles are out of the question, I make a plain enchaud de porc en gelée – sprinkling the joint with a spoonful or two of crushed coriander seeds or a few juniper berries instead of truffles. Not the same I admit, but still superb. In her lovely book 'French Provincial Cooking', Elizabeth David says that truffleless versions are sometimes cooked in south western France at the time of the grape harvest, when slices of bread spread with the delicious dripping and a slice of cold pork topped with a pickled gherkin are distributed to the harvesters for their collation. Lucky vineyard workers!

Metric/Imperial	American
a fine loin of pork weighing 2-2.3kg(4½-5lb)	*4½-5lb pork loin, whole*
a small tin of black truffles	*a small can of black truffles*
2 garlic cloves, cut into slivers	*2 cloves garlic, slivered*
1 small onion, sliced	*1 small onion, sliced*
1 carrot, sliced	*1 carrot, sliced*
a bunch of parsley stalks	*a bunch of parsley stalks*
a generous 150ml(¼pt) white wine	*¾ cup white wine*
a generous 425ml(¾pt) clear meat stock	*2 cups clear meat stock or consommé*
salt and freshly-ground black pepper	*salt and freshly-ground black pepper*

1. Ask the butcher to bone and derind the loin for you, or do this yourself, but be sure to keep the rind and bones which will flavour the beautiful jelly. Starting a day ahead, heat the oven to 180°C (350°F) gas mark 4. Lay the pork on a board. Rub the flesh with a generous seasoning of salt and black pepper, and spike it at intervals with tiny slivers of garlic. Cut the truffles into thick little pieces (carefully reserving their liquor) and lay them at intervals along the inside of the loin. Carefully roll up the meat and tie it firmly in several places with string to make a neat, long bolster shape. Sprinkle the board with salt and pepper and roll the loin to coat the fatty surface with seasonings. Lay the pork in a large roasting pan. Put the bones and rind round it. Cook in the centre of the oven for 45 minutes. By the end of this time the pork fat will be pale gold in colour.

2. Heat the stock, the wine and the liquor from the can of truffles. Add a seasoning of salt and pepper, and pour it around the pork. Tuck in the parsley and sliced vegetables here and there. Cover the roasting pan with a double thickness of foil. Reduce oven temperature to 160°C (325°F) gas mark 3, and cook the pork for 2-2¼ hours more until the meat is cooked to tender perfection.

3. Remove the roasting pan from the oven and leave it, still covered, until cold. The mouthwateringly aromatic smells coming from the pan seem irresistible, but resist opening the parcel one must, for cooling the pork in the steam helps retain all its succulence. When the meat is cold, lift it from the pan, wrap it in the foil to prevent loss of moisture, and store it overnight in a cool place. Discard bones and rind, parsley and vegetables. Scrape the pan juices into a bowl and chill overnight.

4. To serve the pork, remove the string and carve the meat into thin slices. Arrange them, slightly overlapping, on a serving dish. Scrape the solidified dripping(s) from the bowl of juices (save it of course: it is the best dripping in the world). The juices will be set to a soft translucent jelly. Chop this finely with a wet knife and arrange it round the meat.

Serves 10

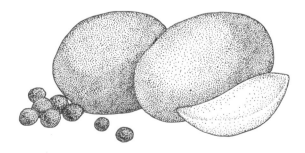

Steak & kidney pudding

Meat puddings are traditional British fare. One reads about them in Dickens, they appear regularly on the menus of gentlemen's clubs and in the City of London taverns, and I always cook one for foreign visitors. Most popular of all English meat puddings is beefsteak and kidney, or 'Kate and Sidney' as it is called in cockney rhyming slang. The delicious addition of oysters was commonplace in eighteenth and nineteenth century England, when oysters were considered an economic means of eking out the steak. Today their inclusion is a sign of luxury. Meat puddings are traditionally cooked with a raw filling, which necessitates boiling them for hours. I find that partially cooking the filling in advance is more convenient, and it makes for a lighter pastry.

Metric/Imperial	American
For the suetcrust pastry:	**For the suet pastry:**
350g(¾lb) self-raising flour	3 cups self-rising flour
175g(6oz) shredded suet	6oz shredded suet
5ml(1 teaspoon) dried mixed herbs	1 teaspoon dried mixed herbs
5ml(1 teaspoon) salt	1 teaspoon salt
For the filling:	**For the filling:**
700g(1½lb) chuck steak	1½lb chuck steak
350g(¾lb) ox kidney	¾lb beef kidney
1 dozen oysters	1 dozen oysters
175g(6oz) small cap mushrooms	6oz small white mushrooms
1 very large onion	1 large onion
50g(2oz) beef dripping	4 tablespoons beef drippings
45ml(3 tablespoons) flour	3 tablespoons all-purpose flour
350ml(12fl oz) beef stock	1½ cups beef stock
5ml(1 teaspoon) lemon juice	1 teaspoon lemon juice
2.5ml(½ teaspoon) Worcestershire sauce	½ teaspoon Worcestershire sauce
a few crushed parsley stalks	a few crushed parsley stalks
a sprig of thyme	a sprig of thyme
a bay leaf	1 bay leaf
salt and freshly-ground black pepper	salt and freshly-ground black pepper

1. Remove skin, fat and core from the meats. Slice the kidneys; cut the steak into 2.5cm (1in) cubes. Chop the onion, wipe the mushrooms clean and cut each in half. Heat half the dripping(s) in a flameproof casserole (Dutch oven) over medium-high heat. Add both meats in batches and fry until well-browned and sealed on all surfaces. Remove with a slotted spoon. Then colour the mushrooms in the hot fat, and remove them with a slotted spoon. Reduce heat slightly, add remaining dripping(s) and the onion and cook, stirring occasionally, for 5 minutes until coloured and slightly softened. Add the flour and cook, stirring to blend it well with the fat and to scrape all the delicious meaty sediment off the base of the pot. Pour on the stock and stir continuously until the sauce is thickened, smooth and comes to boiling. Return the meat and mushrooms to the pot. Add the herbs tied together with string or cotton thread, lemon juice, Worcestershire sauce and a generous seasoning of salt and pepper. Push the ingredients down into the sauce. Cover with a tight-fitting lid and simmer very gently indeed for 1½ hours. Then turn the contents of the casserole into a large bowl. Extract the herbs, and allow the mixture to cool completely. It must be cold when put into the pastry, or the pastry will not cook properly. The sauce should be rich and well-flavoured: the oysters will add piquancy and a certain amount of liquid to thin it later.

2. About 2½ hours before eating the pudding, sift the flour into a large mixing bowl. Add the suet, dried mixed herbs and salt; stir with a palette knife or spatula to mix well. Make a hollow in the middle of the mixture: pour in enough cold water to bind the dough – about 200ml (7fl oz) or 1 scant cup. Gradually draw the dry ingredients into the liquid with the palette knife (spatula). When the liquid is absorbed and well-blended, use your hands to make the dough into a ball and turn it out onto a lightly-floured work surface. Knead the dough lightly for a minute or so until smooth. Divide the dough, making one piece twice as large as the other. Generously butter a 2L (3½pt) or 2 US qt heatproof bowl and a circle of foil at least 5cm (2in) larger in diameter than the top of the bowl. Make a large pleat across the middle of the foil: this is to allow room for the pudding to rise during cooking. Set a trivet in a large boiling pan, half fill with water and bring to boiling point.

3. Roll out the larger piece of pastry 5cm (2in) larger than the top of the bowl. Dust it lightly with flour, fold the pastry in half, then fold again. Put it into the bowl so that the point of the triangle touches the base. Unfold and mould it to the shape of the bowl without stretching. Fold surplus pastry over the rim of the bowl. Open the oysters, add them and their liquor to the meat, then spoon the filling into the pastry, mounding it nicely in the middle. Fold the surplus pastry inward over the filling and brush this rim with cold water. Roll out the smaller piece of pastry to make a lid that will fit neatly inside the top of the bowl. Position it and press lightly to seal it to the damp pastry.

4. Cover the pudding with the greased and pleated foil. Tie it securely with string under the bowl rim, then make two loops of string and attach them, one at each side of the bowl, to help you lower and raise the bowl into and out of the boiling water. Trim away excess foil. Lower the bowl into the pan of fast boiling water, pouring in extra boiling water if necessary: there should be enough to come two-thirds of the way up the sides of the bowl. Cover the pan with a tight-fitting lid and cook the pudding steadily for $1\frac{1}{2}$ hours. Add more boiling water to the pan if necessary during cooking.

5. Lift the pudding out of the pan, dry the bowl and stand it on a warmed plate. Leave for 2 minutes to allow the pudding to settle, then carefully remove string and foil. In keeping with tradition, tie a crisp white linen napkin round the bowl – and the pudding is ready to serve. It is also traditional to take a small sauceboat of freshly-boiled water to the sideboard: if, when the pudding is cut open, the richly-flavoured gravy seems a little too thick, dilute it with a little boiling water. Drying out is unlikely to occur in this quickly-cooked pudding, but the addition of boiling water is often necessary for puddings that have been boiled for 3 hours or more.

Serves 6

†If you feel that oysters are ruined by cooking, add their liquor to the filling before cooking the pudding, then slip the raw shellfish into the dish when you cut the crust open for serving.

Fondue Bourguinonne

The happy-go-lucky, ice-breaking atmosphere of table-top cooking is very appealing, and a fondue Bourguinonne always seems to prove popular with all age groups. From the hostess's point of view it is lovely to share the duties of cooking; for everyone else there is the fun of choosing ingredients and cooking and dipping them to personal taste. The fondue pot will be overcrowded if more than 4 dip in the pot at one time, so I think it is best to allocate 2 forks to each person. While one is spearing the meat and placing in the pot to cook, the second (holding a piece of freshly-cooked meat) can be cooling on the diner's plate.

Metric/Imperial	American
1kg(2¼lb) rump steak	2¼lb beef tenderloin steak
OR 350g(¾lb) rump steak	OR ¾lb beef tenderloin steak
AND 350g(¾lb) pork fillet	AND ¾lb pork tenderloin
AND 350g(¾lb) lean boneless leg of lamb	AND ¾lb boneless lamb loin
sunflower or groundnut oil for frying	sunflower or groundnut oil for frying
a dash of Worcestershire sauce (optional)	a dash of Worcestershire sauce (optional)

For the aubergine purée:	For the eggplant purée:
aubergine weighing 225g(½lb)	½lb eggplant
half a small garlic clove, finely chopped	½ small clove garlic, finely chopped
7ml(1½ teaspoons) lemon juice	1½ teaspoons lemon juice
22ml(1½ tablespoons) sunflower oil	1½ tablespoons sunflower oil
freshly-chopped parsley	freshly-chopped parsley
salt and freshly-ground black pepper	salt and freshly-ground black pepper

For the avocado mayonnaise:	For the avocado mayonnaise:
1 large egg yolk	1 large egg yolk
150ml(¼pt) olive oil	⅝ cup olive oil
15ml(1 tablespoon) lemon juice	1 tablespoon lemon juice
1 very ripe avocado pear	1 ripe avocado
22ml(1½ tablespoons) chopped fresh chives	1½ tablespoons chopped fresh chives
salt and freshly-ground black pepper	salt and freshly-ground black pepper

For the creamy mint sauce:	For the creamy mint sauce:
30ml(2 tablespoons) tarragon vinegar	2 tablespoons tarragon vinegar
a pinch of caster sugar	a pinch of superfine sugar
60ml(4 tablespoons) fresh chopped mint	4 tablespoons fresh chopped mint
a good grinding of black pepper	a generous grind of black pepper
125ml(4fl oz) double cream	½ cup heavy cream

For the skordalia:	For the skordalia:
4 fat garlic cloves, finely chopped	4 large cloves garlic, finely chopped
40g(1½oz) fresh breadcrumbs	1-2 cups fresh bread crumbs
40g(1½oz) ground almonds	scant ½ cup ground almonds
about 105ml(7 tablespoons) olive oil	about 7 tablespoons olive oil
about 15ml(1 tablespoon) lemon juice	1 tablespoon lemon juice
salt	salt

For the mango chutney sauce:	For the chutney sauce:
60ml(4 tablespoons) mango chutney	4 tablespoons peach or other sweet chutney
60ml(4 tablespoons) apricot jam	4 tablespoons apricot jam
22ml(1½ tablespoons) red wine vinegar	1½ tablespoons red wine vinegar

1. To make the aubergine (eggplant) purée, prick the vegetable in two or three places to prevent bursting. Cook under a very hot grill (broiler), turning as necessary, until the skin is black and blistering – about 10-15 minutes. When cool enough to handle, strip away the skin. Chop the flesh into 3 or 4 pieces, put it into a sieve and press with a wooden spoon to extract the juices. Put the flesh into a blender together with the garlic crushed with salt, the lemon juice and oil. Reduce to a smooth purée. Season with pepper, stir in a good quantity of chopped parsley. Turn the purée into a

small bowl, then cover and chill in the refrigerator until ready to serve.

2. To make the avocado mayonnaise, use the egg yolk, olive oil and half the lemon juice to make mayonnaise (as described in detail on *page 127, steps 2-4*). Peel and stone (pit) the avocado, being careful to save the soft green flesh that clings to the skin. Sprinkle with remaining lemon juice, some salt and pepper and mash to a smooth purée. Beat it and the chives into the mayonnaise. Cover and chill until ready to serve.

3. To make the creamy mint sauce, mix the first four ingredients together and let them stand for 10 minutes. Whip the cream softly and fold in the mint mixture. Cover and chill until ready to serve. If steak is the only meat to be used, omit this sauce and make a horseradish sauce instead (see recipe on *page 41, step 3*).

4. To make skordalia, crush the garlic with salt in a mortar with a pestle to make a paste. Soak the breadcrumbs in cold water, squeeze out excess. Gradually pound the crumbs into the garlic. Then carefully blend in the almonds and olive oil, adding them very little at a time (particularly in the case of the oil) in alternate spoonfuls until the sauce is the consistency of mayonnaise. Thin and flavour to taste with lemon juice. Cover and chill until ready to serve.

5. To make the chutney sauce, chop any large pieces of fruit. Mix the chutney with the jam, then stir in the vinegar. Cover and chill until ready to serve.

6. Trim all fat and membrane from the meat(s), cutting the lean into 2.5cm (1in) cubes. Arrange each type on a separate plate (label if wished), cover loosely and keep cool.

7. When ready to serve, fill the fondue pot one-half to two-thirds full of oil. Spice it with a little Worcestershire sauce, if you wish. Heat the oil to 190 °C (375°F) on the stove then transfer the pot carefully to the fondue burner on the table. Maintain temperature by adjusting the flame of the burner as necessary.   *Serves 4*

†The ideal accompaniments to a fondue Bourguinonne are a large mixed green salad and plenty of hot herb bread (this is made in the same way as hot garlic bread – see *page 145, note* – but most of the garlic is replaced by chopped fresh herbs such as tarragon or basil, or a mixture of chives, parsley and dill). As an alternative to a mixed green salad, some people prefer to serve individual dishes of fruit and vegetables – such as slices of dessert apples, button mushrooms, gherkins and capers. If highly-spiced ingredients such as gherkins are used, the sauces are usually less spicy than those suggested here.

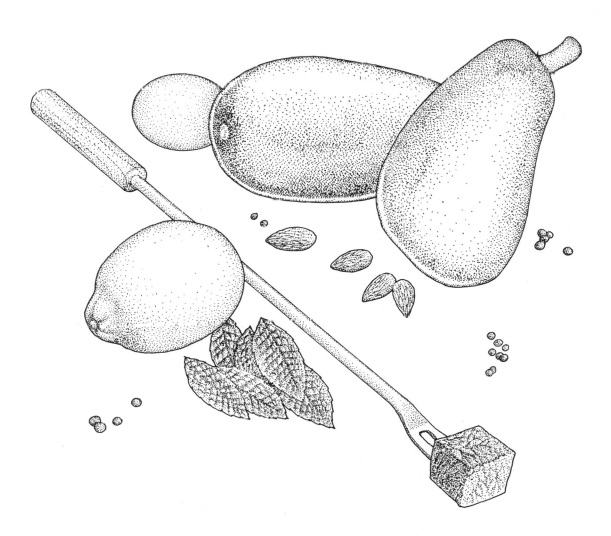

Lamb or pork korma

A korma is a braised Indian dish, much more delicately spiced than a curry or hot stew. Young lamb is particularly suitable for this treatment I think – although pork can also be used. When the ingredients include saffron, almonds and cream, as here, the resulting dish is deliciously fragrant and mild.

Metric/Imperial	American
900g(2lb) fillet or leg of lamb, boned weight	2lb boneless lamb, loin or leg
150ml($\frac{1}{4}$pt) thickened yoghurt (see method)	$\frac{3}{4}$ cup thickened plain yoghurt (see method)
3 garlic cloves	2 cloves garlic
25g(1 oz) fresh ginger root	1 tablespoon grated fresh ginger root
2·5ml($\frac{1}{2}$ teaspoon) chilli powder	$\frac{1}{2}$ teaspoon chili powder
5ml(1 teaspoon) cumin seeds	1 teaspoon cumin seeds
5ml(1 teaspoon) coriander seeds	1 teaspoon coriander seeds
15ml(1 tablespoon) white poppy seeds	1 tablespoon white poppy seeds
OR 15ml(1 tablespoon) sesame seeds	OR 1 tablespoon sesame seeds
a few strands of saffron	a few strands of saffron
65g(2$\frac{1}{2}$oz) ghee or clarified butter (page 62, 3)	5 tablespoons clarified butter (page 62, step 3)
50g(2oz) almond kernels	$\frac{1}{3}$ cup whole almonds
200ml(7fl oz) double cream	1 scant cup heavy cream
salt	salt
275g(10 oz) onions	about $\frac{3}{4}$lb onions

1. For the marinade you need yoghurt (preferably homemade) which has been thickened by hanging up in a cheesecloth bag for 3 hours to allow some liquid to drip away. Chop very finely indeed one of the garlic cloves and half the ginger. Put them into a large mixing bowl. Add the chilli (chili) powder and 45ml (3 tablespoons) of the thickened yoghurt and mix together well. Cut the lamb into small cubes no more than 1.2cm ($\frac{1}{2}$in) square. Put them into the bowl and mix gently until the meat is coated on all sides. Cover the bowl and leave the meat to marinate in a cool place, but not the refrigerator, for 8 hours.

2. About 2 hours before serving Korma, warm the cumin, coriander and poppy or sesame seeds in a

small pan over low heat for a few minutes until they become very aromatic. Set aside. Pound the saffron strands in a mortar with a pestle, pour on 150ml ($\frac{1}{4}$pt) or $\frac{2}{3}$ cup boiling water and set aside to infuse. Blanch the almonds: cover them with boiling water for a minute or two, then drain and slip off the skins. Reserve half the almonds whole, grind the rest to a coarse powder.

3. Chop the remaining garlic and ginger and all the onions very finely indeed. Measure 40g (1$\frac{1}{2}$oz) or 3 tablespoons ghee or clarified butter into a large very heavy-bottomed saucepan. Warm until the fat is melted, add the chopped onions, ginger and garlic and fry, stirring as necessary, for about 10 minutes or until golden. Remove the ingredients from the

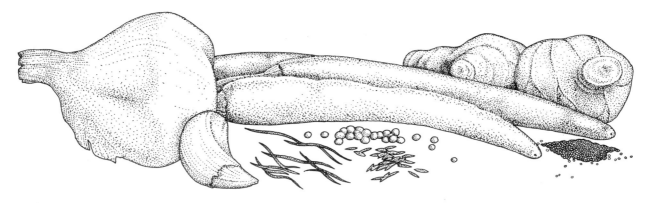

pan with a slotted spoon and reserve on a plate. Add another 15g (½oz) or 1 tablespoon ghee or clarified butter to the pan and increase heat to very high. When really hot, add half the lamb cubes, drained from the marinade. Cook for 6-7 minutes, turning the meat occasionally and scraping the pan to prevent sticking, until the meat surfaces are sealed and a rich brown in colour. Remove the meat from the pan with a slotted spoon and reserve on a plate. Add the remaining ghee or clarified butter to the pan and, when very hot, add the remaining lamb cubes and cook as before.

4. Return the reserved meat to the pan. Pour on the saffron liquid. Let it bubble up and cook over medium heat, stirring occasionally, until the pan is almost dry. Return the onion mixture to the pan. Stir in the remaining yoghurt and any marinade juices left in the mixing bowl. Stir the ingredients together then cook over low heat for 30 minutes. Stir as necessary to prevent sticking and add a little water to the pan if the mixture becomes so dry that there is danger of sticking.

5. When the 30 minutes are up, add the cumin, coriander and poppy or sesame seeds to the pan. Cook, stirring continuously for 1 minute. Add the ground and whole almonds, a seasoning of salt and the cream. Stir once, cover the pan with a very tight-fitting lid and cook over the lowest possible heat (an asbestos mat may be needed) for 25-30 minutes more. Uncover the pan and stir the ingredients once during this time. By the end of cooking the meat should be perfectly tender and coated with a thick aromatic cream. Serve with puris or chappati bread. *Serves 4*

Beef Stroganoff

Named after a Russian nobleman, this dish of tender beef, garnished with a few juicy mushrooms and thin slices of onion, then coated with a delicately-flavoured sour cream sauce, is an excellent choice when you want something special but quick. High-quality meat is essential for such speedy cooking so it is by no means a cheap dish. The secret for success lies in careful control of temperature and timing – the vegetables should be sautéed until they are golden, the beef browned and sealed on the surface but still slightly pink inside.

Metric/Imperial	American
1kg(2¼lb) fillet steak	2¼lb lean top loin steak
225g(½lb) small cap mushrooms	½lb small white mushrooms
275g(10 oz) small onions	about ¾lb small onions
75g(3oz) clarified butter (page 62, step 3)	6 tablespoons clarified butter (page 62, step 3)
5ml(1 teaspoon) cornflour	1 teaspoon cornstarch
275ml(½pt) soured cream	1¼ cups sour cream
10ml(2 teaspoons) French mustard	2 teaspoons French mustard
90ml(6 tablespoons) coarsely-chopped parsley	6 tablespoons fresh, roughly chopped parsley
salt and freshly-ground black pepper	salt and freshly-ground black pepper

1. Trim any fat and membranes from the steak, then cut the meat into very thin strips about 5cm (2in) long and not more than 1cm ($\frac{1}{3}$in) wide. Season the meat with generous grinds of black pepper and set it aside in a cool place. Slice the onions very thinly. Wipe the mushrooms clean, trim stalks level with the caps and slice each one in half. Put a spoonful or so of the soured cream into a small bowl. Add the cornflour (cornstarch), which will help to stabilize the sauce, and beat until smooth. Add the mustard, a generous quantity of salt and pepper and the remaining sour cream and beat until the mixture is very creamy and well-blended. All these preparations (and indeed the preliminary cooking of the onions and mushrooms) can be done in advance of the meal.

2. About half an hour before serving beef, melt half the clarified butter in a large sauté or frying-pan over low heat. Add the sliced onion and cook for 6-7 minutes until slightly softened. Add the mushrooms and increase the heat to medium. Cook, stirring fairly frequently for 3-4 minutes until the vegetables are golden – but not browned or burned.

Lift the vegetables out of the pan with a slotted spoon to drain them well. Keep them hot on a serving dish in a low oven.

3. Increase the heat to high and add the rest of the clarified butter to the pan. Let it foam up and become very hot. When the foam begins to subside add the strips of beef to the pan. Cook briskly for 3-4 minutes, turning the meat as necessary. The aim is to brown and seal the surface of the meat thoroughly but to keep the centre of each strip medium-rare. Immediately reduce heat to medium and return the vegetables to the pan. Cook, stirring, for a few seconds until the ingredients are well mixed together. Slowly pour on and stir in the flavoured sour cream. Let the mixture cook gently for a minute or so until the sauce is really hot and coats the meat and vegetables with a creamy gloss. Quickly turn the contents of the pan onto the warm serving dish, scatter the chopped parsley over the top and serve immediately. Broccoli and triangles of fried bread make delicious accompaniments. Boiled rice or buttered noodles are also popular.

Serves 6

Abbacchio brodettato

Tender, delicately-flavoured lamb is essential for this lovely Roman stew, which seems to me an ideal dish with which to celebrate the arrival of spring. It is traditionally made with lamb so young that it has not fed on grass. Beware using mutton or elderly lamb: their strong flavours would be quite inappropriate here.

Metric/Imperial	American
800kg(1¾lb) lean, boneless young lamb	*1¾lb baby lamb, boneless*
50g(2oz) Parma ham, or unsmoked back bacon	*2oz Italian ham or ready-to-eat Canadian bacon*
1 small onion	*1 small onion*
2 celery stalks	*2 celery stalks*
20ml(4 teaspoons) unsalted butter	*4 teaspoons unsalted butter*
20ml(4 teaspoons) olive oil	*4 teaspoons olive oil*
150ml(¼pt) dry white wine	*⅝ cup dry white wine*
150ml(¼pt) light chicken stock or water	*⅝ cup chicken stock or water*
a few parsley stalks	*a few parsley stalks*
a sprig of oregano	*a sprig of oregano*
15ml(1 tablespoon) lemon juice	*1 tablespoon lemon juice*
2 large egg yolks	*2 large egg yolks*
30ml(2 tablespoons) chopped parsley	*2 tablespoons chopped parsley*
salt	*salt*
freshly-ground black pepper	*freshly-ground black pepper*

1. Discard any fat and cut the lamb into large cubes. Cut the ham or bacon into strips. Finely chop the vegetables. Tie the parsley stalks and oregano together with string.

2. Heat 5ml (1 teaspoon) each butter and oil in a large flameproof casserole (Dutch oven). Add about one-third of the lamb – so that the cubes can lie in a single layer without touching each other – and fry until golden on all sides. Remove the meat with a slotted spoon. Colour the remaining lamb in two more batches, adding another 5ml (1 teaspoon) each of butter and oil to the casserole for each batch. Then add the remaining butter and oil and gently fry the ham or bacon, onion and celery.

3. Return the meat to the casserole. Stir in the wine and bring to a boil. Reduce heat slightly and simmer, uncovered, for 10 minutes so that the liquid reduces considerably.

4. Add the stock or water, the bunch of herbs and a good grinding of pepper. Bring back to simmering point. Reduce heat to as low as possible, cover and cook for 45 minutes, stirring and turning the meat occasionally.

5. Lightly beat the lemon juice, egg yolks and

chopped parsley together in a cup. Stir in a few spoonfuls of liquid from the casserole, then stir the contents of the cup into the casserole. Cook, stirring continuously, for 5 minutes while the sauce thickens slightly. Be careful to keep temperature well below boiling point or the sauce will curdle.

6. Remove the casserole from the heat. Take out the bunch of herbs and squeeze them between two spoons so that the juices drip back into the casserole. Taste the sauce, salt it to taste and add extra lemon and pepper if wished. Serve immediately. *Serves 4*

58

Tournedos & herb butter

Juicily-tender tournedos or filet mignon steaks, topped with pats of melting herb butter, and sitting on circles of crisply-fried bread (which will soak up the delicious meat juices mingled with savoury butter), make a marvellous, very quickly prepared and very elegant dish. Just the thing, I find, to revive jaded appetites for a special occasion.

Metric/Imperial	American
4 tournedos, each about 150g(5oz)	*4 tournedos steaks, round cut from beef fillet*
a little olive oil	*a little olive oil*
half a garlic clove	*half clove garlic*
salt and freshly-ground black pepper	*salt and freshly-ground black pepper*
large bunch of watercress	*large bunch of watercress*
4 fluted rounds of fresh white bread	*4 fluted circles of fresh white bread, steak-size*
clarified butter (page 62, step 3)	*clarified butter (page 62, step 3)*

For the beurre maître d'hôtel:	For the beurre maître d'hôtel:
75g(3oz) unsalted butter at room temperature	*6 tablespoons butter at room temperature*
3 tablespoons (45ml) fresh chopped parsley	*3 tablespoons fresh chopped parsley*
6ml(1 generous teaspoon) lemon juice	*1-2 teaspoons lemon juice*
salt and freshly-ground black pepper	*salt and freshly-ground black pepper*

1. Bring the tournedos to room temperature about an hour before cooking them. Rub the flesh lightly with the cut surface of the garlic clove to impregnate it delicately with the flavour, and brush all over with a little olive oil.

2. To make the maître d'hôtel butter mash and beat the butter until it is pale, smooth and very creamy. Sprinkle on the fresh herbs and lemon juice and beat again until the ingredients are absorbed and the butter evenly-flecked with green. Add some salt and a generous grind of black pepper and beat again. Wet a small sheet of greaseproof or waxed paper and rinse your hands under cold water. Use your hands to shape the savoury butter into a neat can-shaped roll, wrap in the damp paper and chill it in the coldest part of a refrigerator (or pop it briefly into the freezer) until solid.

3. Wash and dry the watercress, divide it into large sprigs discarding tough stems, and keep cool until required. Heat some clarified butter in a pan and fry the rounds of bread until golden and crisp on both sides. Drain well on kitchen paper and keep hot.

4. The tournedos can of course be cooked under a gas or electric grill (broiler) or over charcoal. But I think they taste best (perhaps simply because they look so alluring and professional with a criss-cross finish) if cooked in a ridged grill pan – or dry frying-pan, as it is sometimes called. This looks like a normal very heavy-bottomed frying-pan, except that there are raised ridges running across it: the meat is laid across the ridges (which sear their pattern onto the meat) and the fat drains away into the pan base as the meat cooks.

5. Set the pan over high heat until thoroughly hot. Brush the pan lightly with oil to grease it and prevent sticking. When sizzling add the steaks and cook for about 1 minute to seal and brown the surface. Turn the steaks (using tongs to prevent piercing the meat, which would release precious meat juices). Cook on the second side for 1 minute, still over fierce heat. Then reduce heat to medium, turn the steaks over and lay them at right angles to their previous position to sear them with the criss-cross effect. Cook for 1-4 minutes more depending on the thickness of the steaks and whether you like them rare, medium or well-done. Then complete cooking on the second side in the same way.

6. Lift the cooked steaks out of the pan. Quickly snip and remove the string tied around each. Arrange the hot fried bread on a serving dish, top each piece with a tournedo, sprinkle with a little salt and pepper, and surround them with the watercress sprigs. Cut the herb butter into 8 generous pats, place two on each steak, and serve without delay.

Serves 4

Ceruelles au beurre noire

I include this recipe not only because I rate it very highly but also because I feel that brains are sadly underrated and deserve much wider appreciation. Cooked and served very simply, as here, they make an excellent light dish and are a true delicacy.

Metric/Imperial	American
575g(1¼lb) fresh lamb or calf brains	1¼lb(about 2 pairs) fresh calves' brains
4 lemons	4 lemons
350g(¾lb) butter for clarifying	¾lb butter for clarifying
50g(2oz) unsalted butter	4 tablespoons unsalted butter
120ml(8 tablespoons) olive oil	8 tablespoons olive oil
a small bunch of parsley	a small bunch of parsley
about 60ml(4 tablespoons) capers	4 tablespoons capers
a little plain flour	a little flour
salt and freshly-ground black pepper	salt and freshly-ground black pepper

1. Soak the brains for 3 hours in plenty of cold salted water to help wash away chips of bone and blood. Then rinse the brains under gently running cold water and carefully pull away as much membrane and opaque white bits as you can without tearing the flesh. This is not as difficult as it sounds, although patience and delicacy of handling are necessary. Rinse the brains again. Put them into a saucepan. Add the juice of a lemon, a good seasoning of salt and enough boiling water to cover the brains well. Bring to a bare simmer, cover and poach very gently for 15 minutes for lamb brains, 20 minutes for calf brains.

2. Mix the juice of 2 lemons with 90ml (6 tablespoons) olive oil and a generous grinding of black pepper in a bowl. Lift the poached brains out of the saucepan and into the bowl with a slotted spoon. Turn them gently and leave to absorb the dressing until cold and firm. Then slice the brains thickly and return them to the dressing until ready to cook.

3. Meanwhile clarify the butter for the sauce. Approximately 350g (¾lb) butter will be needed to produce 225g (½lb) clarified butter needed for the recipe. Dice the butter and melt it gently in a small pan. Strain the clear yellow liquid through cheesecloth to get rid of any specks and scum. Discard the milky sediment left in the bottom of the pan. Rinse and dry the pan and return the clarified butter to it.

4. Prepare the remaining ingredients needed to make the sauce: mixing together in a cup the chopped and drained capers, about 90ml (6 tablespoons) chopped fresh parsley, 22ml (1½ tablespoons) lemon juice, a little salt and freshly ground black pepper. Set aside.

5. When ready to cook, drain the slices of brain. Dust them with sifted flour seasoned with salt and pepper and shake off any excess. Heat half the unsalted butter in a heavy-bottomed frying-pan together with 15ml (1 tablespoon) olive oil over medium heat. When the foam begins to subside, add half the brains, laying them in a single layer. Cook for about 3 minutes on each side, until hot and pale gold. Lift the brains out of the pan with a slotted spoon, drain well. Arrange on a hot serving dish and keep warm. Add the remaining unsalted butter to the pan together with another 15ml (1 tablespoon) olive oil. Cook the rest of the brain slices in the same way, drain and keep warm.

6. Reheat the clarified butter over medium heat. It will bubble and crackle, then begin to brown. As soon as it is an even golden brown colour, switch off the heat. Keeping the pan over the source of heat, stir in the caper and parsley mixture. Stand well back as it will bubble up. Quickly pour the sauce over the dish of brains and carry it to the table while still frothing. Serve with steamed French (green) beans and plenty of hot crusty bread. *Serves 4*

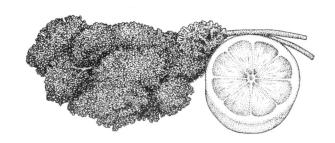

Afelia

This superb Greek recipe is one I cook very frequently. The combination of pork and coriander is exceptionally good, and the warm, spicy aroma that wafts from the cooking pan seems to lure everyone eagerly to the table. I know of no better dish for occasions when you want to serve something that tastes rather special but is very quick and easy to cook.

Metric/Imperial	American
700g(1½lb) fillet of pork	1½lb pork tenderloin
2.5ml(½ teaspoon) black peppercorns	½ teaspoon black peppercorns
15ml(1 tablespoon) coriander seeds	1 tablespoon coriander seeds
5ml(1 teaspoon) soft brown sugar	1 teaspoon light brown sugar
15ml(1 tablespoon) olive oil	1 tablespoon olive oil
6-8 spring onions	6-8 scallions
275ml(½pt) fairly dry red or white wine	1¼ cups medium-dry red or white wine
25g(1 oz) butter	2 tablespoons butter
salt	salt
freshly-ground black pepper	freshly-ground black pepper
freshly-chopped coriander or parsley leaves	freshly-chopped coriander or parsley leaves

1. Trim away and discard any sinew and membrane attached to the meat. Cut the meat up into large cubes and lay them in a shallow dish. Sprinkle the sugar over the meat. Grind the peppercorns and coriander seeds together – either in a peppermill or in a mortar with a pestle – and sprinkle them over the meat. Turn lightly to mix well, cover and leave in a cool place to tenderize and flavour the meat for at least half an hour, or up to 4 hours if more convenient.

2. Choose a heavy-bottomed frying-pan large enough to take the pork cubes in a single layer. About 40 minutes before the meal, measure the oil into it and place over fairly high heat. When the oil is sizzling hot, add the pork to the pan. Fry briskly, turning the meat as necessary, until the pork is well browned and sealed on all sides. It is vitally important that the oil is really hot when the meat is added to the pan and that high temperature is maintained during frying. This is to seal and colour the meat well, and adds greatly to the flavour of the dish.

3. While the pork is browning, trim the spring onions (scallions) and chop them up, green parts as well as white.

4. When the pork is nicely browned, sprinkle the spring onions (scallions) into the pan and push them into the gaps between the meat. Pour the wine into the pan, standing back as you do so for it will bubble up furiously. After a minute or so, reduce the heat under the pan to medium-low.

5. Leave the pork to cook, uncovered, for about 20 minutes, just stirring it occasionally to prevent sticking and to encourage even cooking. By the time the wine has reduced to a few spoonfuls, the meat will be deliciously tender and impregnated with its flavour.

6. Cut the butter up into small dice. Add to the pan together with a few spoonfuls of fresh chopped coriander or parsley leaves. Cook, stirring continuously, for a minute or so until the butter has melted and amalgamated with the wine to make a small quantity of syrupy sauce. Turn off the heat and season the pork with salt and pepper to taste.

7. Turn the pork and its sauce onto a bed of boiled rice or noodles, or serve alone with plenty of hot crusty bread to mop up the exquisite sauce.

Serves 4

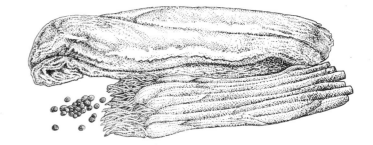

Vitello tonnato

Veal, tuna and anchovies are favourite ingredients in Italian cookery. Here they are combined to make a superb summery dish. In Piedmont vitello tonnato is sometimes offered as a first course, but it is more usual to serve it as a light lunch dish. I like to accompany it with a green salad and plenty of freshly-baked bread to soak up the exquisite sauce. Choose juicy parsley stalks for the braising liquid, as they are richer in flavour than parsley leaves, and use white pepper rather than black, which would speckle, and thus spoil, the pale creaminess of the sauce.

Metric/Imperial	American
1.12kg(2½lb) veal fillet or boned leg of veal	2½lb boneless veal leg rump roast
2 × 50g(1¾oz) cans anchovy fillets	2 × 2oz cans anchovy fillets
150g(5oz) canned tuna fish	¾ × 7oz can tuna fish
25g(1 oz) unsalted butter	2 tablespoons unsalted butter
2 carrots and 2 onions, sliced	2 carrots and 2 onions, sliced
3-4 celery stalks, sliced	3-4 stalks celery, sliced
a few crushed parsley stalks	a few crushed parsley stalks
1 bay leaf	1 bay leaf
275ml(½pt) dry white wine	1¼ cups dry white wine
3 large (no. 2) egg yolks	3 large egg yolks
350-425ml(12-15fl oz) olive oil	1¾-2 cups olive oil
2-3 large lemons	2-3 large lemons
60-75ml(4-5 tablespoons) capers	4-5 tablespoons capers
salt and freshly-ground white pepper	salt and white pepper

1. Start cooking the day before serving the dish. Make a few incisions in the veal and insert into them 4 anchovy fillets cut into small pieces. Tie the meat into a neat shape with string and rub the surface with plenty of pepper. Set aside at room temperature for 1 hour before cooking.

2. Preheat the oven to 160°C (325°F) gas mark 3. While it is warming, melt the butter in a roasting pan on top of the stove. When hot, add the meat and lightly brown it all over. Remove the meat, add the vegetables to the pan and cook them until coloured. Pour out the fat, then return the meat to the pan, laying it on top of the vegetables. Add the bay leaf and parsley. Pour on the wine and, if necessary, some water – the liquid should come about halfway up the vegetables. Cover the pan with foil, place it in the middle of the oven and braise for 2¼ hours. Then cool the cooked veal in the covered pan: this helps to keep the meat beautifully moist.

3. Meanwhile prepare the sauce. Pound the rest of the anchovies to a paste. Do this with a mortar and pestle and it is easier if you add a few drops of lemon juice. Add the tuna and pound again until very smooth. Make a mayonnaise with the egg yolks and

olive oil (*page 127, steps 2-4*). Season it with 30ml (2 tablespoons) lemon juice, a generous grind of pepper and a little salt. Carefully and gradually beat the mayonnaise into the fish paste. Then thin the mixture with some of the strained braising liquid so that the finished sauce is the consistency of thick cream, very smooth and well flavoured. Check and adjust seasoning to taste.

4. Drain and dry the cold veal and remove string. Carve it into thin slices and arrange them, slightly overlapping, in a shallow serving dish. Pour on the sauce, sprinkle on the capers. Cover the dish and chill for at least 8 hours to allow flavours to amalgamate. Bring the dish to room temperature about 30 minutes before serving, and garnish with thin lemon slices.

Serves 6

Pork rillettes

The shrewd way in which the French handle the cheapest of meats is admirably demonstrated by this simple, tasty and very economical pâté – belly of pork (boned spare-ribs) spiked with herbs and spices and reduced to melting tenderness.

Metric/Imperial	American
1.8kg(4lb) fairly lean belly of pork	2 sides lean spareribs, boned (about 5lb)
450g(1lb) pork back fat	1lb fatback
1 dozen juniper berries	1 dozen juniper berries
1 dozen black peppercorns	1 dozen black peppercorns
3 or 4 sprigs each of parsley and lemon thyme	3-4 sprigs each of parsley and thyme
2 bay leaves	2 bay leaves
5-6 large garlic cloves	5-6 cloves garlic
2.5ml(½ teaspoon) freshly-grated nutmeg	½ teaspoon freshly-grated nutmeg
coarse salt	coarse salt
150ml(¼pt) dry white wine or very dry cider	⅔ cup dry white wine or applejack
5ml(1 teaspoon) coriander seeds	1 teaspoon coriander seeds
extra bay leaves and juniper berries to garnish	extra bay leaves and juniper berries to garnish

1. The secret of success with this very economical pâté is to cook the meats and fat very gently indeed until absolutely tender, and to include plenty of delicious flavourings in the cooking pot.

2. Make the pâté at least a day before eating. Heat the oven to 140°C (275°F) gas mark 1. Cut the rind and bones away from the belly of pork (spare ribs), then chop both the meat and the pork back fat into small cubes. Put them into a casserole. Crush the juniper berries with the back of a spoon, then chop them into small pieces. Crush the peppercorns, and crush the garlic cloves with salt. Sprinkle these ingredients among the pork cubes. Stir in the freshly-grated nutmeg – it must be

freshly-grated, ready ground nutmeg simply does not have enough flavour and aroma. Tie together the parsley, thyme sprigs and bay leaves and bury the bunch of herbs among the meat. Pour on wine or cider, cover the dish with foil and a lid. Bake for 4-4½ hours in the centre of the oven.

3. Empty the contents of the casserole into a large strainer placed over a bowl. Press the cubes of meat and fat lightly to help drain off excess liquid fat. Remove and discard the bunch of herbs. Turn half the meat and fat cubes out onto a large plate. Using two forks pull and tear the cubes apart to reduce them to a soft, shredded paste. Shred the remaining meat in the same way.

4. Warm a small frying-pan over moderate heat, add the coriander seeds and cook, shaking the pan occasionally, for a minute or two until the seeds are warmed and smelling aromatic. Remove from the heat, crush the seeds into very small pieces (using either the back of a spoon, or a mortar and pestle, or an empty peppermill). Stir the coriander into the rillettes. Taste to check seasoning and add extra salt, freshly-ground pepper and/or other flavourings to taste.

5. Pack the paste, but do not press it down too firmly, into one large pâté dish or several individual ramekin dishes. Spoon some of the melted fat over the top, decorate with juniper berries and bay leaves, cover and chill. Eat within 8 days. *Serves 10*

Prosciutto al Marsala

This is an adaptation of an Italian recipe traditionally made with an end piece of Parma ham. Gammon or ham is considerably cheaper and frankly I think it is a waste of Parma ham to cook it. Gammon (ham) is beautifully tender cooked by this method and it absorbs the flavours of the sauce very well – a sauce cleverly made by re-using the marinade and thickening it with vegetables cooked with the meat. I find this a useful dish for entertaining: the meat can be soaked and marinated a day ahead, cooked and coated with the sauce in the morning, then simply reheated in the evening.

Metric/Imperial	American
1.15kg(2½lb) lean middle cut gammon	*2½-3lb cook-before-eating semi-boneless ham*
150ml(¼pt) cooking Marsala	*¾ cup cooking Marsala*
60ml(4 tablespoons) olive oil	*4 tablespoons olive oil*
2 large carrots	*2 large carrots*
1 large onion	*1 large onion*
2 celery stalks	*2 stalks celery*
1 bay leaf	*1 bay leaf*
3 black peppercorns	*3 black peppercorns*
a bunch of parsley	*a bunch parsley*
unsalted or very lightly salted chicken stock	*unsalted chicken stock or broth*
salt and freshly-ground black pepper	*salt and freshly-ground black pepper*

1. Soak the gammon (or ham) in cold water for two hours or longer, depending on how salty it is and whether you like a mild or well-salted flavour. Drain the meat and dry it. Rinse and dry the bowl. Pour the Marsala into the bowl, add the meat, and set aside to marinate in a cold place for 4 hours or longer, turning the meat at intervals.

2. The dish can be completely prepared ahead or cooking can start about 2¼ hours before serving. Choose a heavy-bottomed pan into which the ham will fit snugly. Warm the olive oil in it over low heat. Dice the vegetables, add them to the pan and fry for 5-10 minutes until lightly browned. Drain the meat, reserving the Marsala. Lay the meat on top of the vegetables and tuck the crushed parsley stalks, bay leaf and peppercorns beside it. Pour on just enough cold stock to cover the meat. Bring to

simmering point. Reduce heat to the gentlest simmer, cover the pan and cook for 1 hour 10 minutes.

3. Lift the cooked meat out of the pan and let it 'rest' while you prepare the sauce. Transfer 425ml (¾pt) or 2 cups of the cooking liquid to a smaller saucepan and concentrate flavour by fast boiling until reduced by nearly half. Put the reduced liquor into a blender. Remove the vegetables from the cooking pan with a slotted spoon and add to the blender. Blend to a smooth purée. Return the mixture to the small saucepan. Add the reserved Marsala and simmer for a few minutes. Taste the sauce and add salt and pepper (or, if too salty, stir in a few spoonfuls of thick cream). If the sauce seems too thick, thin it with a little more cooking liquor. Remove the rind (if present) from the meat, carve the meat into slices and arrange them, just overlapping, on a serving dish. Pour on the sauce. If the dish is being prepared ahead, set it aside in a cool place.

4. To reheat and thoroughly saturate the meat with the sauce, cover the dish with foil and place it in an oven preheated to 150°C (300°F) gas mark 3 – for 20 minutes if the dish is freshly prepared, for 45-60 minutes if the dish was prepared ahead.

Serves 6

Osso bucho alla Milanese

F ew dishes are more comforting and aromatic than osso bucho, tender veal served with rice that is creamy and fragrant with saffron. A small glass of wine and tomato juice can be used instead of stock for the risotto if you prefer.

Metric/Imperial	American
4 pieces of shin of veal, in 5cm(2in) slices	*2 veal shanks (cut into 2in pieces)*
45ml(3 tablespoons) melted butter	*3 tablespoons melted butter*
10ml(2 teaspoons) olive oil	*2 teaspoons olive oil*
1 small onion, very finely chopped	*1 small onion, very finely chopped*
2 celery stalks, very finely chopped	*2 celery stalks, very finely chopped*
4 large tomatoes, skinned and chopped	*4 tomatoes, skinned and chopped*
150ml(¼pt) dry white wine	*⅝ cup dry white wine*
275ml(½pt) veal or chicken stock	*1¼ cups veal or chicken stock*
salt and freshly-ground black pepper	*salt and freshly-ground black pepper*

For the gremolata:	**For the gremolata:**
1 large garlic clove, finely chopped	*1 large clove garlic, finely chopped*
the finely grated zest of a lemon	*the finely grated rind of 1 lemon*
5 tablespoons fresh chopped parsley	*5 tablespoons fresh chopped parsley*

For the risotto:	**For the risotto:**
225g(½lb) arborio rice	*½lb Italian rice*
1 small onion, finely chopped	*1 onion, finely chopped*
50g(2oz) butter	*¼ cup butter*
a few strands of saffron	*a few strands of saffron*
about 1 litre(1¾pt) veal or chicken stock	*4½ cups veal or chicken stock*
30ml(2 tablespoons) grated Parmesan cheese	*2 tablespoons grated Parmesan cheese*

1. About 2¼ hours before you plan to eat, choose a deep sauté pan (shallow saucepan) or flameproof casserole (Dutch oven) wide enough to spread out the slices of meat in a single layer. Heat it, add the butter and oil, and lightly brown the meat all over. Lay the slices flat so that the bones stand upright and hold the delicious bone marrow safely inside them. Push the onion and celery into the gaps between the pieces of meat and lightly brown them too.

2. Pour on the wine and cook briskly for 10 minutes until reduced to a few spoonfuls. Add the chopped tomatoes and stock. Bring back to simmering point, cover with a well-fitting lid and cook over the lowest possible heat for 1 hour 20 minutes, turning the slices over halfway. Then uncover the pan and continue simmering very gently indeed for 20 minutes more until the meat is absolutely tender and the sauce reduced to a good consistency.

3. About 10 minutes before uncovering the veal pan, start making the risotto. Melt half the butter in a heavy-bottomed pan. Add the onion and cook gently for 5 minutes. Meanwhile bring the stock to a boil. Pound the saffron with mortar and pestle and then soak it in the boiling stock. Add the rice to the onion and stir until coated with fat. Keeping the heat low, add a small ladleful of boiling stock and let the rice simmer, uncovered, until the liquid is almost completely absorbed. Stir the rice lightly to prevent it sticking to the pan base and add another ladleful of boiling stock. Continue adding more stock each time the previous ladleful is absorbed: stir lightly as necessary; do not cover the pan. The rice is ready when it is creamy and tender with just a hint of 'bite' in the centre of each grain – about 20-25 minutes' cooking time. Turn off heat but leave the pan on the stove. Season to taste, stir in the remaining butter and the Parmesan cheese.

4. Finally, season the veal to taste with salt and pepper. Mix the gremolata ingredients together, sprinkle them over the veal and serve immediately.

Serves 4

Crown roast of lamb

Tender, home-produced lamb cutlets (chops) are sweet in flavour, and a crown roast is the most handsome way to present them. Do not cook with a stuffing in the centre of the crown: it will prevent the lamb fat (fell) from crisping really well. Instead fill the crown after roasting with vegetables that have been cooked separately.

Metric/Imperial	American
2 fine best end of neck of lamb, each 6 cutlets	a crown roast of 12 ribs chops
1 garlic clove	1 clove garlic
a little olive oil	a little olive oil
a large bunch of fresh mint	a large bunch of fresh mint leaves
salt and freshly-ground black pepper	salt and freshly-ground black pepper

1. Choose the leanest, meatiest best ends of neck (crown roast) available. Ask the butcher to chine them. This is a saw cut along the length of the back or chine bone which runs at right angles to the tapering cutlet bones; this cut makes it easier to remove the chine bone later. Ask him to make a parallel saw cut across the top, spiky ends of the cutlet bones; this will be done in such a way as to leave the ends hinged to the main part of the joint. The butcher should also skin the meat.

2. About 2¼ hours before serving crown roast, bring the meat to room temperature; 30 minutes later preheat the oven to 220°C (425°F) gas mark 7.

3. Make the best ends of neck up into a crown, if the butcher has not already done this for you. Start by cutting away the hinged bony flap, then remove the chine bone, scraping it away from the

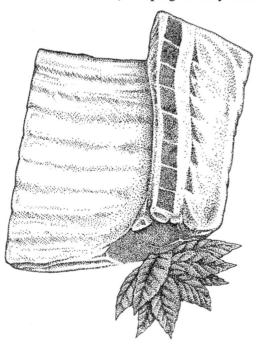

meaty base of the cutlets with a sharp-bladed knife. Cut the thin layer of meat between the cutlet bones to a depth of 2.5cm (1in), scrape the meat away from the bones.

4. Cut the garlic clove into slivers. Make tiny slits in the lamb fat and insert the garlic (if the crown is made up, this means working inside it.)

5. Stand the two joints with the fatty sides facing and all the cutlet bones point upwards. Gently curve the joints to make a crown shape and sew together, stitching the last bone of one joint to the first bone of the other. The meat should bend quite easily but you may have to make one or two nicks here and there in order to curve the joints nicely. Keep cuts to the minimum: they encourage meat juices to leak out and gashes can cause the crown to topple in an unsightly way during cooking.

6. Before putting the meat into the oven, wrap the bare bone tips in foil to prevent them from burning during roasting. Brush the crown all over with a light coating of olive oil. Rub plenty of salt and pepper into the fat.

7. Lightly oil a rack. Place it in a roasting pan and stand the crown on top. Roast for 20 minutes. Reduce oven temperature to 190°C (375°F) gas mark 5 and roast for 35-40 minutes more, until the fat is golden and crisp and the meat tender, succulent and tinged with the palest pink.

8. Transfer the roast to a warmed serving dish strewn with sprigs of fresh mint. Remove the foil from bone tips and decorate with paper frills. Let the meat 'rest' for 10 minutes, fill the cavity with vegetables of your choice and serve. *Serves 6*

Flemish beef stew

H ere is a hearty dish which I find first rate for satisfying cold weather appetites – both deliciously and quite economically. It is the sort of dish I imagine the ice-skaters in Brueghel's wintery paintings might have come home to. Beef, onions and mustard always combine well. The old Flemish idea of using beer to enrich the colour and flavour of the gravy is an excellent one; the curious thing about it is that it tastes very ordinary when added to the casserole (and even halfway through cooking) but the end result is mouthwateringly good and well worth waiting for!

Metric/Imperial	American
1.45kg(3lb) chuck steak or skirt, 5cm (2in) cubes	*3lb beef chuck or rib steak, in 2in cubes*
450g(1lb) onions, coarsely chopped	*1lb onions, coarsely chopped*
3 large garlic cloves, finely chopped	*3 large cloves garlic, finely chopped*
50g(2oz) beef dripping	*4 tablespoons beef drippings*
15ml(1 tablespoon) soft dark brown sugar	*1 tablespoon soft dark brown sugar*
40g(1½oz) plain flour	*⅓ cup all-purpose flour*
575ml(1pt) brown ale	*2½ cups brown ale or dark beer*
75ml(3fl oz) beef stock	*6 tablespoons beef stock*
45ml(3 tablespoons) red wine vinegar	*3 tablespoons red wine vinegar*
salt and freshly-ground black pepper	*salt and freshly-ground black pepper*
freshly grated nutmeg	*freshly grated nutmeg*
1 bay leaf and 2 cloves tied up in cheesecloth	*1 bay leaf and 2 cloves tied up in cheesecloth*

For the topping:
1 French or 2 Vienna loaves
French mustard

For the topping:
1 French loaf
French mustard

1. Switch the oven to 150°C (300°F) gas mark 2, and select a flameproof casserole (Dutch oven) that is large but relatively shallow. A large surface area is important as you will want plenty of room for the delicious bread-and-mustard topping which is added towards the end of cooking, and the slices must lie in a single layer.

2. Heat a little of the dripping(s) in the pot. When it is very hot add about one-third of the cubed beef and fry over medium-high heat until it is browned and sealed on all sides. Remove the meat with a slotted spoon. Brown and seal the remaining cubes of beef in the same way, frying them in batches until really crusty and brown. Add extra dripping to the pot as necessary. When all the meat has been prepared, put the onions, garlic and sugar into the pot. Reduce heat slightly and cook, stirring occasionally, until the vegetables are slightly softened and slightly browned. Sprinkle on the flour and cook, stirring continuously, for 3 minutes or so. Pour on the ale, stock and vinegar and stir well to scrape all the delicious meaty sediment off the bottom of the pot. Continue stirring until the liquids reach boiling point. Season generously with salt and freshly-ground black pepper. Add a generous grating of nutmeg and drop in the cheesecloth bag of herbs and spices. Return the cubes of beef to the pot, pushing them well down into the sauce.

3. Cover the pot with a tight-fitting lid and transfer it to the middle shelf of the oven. Cook the dish of beef at the gentlest possible simmer for about 2½-3 hours or until the meat is perfectly tender. Do not attempt to look at or to taste the carbonnades before a minimum of 2¼ hours have passed or you will be a little bit disappointed – the beer gravy tastes acrid at first, but if you wait until it has properly matured you will be amply rewarded.

4. When the meat is deliciously tender, slice the bread thickly and spread it generously with mustard. Remove the pot from the oven and increase oven temperature to 180°C (350°F) gas mark 4. Extract the cheesecloth bag and squeeze it between two spoons so that the juices drip back into the gravy. Check the gravy for seasoning and adjust to taste. Cover the surface of the casserole with the slices of bread, laying them in a single layer, mustard side up. Then press them lightly down into the gravy so that the bread will begin to soak it up. Return the pot to the oven – without the lid this time – and cook for a further 20 minutes. *Serves 6-8*

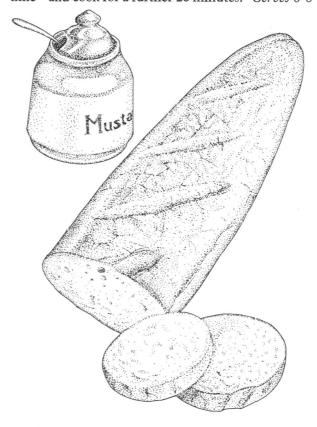

Steak tartare

If, as I do, you like raw steak, this dish is a joy. It is very tasty, nutritious but not fattening, and it involves no cooking. I have, however, on occasion been offered steak tartare that was far too powerfully seasoned for my taste. Since everyone's taste is slightly different, I suggest it is best to make a mild version as described here, and to have tiny bowls of extra chopped onions, chopped capers, quartered lemons, Worcestershire sauce and salt and pepper-mills on the table so that everyone can help themselves to more as and when they wish.

Metric/Imperial	American
700g(1½lb) well-hung rump steak, without fat	1½lb rump or sirloin steak without fat
75g(3oz) peeled onion	3 tablespoons diced onion
30ml(2 tablespoons) capers	2 tablespoons capers
60ml(4 tablespoons) chopped fresh parsley	4 tablespoons chopped fresh parsley
10ml(2 teaspoons) olive oil	2 teaspoons olive oil
5ml(1 teaspoon) lemon juice	1 teaspoon lemon juice
10ml(2 teaspoons) Worcestershire sauce	2 teaspoons Worcestershire sauce
4 small egg yolks	4 egg yolks
salt	salt
freshly-ground black pepper	freshly-ground black pepper

1. The best way to prepare the raw steak and break down meat fibres is either to put the steak through a food processor, or to scrape the meat against the grain with the blade of a knife. If you have no food processor and do not have enough time to reduce the meat by hand, put it through a mincer (grinder). This will, however, cause the meat juices to run.

2. Chop the onion very finely indeed. Drain the capers well and chop them finely. Put both these ingredients into a mixing bowl together with the prepared meat. Add the olive oil, lemon juice, Worcestershire sauce, parsley, a good seasoning of salt and some pepper. Mix together very thoroughly.

3. Divide the mixture into four. Shape each portion into a disc (patty) and make a small hollow in the centre. Put an egg yolk (preferably in half an egg shell) into each hollow. Each person can stir the egg into the steak at table. Garnish with salads.

Serves 4

POULTRY
&
GAME

Duck Bigarade

Bigarade is the French name for Seville or bitter oranges. Their sharp flavour makes this classic and very piquant sauce served with crisply-roasted duck. Sweet oranges, peeled, sliced and mixed with sprigs of watercress make an excellent side salad to accompany the dish.

Metric/Imperial	American
2-2.3kg(4½-5lb) duck, drawn weight	4½-5lb duck, dressed weight
3 Seville oranges	3 tart oranges
50ml(2fl oz) port	4 tablespoons port wine
45ml(3 tablespoons) granulated sugar	3 tablespoons sugar
22ml(1 heaped tablespoon) butter	1 rounded tablespoon butter
22ml(1 heaped tablespoon) plain flour	1 heaped tablespoon all-purpose flour
1 onion	1 onion
1 carrot	1 carrot
1 celery stalk	1 stalk celery
1 bouquet garni	1 bouquet garni
salt and freshly-ground black pepper	salt and freshly-ground black pepper

1. First make a really good stock with the duck giblets. Cook them with the sliced onion, carrot, celery, bouquet garni, a few peppercorns and water in a covered pan for 2-3 hours. Strain, degrease and reduce to 425ml (¾pt) or 2 cups by fast boiling. Season to taste.

2. About 3 hours before serving, heat the oven to 220°C (425°F) gas mark 7. Wipe the duck both inside and out with a damp cloth. Remove and discard the lumps of fat just inside the bird at the tail end. Do not truss the bird as this inhibits even cooking of the leg meat. Prick the bird all over and quite deeply with a skewer or a sharp-pronged fork: this is to enable the fat to run out during roasting, so the finished dish will be crisp and juicy but not greasy. Rub the duck skin generously with salt and pepper and lay the bird on its back on a rack in a roasting pan. A rack is very important to prevent the duck sitting in the fat it exudes during cooking.

3. Roast the bird for 20 minutes. Then reduce the temperature to 200°C (400°F) gas mark 6 and complete roasting, allowing a total of 25-30 minutes per 450g (1lb) for really crisp results. Do not baste the bird at all during roasting, but pour off the fat that collects in the base of the pan every half hour or so.

4. To make the sauce, first measure the port and sugar into a small saucepan. Cook until the sugar dissolves and the mixture becomes a rich mahogany-coloured syrup. Pour on a little of the duck stock and stir until the caramel is dissolved. Then blend in the rest of the duck stock. In a separate, larger pan, make a brown roux with the flour and butter: melt the butter, stir in the flour away from the heat, then cook the mixture until nut brown. Away from the heat, blend in the hot port-flavoured duck stock. Return the pan to the heat, bring to boiling point stirring continuously, then leave the sauce to simmer uncovered for about 10 minutes.

5. Meanwhile thinly pare the rinds from the oranges and cut into narrow shreds or julienne strips. Blanch them for 5 minutes in fast boiling water. Drain, refresh under cold running water, drain again and reserve. Squeeze the orange juice and add it to the pan of gently-simmering sauce. Continue simmering, stirring occasionally, until the sauce is reduced to a good consistency and has rich savoury flavour. Season to taste with salt and pepper, add the blanched strips of rind and, when they are heated through, pour the sauce into a hot sauceboat, cover and keep warm.

6. When roasting time is up, check that the bird is thoroughly cooked by piercing the thickest part of the thigh meat with a skewer: the juices should run clear. If the meat needs a little more cooking, or if the skin is not crisp enough, increase oven temperature to 220°C (425°F) gas mark 7 and roast for 10 minutes or so more before checking again.

7. Divide the roast duck into four portions (as described for chicken, *page 91, step 5*) and serve.

Serves 4

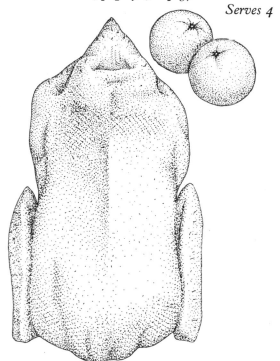

Chicken Kieu

Chicken Kiev, the most famous of all Russian dishes, is beloved of restauranteurs throughout the world. Regrettably, they usually serve a mockery of the real thing: made with tasteless, frozen chicken, overpowering quantities of garlic and faintly rancid butter, coated with some sort of orange grit that masquerades under the name of breadcrumbs and greasily fried in poor quality oil. A true chicken Kiev is made with top-quality, fresh ingredients and the butter contains no garlic, just a delicate flavouring of herbs. It is a lovely dish, and far less difficult to make than most people imagine.

Metric/Imperial	American
the breasts of 2 × 1.3-1.6kg(3-3½lb) roasting chickens with wing bones attached	*the breasts of 2 small roasting chickens, with wings attached*
100g(¼lb) butter, at room temperature	*¼ cup butter, at room temperature*
7.5ml(1½ teaspoons) lemon juice	*1½ teaspoons lemon juice*
10ml(2 teaspoons) fresh chopped tarragon	*2 teaspoons fresh chopped tarragon*
10ml(2 teaspoons) fresh chopped parsley	*2 teaspoons fresh chopped parsley*
5ml(1 teaspoon) fresh chopped chives	*1 teaspoon fresh chopped chives*
salt and freshly-ground black pepper	*salt and freshly-ground black pepper*
plain flour	*all-purpose flour*
2 small eggs, lightly beaten	*2 small eggs, lightly beaten*
about 175g(6oz) fresh white breadcrumbs	*2-3 cups fresh white bread crumbs*

1. To allow plenty of time for chilling, start making the herb butter and preparing and stuffing the chicken breasts a minimum of 3 hours before cooking. First make the herb butter. Beat the butter in a bowl until creamy and very soft. Beat in the lemon juice, fresh herbs and a good seasoning of salt and pepper. Wet a sheet of greaseproof or waxed paper under cold running water and rinse your hands too. Using damp hands shape the flavoured butter into a block, wrap it in the wet paper and chill until solid.

2. Meanwhile prepare the chicken breasts. To do this first lay one bird in front of you. Pull the legs away from the body and cut them off. Using a small sharp knife, cut down the length of the breast, from the tail to the neck. Completely peel back the breast skin on each side of the bird and gently ease out the wish bone. Insert the knife between the flesh and one side of breast bone and, keeping the knife as close to the bone as possible, cut the meat free, gradually working the knife over the rib cage down to the point where the wing joins the body. Cut through the wing joint, so that the wing is attached to the breast meat. Then cut off the wing pinion leaving only the main wing bone attached to the breast meat. Scrape the meat back from the bone so it is clean: after cooking it can be decorated with a paper frill – this looks pretty and will prevent diners' fingers from getting greasy.

3. When all four portions of breast have been removed from the birds, separate the thin fillet of breast meat from each portion. Lay the thin fillets and the main portions between sheets of greaseproof or waxed paper or plastic film and carefully beat flat with a rolling pin. Cut the chilled herb butter into 4 sticks. Lay one along the middle of each main portion, cover with a thin fillet then fold the breast meat over to make a neat, elongated parcel. Dust each parcel with well-seasoned flour, dip in beaten egg to which 15ml (1 tablespoon) water has been added, then coat generously with the breadcrumbs. Lay the prepared chicken portions close to each other, but not touching, on a plate. Cover loosely and chill for a minimum of 2 hours so that the egg and breadcrumb coating sets and seals each parcel very securely.

4. Heat some good oil to 180-185°C (350-360°F) in a deep fat fryer and cook the chicken for 10-15 minutes depending on size. Cook two pieces at a time so they do not touch each other during frying, lower them carefully into the pan and reduce heat if browning too fast. Drain well on paper towels, decorate with paper frills and serve very hot. Each person lifts a portion of chicken from serving dish to dinner plate in the fingers, holding the paper-frilled bone. Do not use a spoon and fork: this risks piercing the meat and releasing a spurt of savoury melted butter.

Serves 4

Raised game pie

Raised pies are so called because the hot-water crust used to make them is raised or moulded by hand across the base and up the sides of the tin in which the pie is baked, then unmoulded for serving. Part of their appeal for me is that they are both homely and elegant, suitable for serving in the fields at harvest time, at home in a scrubbed pine country kitchen or at a chic buffet party. The pastry is crisp and rich but not too crumbly. The filling is beautifully flavoured: slivers of lean game mixed with a good portion of pork fat, aromatic spices and a moistening layer of jellied stock. Pigeon is the traditional farmer's choice of game – but other game birds can be used. Baked in a cake tin (pan) and decorated in the simplest fashion, a raised game pie makes a popular country food: thick slices of it, eaten with crisp lettuce and raw tomatoes, make a substantial and sensibly portable lunch. Baked in an elegantly-fluted mould, raised game pie looks as handsome as it tastes delicious – an impressive centrepiece for the cold supper table.

Metric/Imperial	American
For the hot-water crust pastry:	**For the hot-water crust pastry:**
450g(1lb) plain flour	*4 cups all-purpose flour*
5ml(1 teaspoon) salt	*1 teaspoon salt*
75g(3oz) lard	*6 tablespoons lard*
25g(1oz) dripping or butter	*2 tablespoons dripping or butter*
2 medium-sized eggs	*2 medium-sized eggs*
For the filling:	**For the filling:**
450-500g(1lb-1lb 2oz) skinned and boned	*the meat from 2 pheasants or 5 wild duck, grouse,*
pigeon meat (from 5-6 birds)	*quail or partridge*
275g(10oz) lean ham	*10oz lean ham*
350g(¾lb) hard pork back fat	*¾lb pork back fat, unsalted*
25g(1 oz) canned anchovy fillets	*½ × 2oz can anchovy fillets*
30ml(2 tablespoons) sherry	*2 tablespoons sherry*
2.5ml(½ teaspoon) crushed coriander seeds	*½ teaspoon freshly-crushed coriander seeds*
2.5ml(½ teaspoon) freshly-grated nutmeg	*½ teaspoon freshly-grated nutmeg*
2.5ml(½ teaspoon) ground cinnamon	*½ teaspoon ground cinnamon*
1·5ml(¼ teaspoon) ground cloves	*¼ teaspoon ground cloves*
salt and freshly-ground black pepper	*salt and freshly-ground black pepper*
For the stock:	**For the stock:**
the carcasses of the pigeons used for the filling	*the carcasses of the birds used for meat*
2 pig's trotters, split	*2 pig's feet, split*
1 onion studded with 2-3 cloves	*1 onion studded with 2-3 cloves*
1 carrot	*1 carrot*
2 celery stalks	*2 stalks celery*
12 black peppercorns	*1 dozen black peppercorns*
a large bouquet garni of fresh herbs	*1 large bouquet garni of fresh herbs*
a glass of dry white wine	*a glass of dry white wine*

1. This rich and delicious cold pie can be made in either a cake tin (pan) or in a pie mould. A traditional hinged and fluted pie mould undoubtedly helps to produce professional-looking results but a cake tin (pan) with removable base and, preferably, spring-clip (spring-form) sides is just as satisfactory. Choose a tin (pan) 14-16cm (6-6½in) across and 9-10cm (3½-4in) deep. A removable base and spring-clip sides make it easier to unmould the pie. Once unmoulded, the sides of the pie can be decorated with strips of leftover pastry if you like. The resulting pie will look just as handsome as one made in a traditional fluted mould (shown overleaf on *page 86*).

2. To obtain sufficient meat for the pie filling, you will need 5-6 pigeons (or other small game birds), depending on size. Most of the meat on a pigeon lies in its breast. With the scraps from the thighs plus the bird's liver an average pigeon gives 75-100g (3-4oz) meat. To remove the breast of a game bird, pull back the breast skin, make a cut along the length of the breast bone then, working the knife close to the bone, gradually ease the breast meat free and remove it from the carcass. Reserve the breast meat, together with scraps of meat cut away from the thighs and the livers. Cover loosely and refrigerate until required.

3. The jellied stock can be simmered while the pie bakes, but is best prepared a day ahead, as careful degreasing is easiest when it is cold. Put the bird carcasses and skin into a stock pot. Add the rest of the stock ingredients: cover with plenty of water. Bring to boiling point, skim, then three-quarter

cover the pan and simmer gently for 3-4 hours to extract maximum flavour from the birds and plenty of gelatin from the pig's trotters (feet). Strain, reduce to about 425ml (¾pt) or about 2 cups by fast boiling, then season generously with salt. Cool then chill. Once cold, the surface fat can easily be scraped off, and the stock should be set to a firm jelly.

4. To make the pie filling, mince (grind) the ham, pork back fat and bird livers finely. Cut the reserved breast and thigh meat into tiny slivers (large chunks would make the pie difficult to slice). Chop the anchovy fillets and put them into a mixing bowl. Add the prepared meat, the sherry and spices. Season with a generous grind of pepper and some salt – just a little salt at first because of the salt in the ham and the anchovies. Fry a small ball of the mixture to check flavour (bearing in mind that the pie will be served cold, and chilling tends to mute flavours slightly). Adjust seasoning to taste. Set the filling aside while you prepare the pastry.

5. Hot-water crust is exceptionally easy to make. Liquid and fat are simply brought to the boil then quickly stirred into the dry ingredients. Flour, salt, lard and water are traditional for hot-water crust, but I find that both flavour and texture are improved if part of the lard is replaced with good meat dripping(s) or butter and part of the water with egg yolk.

6. Break one of the egg yolks into a large mixing bowl. Cover it with the sifted flour and salt. Put the chopped lard and dripping(s) or butter into a small saucepan. Add 175ml (6floz) or ¾ cup cold water to the pan. Heat gently until the fats are melted, then bring to a rolling boil. Immediately pour the mixture into the mixing bowl, stirring it in with a wooden spoon. When the dough forms a ball, leaving the sides of the bowl clean, turn it out and knead lightly for 1-2 minutes until smooth. Cover the ball of dough with the upturned mixing bowl and leave it for 15 minutes. Exact timing is important here for care, rather than skill, is necessary to mould hot-water crust successfully. The dough should be just warm enough to be beautifully malleable.

7. While the dough rests, lightly but thoroughly grease the pie mould or cake tin (pan), and place it on a baking tray (sheet). Preheat oven to 220°C (425°F) gas mark 7. Break the remaining whole egg into a cup and beat it lightly, ready to glaze the pie. Assemble a pastry brush, sharp-bladed, small knife and a rolling pin. Roll up a small piece of stiff white card to make a funnel, which can be inserted into the pie to allow steam to escape during baking.

8. When the dough is ready, cut off three-quarters of it and leave the small piece under the upturned bowl to keep warm. Put the large piece into the mould or cake tin (pan). Use your hands to shape it over the base, then work it gradually up the sides of the mould and extend it nearly 1.2cm (½in) above the rim of the mould. Try to work fairly quickly, pressing lightly but firmly, and be sure to make the pastry lining as smooth and even as possible. The slightest crack will allow precious meat juices to leak out during cooking; a thin patch of wall may collapse when the pie is unmoulded. As an added precaution against seepage, brush the pastry lining all over with the leftover egg white.

9. Spoon the filling into the pie, packing it well into the corners and moulding it nicely in the middle. Roll out the remaining pastry to make a lid. Place it on top of the pie, seal well and trim generously. Then gently ease the sealed pastry edges slightly inwards and upwards to make a rim that stands above the mould. This is important because, if the pastry is sealed against the mould, it may stick as it bakes and subsequently tear during unmoulding. Make a large steam hole in the centre of the lid: hold it open by half-inserting the rolled cardboard. Add any leftover egg white to the whole beaten egg and use to glaze the top of the pie. Decorate with pastry trimmings and glaze again. If you are using a cake tin (spring-form pan), reserve some of the decorations to stick to the sides of the pie after unmoulding if you prefer.

10. Bake the pie for 20 minutes, then reduce temperature to 180°C (350°F) gas mark 4 and bake for a further 1¾ hours, reglazing the top of the pie at regular intervals. The pie crust should now be set. Very carefully ease the sides of the mould away from the pie. Glaze the sides of the pie with beaten egg, adding pastry decorations if you like. Cover the top of the pie with greaseproof or waxed paper if already sufficiently browned. Return the pie to the oven, reduce temperature to 160°C (325°F) gas mark 3, and bake for 30 minutes more.

11. Meanwhile set the jellied stock over very low heat to melt, then set aside: it should be cool but not set when added to the pie. This will fill up any gaps in the pie caused by meat shrinkage. It adds flavour and texture and, when set, makes the pie easier to slice. Insert a small funnel into the rolled cardboard in the pie top and spoon in, slowly and carefully, as much of the stock as the pie will absorb without flooding the top. Using a fish slice (pancake turner) and a metal spatula, carefully transfer the pie to a serving dish. Put it into a cold place but do not cover the pie until it is completely cold – this takes about 4 hours – or condensation will spoil the pastry. Serve the pie next day with accompanying salads. *Serves 8-10*

Paella Valenciana

Paella is synonymous with Spanish cookery for most people who have visited Spain, and tourists are usually treated to extravagant versions which include lobster. Far simpler paellas are more commonplace and some include no fish or meat at all. Paella Valenciana is the name usually given to a paella that contains both meat and fish. The choice of ingredients can be varied to suit your taste and purse, and this is part of the charm of the dish.

Metric/Imperial	American
900g(2lb) chicken drumsticks	2lb chicken drumsticks
700g(1½lb) large boiled prawns in their shells	1½lb large shrimp, in their shells
700g(1½lb) squid	1½lb squid
2.3L(2 quarts) mussels	2-3qt mussels
225g(½lb) chorizo sausage	½lb chorizo or highly-seasoned sausage
700g(1½lb) long-grain rice	3¼ cups long-grain rice
450g(1lb) red peppers, seeded and cut into strips	1lb red peppers, seeded and cut into strips
1 Spanish onion, finely chopped	1 Bermuda or sweet onion, finely diced
2 large garlic cloves, crushed	2 large cloves garlic, crushed
2 generous pinches of saffron strands	2 generous pinches saffron
120ml(8 tablespoons) olive oil	8 tablespoons olive oil
well-flavoured chicken stock	well-flavoured chicken stock or broth
a handful of small black olives	a handful of small black olives
3 lemons, cut into quarters	3 lemons, quartered
salt and freshly-ground black pepper	salt and freshly-ground black pepper

1. To prepare the squid, first pull the head part and tentacles away from the body or bag. Remove from inside the body the hard transparent 'pen' (so called because it is shaped like an old-fashioned quill pen). Peel away the purplish-red membrane which covers the body. Wash the squid very thoroughly inside and out under cold running water. Chop the tentacles from the head and discard the head. If the squid are really small, leave the tentacles as they are and keep the body as it is. Otherwise cut the body into rings and the tentacles into short lengths.

2. Pound the saffron strands in a mortar with a pestle. Prepare the mussels and open them as described on *page 3, steps 1-4* but use a small glass of water in place of the wine. Discard any that do not open, reserve the rest. Strain the hot mussel liquid through a cheesecloth-lined strainer to extract grit. Pour it onto the pounded saffron and leave to soak. Slice the sausage. Reserve a few whole prawns (shrimp) for garnish, peel the rest.

3. A paella pan is traditional but you can use a wok, a really large frying-pan or a wide flameproof casserole instead. Starting just under an hour before the meal, measure the olive oil into it, add the prepared squid and place over fairly high heat. Starting to cook with cold oil helps to tenderize squid. Fry for 8-10 minutes, stirring the pieces.

Remove the squid with a slotted spoon and reserve. Add the chicken pieces to the pan and fry for 10 minutes until the skins are a rich brown all over.

4. Reduce heat. Add the onion, garlic and peppers to the pan. Cook gently, stirring occasionally for 7-8 minutes until the vegetables are slightly softened. Meanwhile, in a separate pan bring to boiling the mussel-flavoured saffron liquid plus as much well-flavoured chicken stock as is necessary to make a total of 1.7L (3pt) or about 8 cups. Pour the rice into the paella pan and cook, stirring, for 2-3 minutes. Pour on the boiling liquid, add a good seasoning of salt and pepper. Stir in the squid, prawns (shrimp) and sausage. Cover the pan with a double thickness of foil. Reduce heat as low as possible and cook gently for 15 minutes until most of the liquid is absorbed. Then lay the mussels and olives on top of the rice mixture. Cover again and continue cooking very gently for a further 5 minutes: the mussels and olives will be heated by the steam rising from the dish. Then uncover the pan. Stir the mussels and olives into the paella. If some liquid still remains in the pan, increase the heat slightly and cook a few minutes longer until it evaporates. Arrange the reserved prawns (shrimp) and wedges of lemon on top. Paella is best served as soon as cooked, but it can be kept warm in a low oven for about half an hour.

Serves 8-10

Tandoori chicken

This Indian method of cooking chicken produces succulent meat that is delicately impregnated with delicious aromatics, sealed under a surface crust of well-flavoured paste. For authenticity, the chicken should of course be cooked in a traditional tandoori clay oven. But very respectable results can be achieved using a modern gas or electric oven. This is one of the very best and easiest ways I know of making mass-produced chicken taste really good.

Metric/Imperial	American
1.6kg(3½lb) roasting chicken, drawn weight	*3½-4lb roasting chicken*
5ml(1 teaspoon) hot chilli powder	*1 tablespoon chili seasoning*
30ml(2 tablespoons) fresh lime or lemon juice	*2 tablespoons fresh lime or lemon juice*
10ml(2 teaspoons) cumin seeds	*2 teaspoons cumin seeds*
10ml(2 teaspoons) coriander seeds	*2 teaspoons coriander seeds*
15g(½oz) fresh ginger root	*1 tablespoon fresh root ginger, finely chopped*
3 garlic cloves	*3 garlic cloves*
2.5ml(½ teaspoon) paprika	*½ teaspoon paprika*
45ml(3 tablespoons) thickened yoghurt (pg 54, st 1)	*3 tablespoons thickened yoghurt (page 54, step 1)*
15ml(1 tablespoon) tomato purée	*1 tablespoon tomato purée*
1 fresh, skinned red pepper	*1 fresh, skinned red pepper*
OR 1 canned red pepper	*OR 1 canned red pepper*
2.5ml(½ teaspoon) red food colouring	*½ teaspoon red food coloring*
50g(2oz) ghee	*4 tablespoons ghee*
OR about 100g(¼lb) unsalted butter	*OR ½ cup unsalted butter*
2 lemons, quartered, to garnish	*2 lemons, in wedges, to garnish*
parsley or coriander leaves to garnish	*parsley sprigs to garnish*

1. Starting a day ahead, cut off the parson's nose (fat sac at the tail end), the scaly chicken legs and the meatless wing tips. Skin the chicken completely. This is easiest to do if you first make a cut in the loose neck skin then gently pull it free of the breast, over the legs and wings, and then away from the back. Prick the flesh deeply all over with a larding needle or skewer and make three deep slashes with a knife across each side of the breast, then slash the thigh meat in two or three places. This is to allow the aromatics to seep into and to flavour the meat really well. Sprinkle the chilli powder (chili seasoning) over the bird, pour on the citrus juice, then brush the mixture all over the bird and deep into the cuts. Set aside.

2. Warm the cumin and coriander seeds in a small pan over low heat for a few minutes to bring out their aromas. Pound the seeds with mortar and pestle and put them into a blender goblet. Peel and chop the ginger very finely, and crush the garlic. Add to the blender with the paprika, thickened yoghurt, tomato purée and red pepper, and reduce the mixture to a paste. Then stir in the red food colouring. Spread the paste all over the bird, again pushing the mixture deep into the slashes. Cover and refrigerate for 24 hours to flavour and tenderize the chicken very thoroughly.

3. Preheat the oven to 200 °C (400 °F) gas mark 6. Pour a little water into a roasting tin (pan), just enough to cover the base: this is to prevent the meat juices from burning during roasting. Put a rack in the roasting tin and stand the chicken on it. Spoon on any of the paste remaining in the marinade bowl.

4. Clarified butter is easily prepared at home, although ghee can be bought where there are Indian shops. Melt unsalted butter in a small pan over low heat, then strain through a cheesecloth-lined sieve to remove the impurities. Leave the milky sediment in the pan. It is these sediments that cause spluttering and burning in cooking. Drizzle the melted ghee or clarified butter over the bird. Roast for 1 hour basting occasionally. Then increase heat to 230 °C (450 °F) gas mark 8 and roast for a further 5-10 minutes to crisp the crust.

5. To divide the chicken into four portions, first cut the bird in half lengthways, along the breast and backbone. A sharp knife can be used or, easier still, poultry shears or good kitchen scissors. Then cut each half across in a diagonal line so that each portion includes some breast meat. Serve very hot, sprinkled with salt and chopped fresh coriander or parsley leaves and garnished with wedges of lemon.

Serves 4

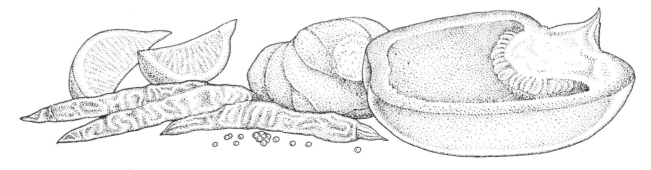

Traditional roast pheasant

Pheasants are the most strikingly handsome game birds: the cock bird has beautiful green head feathers and all the shades of autumn in his long sweeping tail. In days when a variety of roasted birds were served at the same meal, pheasant was decorated with its own tail feathers just before serving, so that the dish was immediately identifiable to the diners. Such decorations are rarely used today, but roast pheasant remains a special treat – providing the birds are young. Look for pale legs in the hen bird, short rounded spurs on the legs of the cock, and flight feathers that are rounded and downy underneath. A good bird will serve 3-4.

Metric/Imperial	American
a brace of young pheasant	*2 young pheasants, dressed*
a large handful of coarse fresh breadcrumbs	*a large handful coarse fresh bread crumbs*
about 50g(2oz) melted butter	*about 4 tablespoons melted butter*
4 rashers fat, unsmoked bacon	*4 thick slices bacon*
75g(3oz) unsalted butter	*6 tablespoons unsalted butter*
150ml(¼pt) dry red wine	*¾ cup dry red wine*
150ml(¼pt) good stock from the giblets	*¾ cup well-flavoured stock made from the giblets*
a little plain flour	*a little flour*
a squeeze of lemon juice	*a squeeze of lemon juice*
salt and freshly-ground black pepper	*salt and freshly-ground black pepper*

For the game chips:	For the game chips
700g(1½lb) potatoes	*1½lb potatoes*
oil for deep frying	*oil for deep frying*

1. First prepare the potatoes that will accompany the roast birds. Choose potatoes of even shape and size for minimum wastage. Peel them, cut off the rounded ends and shape so that each slice will be approximately the same in diameter. Cut the potatoes into paper-thin slices, using a mandolin if you have one. Soak the slices in plenty of cold water for 1 hour to remove starch, then drain and dry very thoroughly. Washing and drying the potatoes is essential: if starchy they will stick during frying, if wet they will cause dangerous spluttering when put into the hot oil.

2. About 1½ hours before serving the pheasants, preheat the oven to 220°C (425°F) gas mark 7. Rub the skins of the pheasants with salt and pepper. Season the body cavities too, and stuff them with the breadcrumbs well soaked in the melted butter. Lay the bacon rashers across the breasts and tie them securely. The bacon, like the buttered crumbs, is a precaution against the meat drying out.

3. When they are ready, melt unsalted butter in a roasting pan. When hot, add the pheasants and fry until nicely browned on all sides. Lay the pheasants on their backs and transfer the roasting pan to the oven. Roast the birds for a total of 45-60 minutes depending on size. Baste frequently with the buttery pan juices and pour the wine into the pan after 30 minutes. About 8 minutes before the end of roasting time, remove the bacon (cook's perk to eat it!). Baste the breasts, dredge lightly with flour and baste again so that the skin will brown. Check that the birds are properly cooked by piercing the thigh meat with a skewer: the juices should run clear.

4. Cook the game chips while the pheasants are roasting. Heat oil in a deep fat fryer to 198°C (395°F). Fry the potato chips in batches, pushing the slices gently round the frying-basket so that they remain separate. They will cook very quickly and are ready as soon as crisp and a rich golden colour. Drain on plenty of crumpled paper towels, pile onto a hot serving dish, sprinkle with salt and keep hot. Do not cover them or they may become soggy.

5. Transfer the roasted game birds to a hot serving dish and 'rest' in a warm place. Add the giblet stock to the pan juices and place the pan over direct heat. Cook, stirring and scraping the mixture until it bubbles up and reduces to a well-flavoured gravy. Season with salt and pepper, and sharpen with a squeeze of lemon juice if you like. Pour the gravy into a hot gravy boat. Garnish the pheasants with the game chips and some watercress, and serve.

Serves 6-8

Chicken saté

Indonesia (or the Dutch East Indies as it used to be called when part of the Dutch Empire) is situated off the continents of India and China, so it is not surprising to find that Indonesian cookery bears the influence of both Indian and Chinese cuisines. The spiciness of the former is fused with the delicacy of the latter to exquisite effect – and nowhere is this better illustrated than in chicken saté, which might well be called the national dish of Java.

Metric/Imperial	American
900g(2lb) chicken breasts	*2lb chicken breast meat*
30ml(2 tablespoons) black treacle	*2 tablespoons blackstrap molasses*
30ml(2 tablespoons) peanut oil	*2 tablespoons peanut oil*
30ml(2 tablespoons) fresh lime or lemon juice	*2 tablespoons fresh lime or lemon juice*

For the peanut sauce:	**For the peanut sauce:**
65g(2½oz) peeled onion	*2-3 tablespoons finely chopped onion*
2 garlic cloves	*2 cloves garlic*
22ml(1½ tablespoons) peanut oil	*1½ tablespoons peanut oil*
3ml(¾ teaspoon) chilli powder	*¾ teaspoon chilli powder*
22ml(1½ tablespoons) black treacle	*1½ tablespoons blackstrap molasses*
22ml(1½ tablespoons) fresh lime or lemon juice	*1½ tablespoons fresh lime or lemon juice*
22ml(1½ tablespoons) soy sauce	*1½ tablespoons soy sauce*
90ml(6 tablespoons) peanut butter	*6 tablespoons peanut butter*
salt	*salt*

1. Chicken sate is best served alone as a first course I think – miniature kebabs suspended across a tiny bowl of sauce for each person look very inviting and taste very appetizing. Chicken saté can also be served with fried bananas and boiled rice as a main dish, and it is sometimes served as part of a Rijstafel (a feast which consists of some 40 dishes – admirably executed by Indonesian restaurants, but not really practical for preparing in a domestic kitchen).

2. Starting about $4\frac{1}{2}$ hours before serving, warm the treacle (molasses) to make it runny by standing the container in a pan of hot water. Carefully skin and bone the chicken breasts. Separate the thin fillet of meat from the thick fillet. Place the thick fillets side by side between sheets of plastic film, greaseproof or waxed paper and beat lightly with a rolling pin to flatten them slightly. Cut all the chicken meat into narrow strips about 2.5×1.2cm ($1 \times \frac{1}{2}$in). Measure 30ml (2 tablespoons) each black treacle (molasses), lime or lemon juice and peanut oil into a mixing bowl. Stir vigorously to mix, then add the chicken and turn to coat all over with the mix-

ture. Cover and marinate in a cool place, but preferably not the refrigerator, for 4 hours.

3. Starting about 20 minutes before the meal, reduce the onions and garlic to a purée in a blender together with the oil. Put the mixture into a small pan and cook over low heat for 10 minutes or until softened but not coloured. Add the remaining sauce ingredients and as much water as is needed to make a thick sauce. Cook, stirring continuously, over medium heat until the sauce is hot, smooth and glossy. Set aside and keep hot.

4. Preheat the grill (broiler) until very hot. Slide the marinated strips of chicken onto small skewers, ribbon fashion, spreading out the strips so they are almost flat. Place on the rack of the grill (broiler) pan, pour on the marinade and cook for about 5 minutes, turning the kebabs as necessary, until tender and browned. Meanwhile quickly reheat the sauce, divide it between warmed individual bowls. Arrange the skewers across the bowls and serve immediately. *Serves 6-8 as a first course.*

French roast chicken

Roast chicken is like the little girl in the nursery rhyme who had a curl in the middle of her forehead: when it is good it is very, very good and when it is bad it is horrid! A plump, fresh chicken, roasted in the French manner, is a simple but very real pleasure: the skin is a crackle of gold, the flesh is juicily tender, and the exquisite smells wafting from the oven foretell of the treat to come. The trick of stuffing the breast cavity with seasoned butter, and roasting the bird breast downwards for the major part of cooking time is, I think, the key to success – as the butter melts it seeps into the lean breast meat keeping it beautifully succulent. Use plenty of butter and baste regularly.

Metric/Imperial	American
1.8kg(4lb) roasting chicken, drawn weight	4lb roasting chicken
125g(¼lb) unsalted butter	¼lb unsalted butter
a few sprigs of tarragon	a few sprigs of tarragon
salt and freshly-ground black pepper	salt and freshly-ground black pepper
a generous glass of red or white wine	a wineglass of red or white wine
1 carrot, chopped	1 carrot, chopped
half an onion, chopped	half an onion, chopped
1 celery stalk, chopped	1 stalk celery, chopped
watercress to garnish	watercress to garnish

1. About 2½ hours before you plan to eat the chicken, mash 25g (1oz) or 2 tablespoons of the butter until soft, flavouring it with a good seasoning of salt and freshly-ground black pepper. Wipe the chicken inside and out with a damp cloth. Remove the fat from inside the bird at the tail end. Put the tarragon into the body cavity, first crushing it lightly to bruise and release fragrance, and add the seasoned butter. Rub the chicken skin generously with salt and pepper, then smear it all over with 50g (2oz) or 4 tablespoons of softened butter, taking particular care to coat the thighs generously.

2. Preheat oven to 200°C (400°F) gas mark 6. Put the chicken giblets into a small saucepan together with the chopped vegetables. Add the glass of wine and 425ml (¾pt) or 2 cups water. Bring to boiling point, cover and simmer for 1¼ hours to make giblet stock for the gravy.

3. Put a rack in the roasting pan. Lay the chicken on one side of its breast on the rack. Put the pan into the oven and immediately reduce heat to 190°C (375°F) gas mark 5. Roast for 30 minutes, basting the bird with the buttery juices every 10 minutes. Turn the chicken onto the other side of its breast and roast for 30 minutes more, again basting regularly. Then increase oven temperature to 200°C (400°F) gas mark 6, lay the chicken on its back on the rack and roast for 20-25 minutes until the breast skin is golden and crisp. Spluttering sounds and delicious smells will indicate that the chicken is ready, but check that the meat is thoroughly cooked by piercing the thickest part of the thigh with a skewer: the juices should run clear and colourless. If the juices are still pink, reduce the oven heat slightly and cook the chicken a few minutes more.

4. Strain the giblet stock, reserving the chicken liver. Return the liquid to the pan and fast boil until reduced to 150ml (¼pt) or ⅔ cup. Season to taste with salt and pepper. Chop the chicken liver into small pieces.

5. Lift the roasted chicken out of the pan, tilting it so that the buttery juices in the body cavity run back into the pan. Lay it on a warmed serving dish and put in a warm place to 'rest' for 15 minutes or so before serving and carving. Meanwhile finish the gravy. Add the remaining butter to the roasting pan and place it on top of the stove over medium heat. Add the chopped chicken liver and the reduced stock. Cook, stirring occasionally, until the butter and wine-flavoured stock are well-blended, bubbling together and reduced slightly to make a small quantity of very savoury rich gravy. Pour into a warmed sauceboat or gravy bowl. Garnish the chicken with bunches of crisp watercress and serve. *Serves 4-6*

Venison pie

The flavour of venison is rich, gamey and sweet, characteristics which are heightened by the inclusion of prunes and port in this delicious and very English pie. Buttery puff pastry makes a lovely crisp topping, and the richness of the whole is sensibly contrasted by the old-fashioned forcemeat balls – tiny piquant mouthfuls of anchovy, lemon and parsley.

Metric/Imperial	American
700g(1½lb) stewing venison, boneless weight	1½lb boneless venison
puff pastry made with 175g(6oz) flour	puff pastry made with ¾ cup flour
OR 350g(12oz) packet of puff pastry	OR 1 package refrigerated dinner roll
12 pitted Californian prunes	12 large pitted prunes
125g(¼lb) smallish cap mushrooms	¼lb small mushrooms
1 large onion	1 large onion
150ml(¼pt) port	⅝ cup port wine
10ml(2 teaspoons) lemon juice	2 teaspoons lemon juice
225ml(8floz) beef stock	1 cup beef stock
25g(1oz) butter	2 teaspoons butter
30ml(2 tablespoons) oil	2 tablespoons oil
45ml(3 tablespoons) plain flour	3 tablespoons all-purpose flour
salt and freshly-ground black pepper	salt and freshly-ground black pepper

For the forcemeat balls:

Metric/Imperial	American
50g(1¾oz) can anchovy fillets	2oz can anchovy fillets
25g(1 oz) shredded suet	2 tablespoons suet, shredded
25g(1 oz) streaky bacon, finely minced	2 tablespoons bacon, finely minced
50g(2oz) fresh brown breadcrumbs	about 1 cup fresh wholewheat bread crumbs
45ml(3 tablespoons) fresh parsley	3 tablespoons fresh parsley
the zest of a large lemon	grated rind of 1 large lemon
1 medium-sized egg	1 medium-sized egg

1. Soak the prunes overnight in the port. Drain them next day, reserving fruit and liquor separately.

2. Prepare the pie filling ahead. Remove fat and gristle from the venison and cut the meat into 2.5-4cm (1-1½in) cubes. Heat the butter and oil in a flameproof (metal-based) casserole. Add the meat in batches and fry until well browned on all sides. Remove with a slotted spoon. Chop the onion finely; halve the mushrooms. Add them to the pot and cook until they colour. Remove the mushrooms and reserve them. Stir in the flour and, when well blended with the fat, pour on the prune liquor, stock and lemon juice. Bring the sauce to boiling point, stirring continuously. Return the meat to the pot, and add a good seasoning of salt and pepper. Reduce heat to very low, cover the casserole and simmer gently for 1½ hours.

3. Meanwhile prepare the forcemeat balls. Chop the anchovy fillets into tiny pieces. Mix them well with the minced bacon, suet, breadcrumbs, parsley, lemon zest (rind) and some ground pepper (but no salt in view of the bacon and anchovies) and most of the beaten, raw egg – but reserve a little for glazing the pastry. Divide the forcemeat into 12 pieces and roll each piece into a small ball.

4. When the initial cooking of the venison is completed, remove the casserole from the heat and turn the contents into a deep pie dish (pan) of 1.4L (2½pt) or 6-7 cups capacity, standing a pie funnel (or inverted demitasse cup) in the centre of the dish. Set the dish aside until the venison is cooled: if the venison is hot when the puff pastry lid is added the pastry will become soggy during cooking.

5. About 1¼ hours before serving, preheat the oven to 220°C (425°F) gas mark 7 and place a baking tray on the middle shelf. Check the venison sauce for seasoning and adjust if necessary. Bury the mushrooms, prunes and forcemeat balls here and there in the mixture. Roll out the pastry until it is 3cm (1¼in) larger all around than the top of the pie dish (pan). Cut off an outer 2.5cm (1in) strip from the pastry and press it onto the rim of the pie dish. Dampen the pastry strip. Lay the pastry lid on top of the pie. Press the pastry edges to seal them and cut away excess. Glaze with egg, decorate with pastry trimmings and glaze again. Stand the pie on the hot baking tray and bake for 25 minutes. Then reduce oven temperature to 160°C (325°F) gas mark 3, cover the pie with a piece of damp greaseproof or waxed paper to prevent the pastry from over browning; bake 30 minutes more. *Serves 4-6*

Terrine of duck

I always feel reassured when I have a good home-made terrine or pâté in store – they are so useful for picnic lunches and buffet parties as well as making a popular first course for dinner. This one includes juniper berries and orange to offset the sometimes over-rich flavour of duck, and it is a fine way to stretch one duck to feed eight people.

Metric/Imperial	American
2kg(4½lb) duck, drawn weight	4½lb duck
60ml(4 tablespoons) brandy	4 tablespoons brandy
225g(½lb) pork belly, boned and de-rinded weight	½lb boneless pork spare rib
225g(½lb) pig's liver	½lb pig's liver
1 small onion	1 small onion
1 orange	1 orange
8 juniper berries	8 juniper berries
25g(1 oz) pistachio nuts, shelled weight	2 tablespoons shelled pistachio nuts
2.5ml(½ teaspoon) dried lemon thyme	½ teaspoon dried lemon thyme
75g(3oz) fresh white breadcrumbs	about 1½ cups white bread crumbs
225g(½lb) pork back fat	½lb pork back fat, unsalted
salt and freshly-ground black pepper	salt and freshly-ground black pepper

1. Starting at least 4 days before you plan to eat the terrine, cut through the skin of the duck's breast and remove the breast meat. Discard skin and slice the breast meat into thin strips. Put into a small bowl, pour on the brandy and marinate for several hours.

2. Cut the remaining meat off the duck, again discarding skin and fat, and reserving the bones. Use all the bones and giblets (excluding the duck liver) to make a fine stock.

3. Mince (grind) the meat from the duck carcass together with the duck liver, pork meat, pig's liver and chopped onion. Put them in a bowl and add the juice and finely grated zest (rind) of the orange, the nuts, lemon thyme and a generous seasoning of salt and pepper. Crush the juniper berries between two spoons, chop into small pieces and stir into the meat, together with the breadcrumbs. When every-

thing is well blended, fry a small nugget of the mixture to check seasoning, and adjust to taste.

4. Preheat the oven to 180 °C (350 °F) gas mark 4. Cut the pork back fat into 6mm (¾in) slices and then into neat long strips. Lay strips of the fat in parallel lines diagonally across the base of a 1.4L (2½pt) terrine or pâté dish (6 cup mould). Repeat at an angle to make a lattice pattern, then press strips of fat up the sides of the dish.

5. Stir the duck breast meat and the marinade liquid into the rest of the ingredients; mix well. Pack the mixture into the prepared dish and top with a lattice of pork back fat. Cover the dish with greaseproof or waxed paper and foil, stand the dish in a roasting pan and add enough boiling water to come halfway up the sides of the dish. Cook for 2½-3 hours.

6. Fit a very thick piece of cardboard over the foil-covered terrine, press with weights on top and leave in a cold place overnight.

7. Reduce the duck stock to a few syrupy spoonfuls and allow to cool slightly. Uncover the terrine, scrape off excess fat and coat the meat with the syrupy glaze. Cover and mature for 3 days before eating (it will keep for 10 days in the refrigerator). Decorate with thin slices of unpeeled orange just before serving. *Serves 8*

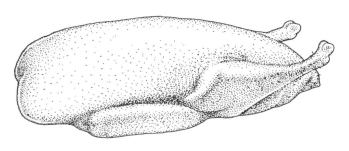

Poule-au-pot

When King Henry IV of France expressed the wish that every family in his realm might be rich enough to eat chicken every Sunday, he was apparently specifically referring to this dish – in which broth and main course are cooked in one pot. Made with a scraggy boiling fowl and hearty vegetables such as cabbage and turnips it makes a plain but nourishing dish. But made with a plump roasting chicken, accompanied by a lovely selection of young spring vegetables and a delicately flavoured sauce, it is certainly a dish to set before a king.

Metric/Imperial	American
2.3kg(5lb) roasting chicken, drawn weight	5lb roasting chicken
the thinly-pared rind of a lemon	the thinly pared rind of 1 lemon
1 large carrot	1 large carrot
2 celery stalks	2 stalks celery
1 large onion	1 large onion
a large bouquet garni	a large bouquet garni
4 coriander seeds	4 coriander seeds
4 black peppercorns	4 black peppercorns
salt and freshly-ground black pepper	salt and freshly-ground black pepper
25g(1 oz) unsalted butter	2 tablespoons unsalted butter

For the vegetable accompaniment:	For the vegetable accompaniments:
450g(1lb) small new potatoes	1lb whole baby white potatoes
450g(1lb) young leeks	1lb young leeks
225g(½lb) stringless French beans	½lb green beans, French-style
225g(½lb) mangetout peas	½lb snow peas
225g(½lb) broccoli	½lb broccoli
225g(½lb) whole baby carrots	½lb whole baby carrots

1. About 2 hours before serving, prepare the chicken. Remove the fat sac from inside the chicken at the tail end. Wipe the bird inside and out with a damp cloth. Put the lemon rind in the body cavity and add a good seasoning of salt and pepper. Rub the chicken skin all over with salt and pepper too.

2. Choose a heavy-bottomed pan which fits the bird snugly. Put butter into the pan over medium heat. When melted, add the chicken and fry briefly, turning as necessary, until the skin is pale gold on all sides. Lift the chicken out of the pan and put the chopped vegetables and chicken giblets into it. Replace the chicken, laying it breast upwards on top of the vegetables. Add the coriander, peppercorns and bouquet garni. Pour on enough hot water to cover the chicken thighs completely. Bring to boiling quickly, then reduce heat, cover the pan with a tight-fitting lid and leave to simmer gently for 1 hour 40 minutes. The tender breast of a roasting chicken will cook in the rising steam, while the tougher leg and wing meat are tenderized in the simmering liquid.

3. Meanwhile prepare the accompanying vegetables. Scrub but do not peel the young potatoes and carrots and leave them whole. Trim and thoroughly wash the slim young leeks, again leaving them whole. Trim the broccoli, beans and pea pods.

4. About half an hour before the chicken is ready, start cooking the vegetables. Steaming is preferable to boiling as it retains flavour, texture and vitamins better. Several types of vegetable can be cooked together: add those that take longest first, then the quicker cooking varieties and finally the pea pods.

5. Transfer the cooked chicken to a hot serving dish, tilting as you lift it from the pan so that the liquid inside drains back into the pan. Let the bird rest for 10 minutes or so before carving and serving. Meanwhile finish cooking the accompanying vegetables and arrange them in colourful groups, like the spokes of a wheel, on a large warmed serving dish. Moisten with a little cooking liquid (save the rest for soup). Serve accompanied by a large bowl of Hollandaise sauce (*page 143, steps 3-5*). *Serves 6-8*

Chicken galantine

hen I want a splendid showpiece for a buffet supper, but my housekeeping budget is sadly depleted, I usually turn to this recipe – a boneless chicken, stuffed then set in its own jelly. It is fine tasting, very handsome looking, yet remarkably inexpensive. It is true that boning a chicken is a fiddly job but it is not as complicated in practice as it appears on paper. The important things are to arm yourself with a very sharp knife (a small one is easiest) and to allow yourself plenty of time.

Metric/Imperial	American
1.35kg(3lb) roasting chicken, drawn weight	*4lb roasting chicken*
900g(2lb) knuckle of veal, chopped	*2lb veal knuckle, chopped*
2 Spanish onions, each studded with 2 cloves	*2 Bermuda onions, each studded with 2 cloves*
2 large carrots, chopped	*2 carrots, chopped*
1 leek, trimmed and sliced	*1 leek, trimmed and sliced*
2 celery stalks with leaves, sliced	*2 celery stalks (with leaves), sliced*
a glass of dry white wine	*1 glass of dry white wine*
a large bouquet garni	*1 large bouquet garni*
12 black peppercorns	*12 black peppercorns*
175g(6oz) pie veal	*about ¼lb ground veal*
175g(6oz) ham	*about ¼lb ham*
50g(2oz) fresh breadcrumbs	*1 cup fresh bread crumbs*
20ml(1 heaped tablespoon) fresh tarragon	*1 heaped tablespoon fresh tarragon*
OR 10ml(2 teaspoons) dried tarragon	*OR 2 teaspoons dried tarragon*
10ml(2 teaspoons) coriander seeds	*2 teaspoons coriander seeds*
5ml(1 teaspoon) fresh chopped lemon thyme	*1 teaspoon fresh chopped lemon thyme*
OR 2.5ml(½ teaspoon) dried lemon thyme	*OR ½ teaspoon dried thyme*
a pinch of ground cloves	*a pinch of ground cloves*
the grated zest of a small lemon	*the grated rind of a small lemon*
125ml(¼pt) dry sherry or brandy	*½ cup dry sherry or brandy*
salt and freshly-ground black pepper	*salt and freshly-ground black pepper*
1 large egg, separated	*1 large egg, separated*
15-25g(½-1oz) gelatine powder (optional)	*½-1oz gelatin (optional)*
olives, cucumber peel, lemon zest	*olives, cucumber peel, lemon rind*
AND/OR fresh tarragon leaves to garnish	*AND/OR fresh tarragon leaves to garnish*

1. Starting at least a day ahead, remove the giblets from the chicken. Wipe the bird inside and out with a damp cloth. Cut off the wings at the second joint and the legs at the first joint. Lay the chicken on its breast and cut through the skin along the length of the backbone with a small sharp knife. This is the only point at which the skin should be cut. From now on the aim is to remove all the bones without once cutting or piercing the skin at all. Holding the knife flat against the backbone, gradually work the blade down the carcass freeing the flesh and skin from the bones on both sides of the bird.

2. When you reach the legs, sever the joints which attach the thigh bones to the carcass. Holding the drumstick with one hand, use the knife to work the leg flesh away from the bone, then remove the bone completely. Loosen the flesh up the wing bones towards the body. Sever the wing bones at the point where they join the carcass and remove them. Ease the flesh gently away from the rib bones until the carcass is completely freed, then lift it out. Cut off the fatty tail end and turn the legs and wings inside out, pushing them into the body. Cover the chicken loosely and refrigerate it.

3. Make the stock. Wash the veal thoroughly under cold running water. Blanch it by placing it in a large pan of cold water, bring slowly to boiling point, then drain and rinse again thoroughly. Return the veal bones to the cleaned-out pan. Add the chicken carcass and giblets, the onions, carrots, leek, celery, wine and enough cold water to cover generously. Bring slowly to the boil. Skim off scum, add the bouquet garni and peppercorns. Reduce heat to very low, half-cover the pan and simmer gently for 2½-3 hours. Then strain the liquid through a cheese-cloth lined strainer, season with a little salt and cool. When cold, scrape off surface fat.

4. To make the forcemeat, first put the veal and ham through a food processor or the fine blade of a mincer (grinder). Put them into a bowl with the breadcrumbs, tarragon, coriander, thyme, 45ml

(3 tablespoons) sherry, lemon zest (rind) and ground cloves. Season well with salt and pepper. Add the egg yolk and beat until smooth and well blended. Roll a tiny piece of the mixture into a ball, fry it, then check seasoning and adjust accordingly.

5. Lay the boned chicken skin-side down and season the meat generously with freshly ground coriander, pepper and salt. Mound the forcemeat down the middle of the bird. Fold the ends of the bird over the stuffing, then the sides, to make a neat bird-shaped parcel completely enclosing the forcemeat. Sew the joins securely with a trussing needle and strong cotton thread or fine string. Wrap the bird in a double layer of cheesecloth and tie firmly with string at each end.

6. Choose a heavy-bottomed pan into which the chicken will fit snugly; it should be deep enough to cover the chicken completely in stock but not too wide. Put the bird into the pan. Pour on all but 45 ml (3 tablespoons) of the remaining sherry and enough stock to cover the chicken. Bring quickly to boiling point, reduce heat to a gentle simmer, cover with a well-fitting lid and poach for 1½ hours. Lift the cooked chicken out of the pan, drain it well and place on a large plate. As soon as it is cool enough to handle, tighten and adjust the cloth wrappings. Put another plate on top of the bird and weight it. Set aside until the bird is cold, then refrigerate. Strain the stock through cheesecloth, cool it quickly then chill it.

7. Scrape the surface fat off the chilled stock and check whether the liquid has set to a firm jelly, then measure and taste the stock. Reduce by fast boiling and add extra seasoning if necessary; about 700ml (1¼pt) or 3 cups of well-flavoured jellied stock will be needed for the aspic. If the stock is insufficiently jelled, it will have to be boosted with gelatine powder after clarifying.

8. To clarify the stock, put it into a pan. Add the remaining 45 ml (3 tablespoons) sherry, the egg white and crushed egg shell. Place over low heat. Whisk continuously until the mixture approaches simmering point, when a white foamy scum will rise to the surface. Stop whisking, allow the mixture to reach boiling point, immediately switch off heat

but leave the pan where it is for 10 minutes. Specks and impurities in the liquid will be drawn up, attracted like moths to a candle, into the foam. Gently slide the contents of the pan into a strainer lined with damp cheesecloth over a bowl. The liquid should now be a sparkling aspic but, if its setting quality was poor when last tested, blend in 15g (½oz) gelatine powder or more dissolved in a spoonful or two of the liquid. Place the bowl of aspic over a bowl of ice cubes to cool it quickly.

9. Meanwhile remove the chicken wrappings and carefully pull out the stitches. Lay the bird on a rack, breast up, on a baking tray, and prepare the decorations. Stoned (pitted) and halved black olives, tarragon leaves, strips of cucumber peel and lemon rind are traditional ingredients: simple designs look best. When the aspic is cold and has the syrupy consistency of raw egg whites, spoon a little of it along the top of the bird and let it trickle down to coat the sides. When the bird is completely covered with a thin even layer of aspic, arrange the decorations on top and refrigerate until set. Carefully spoon a second coat of aspic over the bird and chill again. Pour any leftover aspic into a shallow dish and chill until firmly set.

10. Transfer the galantine to a serving dish. Turn the dish of aspic out onto a sheet of wet greaseproof or waxed paper and chop it with the full length of a knife blade dipped in cold water. Arrange the chopped golden jelly around the galantine. Serve with salads. *Serves 6-8*

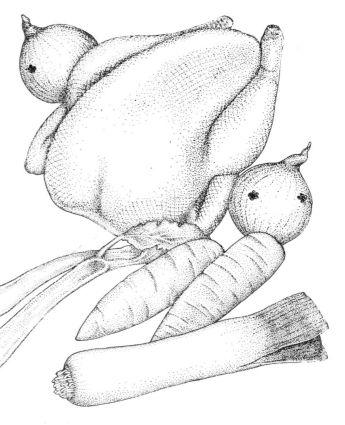

FISH
&
SHELLFISH

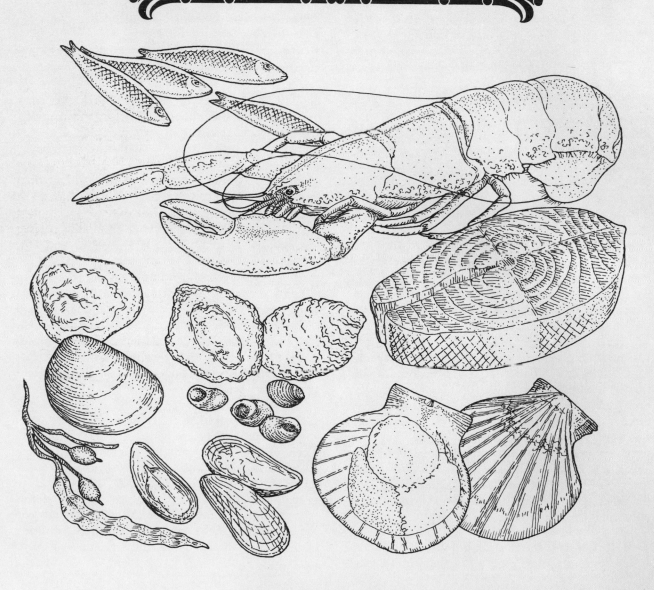

Coquilles St Jacques

Fresh scallops have exquisite flavour and beautifully plump flesh that is both tender and firm. Frozen scallops are only pale imitations, often tough, nearly always watery, and not really worth using for a dish such as this, which makes a deliciously-appetizing first course. I serve it in deep curved scallop shells. Mushrooms make fine companions for scallops and are included in many scallop recipes. Here the mushrooms are chopped and mixed with garlic and parsley to make an old-fashioned 'fines herbes' beloved of the French. It is a delicious mixture and particularly good with fried scallops.

Metric/Imperial	American
10 large, fresh scallops	*10 large scallops*
115g(¼lb) mushrooms	*¼lb mushrooms*
90ml(6 tablespoons) fresh chopped parsley	*6 tablespoons fresh chopped parsley*
15ml(1 tablespoon) fresh chopped chives	*1 tablespoon fresh chopped chives*
1 garlic clove	*1 clove garlic*
half a lemon	*half a lemon*
salt and freshly-ground black pepper	*salt and freshly-ground black pepper*
65g(2½oz) unsalted butter	*5 tablespoons unsalted butter*
75g(3oz) fresh white breadcrumbs	*2 cups fresh white bread crumbs*
clarified butter (page 62, step 3)	*clarified butter* (page 62, step 3)

1. Carefully remove the scallops from their shells. Gently pull away and discard the black intestinal thread. Wash the scallops to remove any traces of sand or grit, and pat them dry. Carefully and gently separate the coral roe or lip away from the white flesh of each scallop, pulling it away with your fingers. Put the coral roes into a bowl. Cut off and discard the very white piece of muscle attached to each scallop. Slice each whole disc of scallop across to halve it, then chop each half into four. Add them to the bowl. Squeeze the lemon juice over the scallops. Add the grated lemon zest (rind) and a good seasoning of salt and freshly-ground black pepper. Set the bowl aside in a cool place for 20 minutes or so.

2. Meanwhile, heat some clarified butter in a frying-pan. When very hot add the fresh breadcrumbs and fry them until golden and crisp. Drain them very thoroughly on crumpled paper towels and keep them very hot – spreading them out on a baking sheet or tray and placing them in a fairly low oven until required. Do not cover the crumbs or condensation will occur and make them soggy. Also wash four of the deep curved scallop shells (which form the other side of the shell) and warm them to use as individual serving dishes.

3. Wipe the mushrooms clean but do not peel them. Chop them into small pieces. Put them into a small bowl. Crush the garlic and add it to the bowl together with the chopped parsley and snipped chives. Mix together well and set aside until required.

4. About 10 minutes before you plan to eat, turn the scallops into a sieve placed over a small bowl to drain off the lemon juice. Put the unsalted butter into the cleaned-out frying-pan and place it over medium-low heat until the fat is melted and hot. Add the white pieces of scallop to the pan and fry them for 3 minutes, turning them occasionally to stiffen and slightly colour the flesh on all sides. It is important to cook them fairly gently and not to cook them too long or the texture will become tough. Add the coral roes to the pan and cook for 2 minutes more, turning them halfway through this time. Lift the scallops out of the pan with a slotted spoon and keep them warm.

5. Increase the heat to fairly high. Add the mushroom, parsley, chive and garlic mixture to the pan. Cook, stirring for 2-3 minutes. Draw the pan to one side. Stir in the scallops, add 5ml (1 teaspoon) of the lemon juice and season with salt and pepper to taste. Place the pan over the heat for just a few seconds more. Then divide the mixture between the four scallop shells. Garnish each with a scattering of the crisply fried crumbs, and serve immediately.

Serves 4

Fried whitebait

Many English, myself included, consider very crisply fried whitebait a great delicacy. To eat tiny fish whole, in one scrunchy bite, may seem eccentric to anyone who has not tried it but, once tasted, feasting on fried whitebait can easily become something of an addiction.

Metric/Imperial	American
450g(1lb) whitebait	*1lb small herring or sprat minnows*
flour seasoned with salt and pepper	*flour seasoned with salt and pepper*
salt	*salt*
cayenne pepper	*cayenne pepper*
a large lemon, quartered	*1 large lemon, quartered*
a bunch of parsley	*a bunch of parsley*

1. Put the tiny whole fish into a colander and dip into a sinkful of cold, salted water to rinse them thoroughly; this method ensures that the delicate little fish do not get bruised. Drain well and pat dry, using plenty of paper towels. Dust the fish with flour seasoned with salt and freshly-ground black pepper, taking care that each fish is evenly and well coated. Then gently shake off surplus flour.

2. Immediately heat some oil in a deep-fat fryer, clipping a thermometer to the side of the pan. The oil should only come one-third of the way up the side of the pan. It is an unnecessary extravagance, and can be dangerous, to use too much oil. When the oil temperature reaches 190°C (375°F), dip a fine-meshed frying basket into the pan to heat and to coat it with oil, so that the fish will not stick (it must be fine-meshed or the fish could slip through).

3. Lift the basket out of the pan, put a small handful of whitebait into it, and lower it into the hot oil. Fry for about 1½-2 minutes (small herrings or sprat minnows may need longer), shaking the pan gently every now and then to prevent the fish sticking to each other. Lift out the basket as soon as the fish are golden and very crisp. Hold the basket over the pan for a few seconds so that surplus oil drips back into the pan. Turn the fried whitebait out onto crumpled paper towels to drain them. Then transfer them to a hot plate and keep warm in a low oven. Return the frying basket to the pan and check that the oil regains correct frying temperature before cooking the next batch of whitebait in the same way.

4. When all the fish are cooked, sprinkle them with salt and a little cayenne. Serve immediately, piping hot and garnished generously with parsley sprigs and wedges of juicy lemon. *Serves 4 as a first course*

†The accompanying parsley sprigs can be deep-fried too. This looks pretty and tastes delicious, but it is important that the parsley is completely dry when it is put into the oil. Switch off the heat and allow the oil to cool slightly when you have finished cooking the whitebait. Place individual parsley sprigs around the edge of the bottom of the basket. Holding the basket at arm's length, lower it into the pan. Fry only as long as is needed to crisp the parsley: it should retain some freshness and green colour.

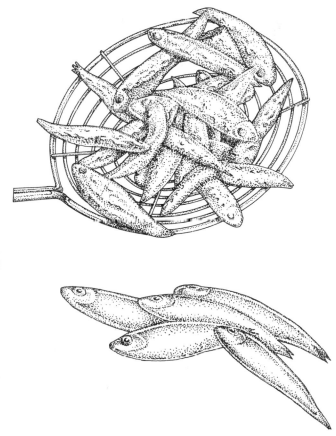

Gravad lax

This ancient Swedish method of pickling fish, delicately but distinctively flavoured with dill, is now popular throughout Scandinavia. It is remarkably little effort to prepare, and makes a lovely (and considerably cheaper) alternative to smoked salmon. Trout and mackerel can be prepared the same way.

Metric/Imperial	American
900g(2lb) tail end or middle cut of salmon	*2lb piece salmon*
For the pickle:	**For the pickle:**
5ml(1 teaspoon) black peppercorns	*1 teaspoon black peppercorns*
20ml(4 teaspoons) coarse salt	*4 teaspoons coarse or sea salt*
20ml(4 teaspoons) granulated sugar	*4 teaspoons sugar*
a pinch of saltpetre (optional)	*a pinch of saltpeter (optional)*
a bunch of fresh dill	*a bunch of fresh dill*
OR 30ml(2 tablespoons) frozen or dried dillweed	*OR 2 tablespoons dried dill*
For the mustard sauce:	**For the mustard sauce:**
2 large (no. 2) egg yolks	*2 large egg yolks*
30ml(2 tablespoons) caster sugar	*2 tablespoons superfine sugar*
60ml(4 tablespoons) French mustard	*4 tablespoons French mustard*
60ml(4 tablespoons) white wine vinegar	*4 tablespoons white wine vinegar*
225ml(8fl oz) olive or sunflower oil	*1 cup olive or sunflower oil*
salt and freshly-ground black pepper	*salt and freshly-ground black pepper*

1. Starting at least a day before you plan to eat the fish, crush the peppercorns with the back of a wooden spoon. Mix them with the salt, sugar and saltpetre if used. Saltpetre can be bought from chemists or drugstores and is used to retain the colour of the fish. Chop the dill coarsely (dillweed is a name given to dill leaves when frozen or dried and is very different from dill seed).

2. Cut the salmon in half lengthways to make two long fillets; lift out the backbone carefully. Sprinkle a quarter of the spice mixture in a dish and add some of the dill. Lay one piece of salmon, skin side down, on the dish. Strew it with half the spice

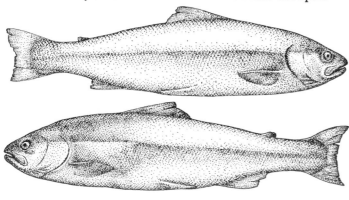

mixture and more dill. Cover with the second piece of salmon, skin side up (and placing the thick end over the thin end of the first piece if a tail cut is used). Sprinkle on the remaining spices and dill. Cover with a board and put heavy weights on top. Leave in a cold place – but not the refrigerator – for about 24 hours (no less than 16 hours and no longer than 4 days).

3. To make the mustard sauce – which is far quicker than mayonnaise – beat the egg yolks, sugar and mustard together with a balloon whisk. Beat in the vinegar, then gradually blend in the oil, and season to taste with salt and pepper. Pour the sauce into a bowl.

4. Remove the salmon from the pickle, gently scrape off the spices and dill, then carve the fish in very thin slices exactly as though carving smoked salmon. Arrange on a dish and garnish with wedges of lemon. Serve as a light main dish with the accompanying mustard sauce. Hot new potatoes steamed in their skins, and a dish of paper-thin cucumber slices, sprinkled with fresh chopped dill leaves and freshly-ground pepper, are traditionally served at the same time. *Serves 6*

Quenelles & Nantua sauce

Quenelles are the most aristocratic dumplings in the world. Pike is the traditional fish used for making quenelles – and I know of no better way to cook this fine-tasting but unbearably bony fish. The fish is reduced to a purée and is then blended with a partner before being formed into egg-shapes between two spoons. Choux paste or a bread panada (both of which are good) can be used for this, but quenelles made with cream and egg white are infinitely superior, a true delicacy which is a delight to eat: mouthwatering, feather-light and with creamy, just-soft centres.

Sauce Nantua is the classic and delectable accompaniment for quenelles. To be correct, and for the best flavour, this sauce should be made with freshwater crayfish. But, unless you are lucky enough, as I am, to live in an area with chalk and limestone streams, their natural habitat, you will probably have to use prawns (shrimp) instead. Not the same thing, of course, they will make a very special sauce nonetheless.

Metric/Imperial	American
For the quenelles:	**For the quenelles:**
450g(1lb) pike	450g(1lb) pike or pikelet
90ml(6 tablespoons) double cream	6 tablespoons heavy cream
2 large (no. 2) egg whites	2 large egg whites
salt and freshly-ground white pepper	salt and freshly-ground white pepper
For the sauce Nantua:	**For the sauce Nantua:**
225g(½lb) freshly-boiled freshwater crayfish	½lb freshly-boiled crayfish
OR 225g(½lb) prawns, weighed in their shells	OR ½lb shrimp, in the shell
90g(3½oz) unsalted butter	7 tablespoons unsalted butter
22ml(1½ tablespoons) plain flour	1½ tablespoons
275ml(½pt) good fish stock (page 10, steps 1-4)	1¼ cups fish stock (page 10, steps 1-4)
50g(2oz) mushrooms	½ cup chopped mushrooms
5ml(1 teaspoon) lemon juice	1 teaspoon lemon juice
1 large (no. 2) egg yolk	1 large egg yolk
75ml(5 tablespoons) double cream	5 tablespoons heavy cream

1. Start to prepare quenelles several hours before the meal. Successful quenelles depend on using the correct proportions of fish to cream and egg white, so it is vital to measure the ingredients accurately. Pike weighing about 450g (1lb) will be required to yield 225g (½lb) boned and skinned flesh to make this recipe. Allow yourself plenty of time for removing all the nasty little bones. Chop the measured raw fish roughly and put it into a blender with the cream and blend until reduced to a very smooth purée. Scrape the mixture out of the blender goblet into a shallow dish and season it with salt and freshly-ground white pepper. Using a fork stir in the raw, unwhisked egg whites, adding a spoonful or so at a time. When the egg whites are absorbed and well-blended into the mixture, chill it for several hours to dry and firm it a little before being shaped and poached.

2. It is also practical to prepare well ahead of the meal the velouté base that goes to make the delectable sauce Nantua. For the velouté, first melt 40g (1½oz) or 3 tablespoons butter in a saucepan over low heat. Away from the heat stir in the flour. Return the pan to low heat and cook, stirring, for 3-4 minutes until pale gold. Away from the heat, gradually blend in the fish stock. Chop the mushrooms finely and add them to the pan. Cook over low heat stirring continuously until thickened and simmering. Then cover the pan and let it simmer gently for 5 minutes, uncover it again and let it simmer for 5 minutes more. Turn off the heat but leave the pan on the stove. Stir in the lemon juice, add a good seasoning of salt and freshly-ground white pepper. Let the sauce stand for 10 minutes before straining it through a sieve to extract the mushroom pieces. Press the mushrooms with a wooden spoon to encourage all their delicious juices to drip through the sieve into the sauce. Cover the velouté with a circle of buttered waxed paper to prevent a skin from forming on the surface, and set it aside.

3. Make the shellfish butter ahead. Peel and clean all the crayfish or prawns (shrimp), by pulling off the heads and then putting your thumb under the legs on one side, to peel upwards over the back. Hold the exposed pink body and nip the tail with the other hand, while pulling the body free. Crush the shells and heads; if using crayfish, make sure they are broken into pieces. Dice the remaining butter, put it into a saucepan together with the crushed shells. Place the pan over very low heat and cook gently for 5 minutes until the butter has melted, the shells are warmed and coated with fat. Scrape the contents of the pan into the blender. Add 15ml (1 tablespoon) boiling water and blend to pulverize the shells and, in so doing, to thoroughly infuse the butter with their delicious flavour. Scrape the mixture out of the blender goblet (if it has stiffened warm it over low heat to melt the butter again), then strain it through a cheesecloth lined strainer to separate shell from butter. Press the shells with a wooden spoon to extract maximum juices. Set the shellfish butter aside. Select 4 of the smallest crayfish or a dozen prawns (shrimp) to use whole for garnish, chop the rest finely. Reserve the whole and chopped shellfish separately in covered bowls.

4. When you are ready to cook the quenelles, about 20 minutes before eating them, place a pan of fish stock or salted water over low heat. A large fairly shallow pan, such as a sauté pan, is best: depth is unnecessary but a large surface area will enable you to poach the quenelles in one or two batches only; this is desirable as quenelles should be eaten as soon as possible after cooking. Have a warmed serving dish ready. Place the pan of velouté close to the stove. Beat the egg yolk with the cream in a cup and place it close at hand, with the bowls of shellfish butter, whole shellfish and chopped shellfish.

5. Using two dessertspoons, shape the quenelle mixture into 12 fat blobs inverting the top spoon to smooth the top of the quenelle. Poach them in batches in the barely-simmering liquid, spacing them sufficiently far apart not to touch each other. They will need 6 minutes cooking time and should be flipped over with a slotted spoon after the first 3 minutes. It is of the utmost importance to keep the liquid at the barest simmer; it should hardly tremble. If the liquid is agitated, the quenelles will disintegrate. Lift the quenelles out of the pan gently, using a slotted spoon, blot them on paper towels and keep warm.

6. While the last batch of quenelles is poaching, start gently reheating the basic velouté sauce. When the quenelles are all cooked, carefully whisk the shellfish butter into the sauce, then stir in the chopped shellfish. When the sauce reaches simmering point, beat a few spoonfuls of it into the egg and cream liaison, then carefully blend the contents of the cup into the sauce pan. Cook gently, stirring continuously, without allowing it to boil, until the sauce is very hot. Away from the heat check seasoning and adjust to taste. Pour the sauce over the quenelles. Quickly garnish with the reserved whole shellfish and serve immediately.

Serves 4

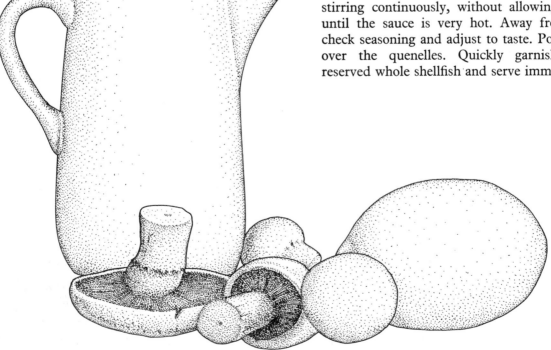

Dressed crab

C rab is a luxury, but happily a luxury one can indulge in without feelings of guilt – for whereas lobster and even scallops are outrageously expensive, crab is reasonably priced. Its sweet salty shellfish flavour is exquisite and best when very simply served as here. I admit to feeling mildly squeamish about cooking a crab the first time I did so, and somewhat daunted by the length of time it takes to dress crab. But greed soon overcame squeamishness – crab prepared at home tastes *so* superior to shop-prepared crab – and the miser in me now delights in the challenge of seeing just how much sweet-flavoured crabmeat I can pick from the shell.

Metric/Imperial	American
2 live crabs, each 1.1-1.4kg (2½-3lb)	*2 × 2½-3lb live hard-shell crabs*
a few spoonfuls of vinaigrette dressing	*a few spoonfuls of vinaigrette dressing*
OR a few spoonfuls of mayonnaise (page 127, 2)	*OR a few spoonfuls of mayonnaise (page 127, 2)*
French mustard	*French mustard*
lemon juice	*lemon juice*
olive oil	*olive oil*
salt and freshly-ground black pepper	*salt and freshly-ground black pepper*
parsley sprigs	*parsley sprigs*

1. The fresher the crab the sweeter it tastes: to be sure it is fresh, buy live crab and cook and dress it yourself! Buy direct from a crab fisherman if possible, or a fishdealer known to get regular supplies. Choose your crabs as soon as fresh deliveries arrive. Bypass any crabs with damaged shells, missing claws or legs, and any that do not react with healthy vigour when touched! Do not be tempted to buy one giant or king crab instead of two smaller ones: it would mean less work but the texture and flavour of very large crabs is nearly always disappointing. Choose crabs which feel heavy for their size (lightness in proportion to size is a sign that the crab has been out of the sea for some time, living off stored nourishment). To pick a crab up, stretch your hand across its back so that the claws cannot reach you. Then shake it gently to check that the weight is all meat, not seawater.

2. Always cook and eat crab on the day you buy it. Fish sellers usually plunge crab into boiling water to kill it. It is far less distressing for cook and creature to use the method recommended by the Royal Society for the Prevention of Cruelty to Animals in Britain. Place the crab into a very large pan indeed. Fill it with seawater or very heavily-salted cold water – 200g (7oz) salt for every 2.3L (4pt) water (about ⅔ cup salt for each 2qt of water). Cover the pan with a lid and weigh it down so that the crab cannot push off the lid. Put the pan over the lowest possible heat and bring it to boiling point very slowly indeed. A very gradual increase in warmth makes crab feel a bit woozy; it will faint as the temperature rises and die in its sleep long before the water is hot enough to cause it pain. Once boiling point is reached, simmer the crab for 20-30 minutes depending on size. Remove the cooked crab from the pan and leave to cool.

3. Dressing a crab simply means separating the meat from the bone and seasoning it. A commercially-dressed crab will probably include malt vinegar, which can kill fine shellfish flavour, and the meat is invariably padded out with breadcrumbs. If you spend time on picking the bones really clean, there will be so much crabmeat to pile into the shell for serving that there is no need for, and indeed no room for, extra bulk. Assemble a large chopping board, a sharp knife and two bowls (one for the white meat and one for brown meat), nutcrackers or a hammer for cracking the claws and legs, a coffee spoon and a skewer or larding needle for picking out meat from small nooks and crannies of shell.

4. First, twist the crab legs and claws away from the body. Crack the claws and legs open and pry out the meat, taking care to discard little chips of bone and membrane. If the crab is really fresh, it will contain lots of creamy pink curd and the tips of claw meat will be very tender and moist.

5. Next, separate the body section from the hard back shell. To do this, lay the crab on its back with the tail end facing you. Holding the shell down with your fingers, use your thumbs to lever and push the body section up and out of the back shell. Set the body section aside while you deal with the back shell.

6. Remove and discard stomach sac from the head end. Scrape curd and meat from the shell. Trim the shell by tapping along the natural curved line marked on it: this is the dividing line between very hard and relatively thin (soft) shell. The softer shell should break away quite easily, leaving you with a handsome 'bowl' of back shell which can be washed, dried and rubbed with a little oil to make a dish in which to serve the crabmeat.

7. Return to the body and pull off and discard the feathery-grey gills which are attached on either side. These are sometimes called 'dead man's fingers' and are inedible. Scrape the creamy brown meat with a spoon. Now for the fiddly but very rewarding task of seeking out the white meat which lies hidden in the maze of thin shell. This is where the major part of the sweetest white crabmeat lies and it is amazing just how much meat a skilfully-wielded skewer or larding needle will yield. Split the body section in half, head to tail end, with a firm blow with a sharp knife. This gives greater

access into the interior of the body and makes the job of prying the meat out considerably easier.

8. When the skeleton is picked clean, shred the white meat with a pair of forks. Season it to taste with a spoonful or so of mayonnaise or vinaigrette dressing and a little salt and freshly-ground black pepper. Cream the bowl of dark meat with a spoon, seasoning it with a few drops of olive oil, a squeeze of lemon juice and a little salt and freshly-ground black pepper and French mustard.

9. Pile the prepared crabmeat back into the shells, packing the white meat down either wide of each shell, then mound the dark meat down the centres. I believe strongly that decorations should be kept to the minimum; plainly-dressed crabs look and taste better than those which are too elaborate, so I

simply mark the dividing lines between white and dark meats with tiny sprigs of fresh parsley. Some cooks like to add chopped egg whites, mimosa-style egg yolk garnishes, piped mayonnaise and other fancy trimmings. Eggs and mayonnaise go well with the sweet salty fresh flavour of crab, but I think these ingredients are far better served separately. I always accompany dressed crab with a cucumber salad, plenty of good brown bread (fresh whole wheat bread) and fresh, unsalted butter. If appetites are copious, or if the crabs have yielded less meat than I hoped, I also bring to the table a bowl of mayonnaise and a dish of hard-boiled eggs, halved and sprinkled with a handful of fresh chopped parsley. This makes a feast of a meal. No first course is necessary and all that will be needed to follow is, say, a bowl of fresh cherries on ice or a dish of freckled, ripe apricots. *Serves 8*

Sole Colbert

D over sole is a prince among fish. I like it best of all fried à la meunière (in butter) but here is another excellent way to fry it, which I have chosen for two reasons. First, I find that many people appreciate being served fish without bones (and the method used here cleverly cooks sole on the bone in such a way that the bones can be removed in seconds just before serving). Second, I particularly like the savoury butter after which the dish is named, an unusual one for fish in that it includes glazed meat juices.

Metric/Imperial	American
4 fine sole, each weighing 275-350g(10-12oz)	4 × 10-12oz sole
a little plain flour	plain flour
2 medium-sized eggs	2 eggs
dried white breadcrumbs	dry white bread crumbs
salt and freshly-ground black pepper	salt and freshly-ground black pepper

For the Colbert butter:	For the Colbert butter:
115g(¼lb) unsalted butter	½ cup unsalted butter
15ml(1 tablespoon) fresh chopped tarragon	1 tablespoon fresh chopped tarragon
30ml(2 tablespoons) lemon juice	2 tablespoons lemon juice
45ml(3 tablespoons) fresh chopped parsley	3 tablespoons fresh chopped parsley
5ml(1 teaspoon) finely-grated lemon zest	1 teaspoon finely-grated lemon rind
15ml(1 tablespoon) meat jelly, from dripping	1 tablespoon meat juice from roast beef
salt and freshly-ground black pepper	salt and freshly-ground black pepper

I. When buying fish for this dish, be sure to first measure the width of your frying-basket. If the fish are too large for it, the appearance will be spoiled. Ask the fishmonger (dealer) to remove the dark fish skin or do this yourself. Make a cut just above the tail. Ease the skin a little with the point of a knife. Dip your fingers in salt. Hold the tail firmly with one hand, grip the skin with the salted fingers of your other hand and pull it away as though ripping off adhesive tape. Trim fins and tail as necessary to fit your frying-basket. Cut the flesh along the length of the backbone on the skinned side. Slide the knife under the flesh close to the backbone and gently ease the flesh away from the bone, until fillets are attached only at the head, tail and fins. Then snip through the backbone with scissors near the head, in the middle and near the tail, and roll back the cut edges of the fillets a little to make an opening in the fish. This cutting and shaping is to make it very simple to remove the bone after cooking and to provide a pocket in which to place the butter.

2. Sprinkle the sole all over with salt and freshly-ground black pepper, then dust them with a little flour. Holding the fish by their tails, dip them, one at a time in the eggs beaten lightly with a spoonful of water, and coat them generously with breadcrumbs. Set aside in a cold place, lightly covered with grease-proof or waxed paper, for an hour to firm the egg and crumb coating.

3. Meanwhile beat the lemon, the jellied meat juice, herbs, salt and pepper into the softened butter. Using wet hands and a sheet of greaseproof or waxed paper damped with cold water, shape the butter into a roll, wrap it and put it on ice until solid.

4. About 35 minutes before serving fill a deep-fat fryer one-third full of oil. Clip a thermometer to the side of the pan and heat to 190 °C (375 °F). Dip the basket into the pan, remove it, add one fish, cut side up, and lower it in to the pan again. Fry for 3-4 minutes until the sole is cooked through and the surface is golden. Drain the fish on crumpled paper towels on a baking tray and keep hot while you cook the rest of the fish. (As the fish have to be cooked one at a time it is inadvisable to choose this dish for a large party.) When all the fish are cooked, use a sharp knife to ease out the backbones. Transfer the fish to a serving dish. Slice the chilled butter into pats and arrange 3 or 4 in the opening of each fish. Serve immediately. *Serves 4*

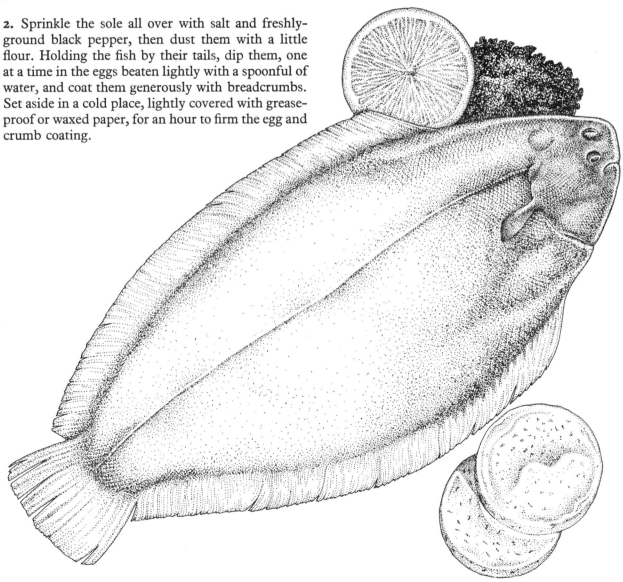

Taramasalata

The creamy-pink fish paté that the world has come to know and love is, ironically, only a variation on the original Greek dish. Strictly speaking it should be, as the name implies, a salad of tarama – the salted roe of grey mullet, a fish which is rarely found outside the Mediterranean. The fact that we have adapted the dish to fish that are locally available always seems to me the best of all testimonials to its excellence. And, whether you use the authentic tarama or smoked cod's roe, this distinctive pâté always proves a much appreciated first course for dinner, an attractive buffet party item and a good choice for a picnic.

Metric/Imperial	American
175g(6oz) salted grey mullet roe	*6oz salted grey mullet roe*
OR 175g(6oz) smoked cod's roe	*OR 6oz smoked cod's roe*
175-200ml(6-7fl oz) olive oil	*¾-1 cup olive oil*
50g(2oz) fresh, crustless white bread	*2 slices fresh white bread, crusts removed*
1 very large garlic clove, finely chopped	*1 very large garlic clove, finely chopped*
about 30ml(2 tablespoons) lemon juice	*about 2 tablespoons lemon juice*
a little salt	*a little salt*
freshly-ground black pepper	*freshly-ground black pepper*
2 lemons, cut into quarters, to garnish	*2 lemons, quartered, to garnish*
a few small black olives to garnish	*a few small black olives to garnish*

1. The traditional way to make taramasalata involves pounding the fish roe in a mortar with a pestle. This is time-consuming but does give very smooth results. Today the ingredients are more often puréed in a blender. This is certainly very quick but it does not, in my opinion, give such good results. Moreover I find it wasteful since a certain amount of the precious fish paste sticks firmly to the blades and is impossible to scrape out of the blender goblet. So you either have to forgo a surprisingly large portion of the pâté, or you can wash it out with extra lemon juice and olive oil – but this of course alters the balance of flavours and texture. I find the most practical method is to use a fork and a soup plate – not so speedy as using a blender, but rather quicker than using pestle and mortar and just as thorough.

2. Put the roe into a small bowl. Pour on freshly-boiled water to cover and set aside for 3-4 minutes:

this will loosen the skin and marginally reduce the saltiness of the roe. Drain the roe and pat it dry with paper towels. Make a nick in the skin with the point of a sharp knife, peel it away and discard. Break the sticky roe in to small pieces and put it into a large soup plate. Add a spoonful or so of the measured olive oil to moisten the roe, then mash very thoroughly with a fork, first breaking the roe down to coarse 'crumbs', then adding a little more oil and reducing it to a smooth, very thick paste.

3. Break the bread into pieces, put into a blender and reduce to fine crumbs. Turn the crumbs into a second large soup plate, add 60ml (4 tablespoons) cold water and mash to a paste with a fork. Crush the garlic with a very little salt. Add it to the bread together with a spoonful or two of olive oil. Mash again until the ingredients are well-blended and very smooth. Add a spoonful of the prepared roe and mash it into the bread mixture. Gradually incorporate the rest of the roe, mashing and beating the

mixture with a fork until perfectly smooth and well blended. Beat in the lemon juice, then as much of the remaining olive oil as is necessary to make a smooth thick cream. Add the oil just a spoonful or so at a time (as when making mayonnaise) and check that it is properly absorbed before adding the next spoonful. Eat a tiny piece of the mixture to check seasoning and add extra garlic, salt or a squeeze of lemon juice to taste.

4. Spoon the taramasalata into a shallow dish, smoothing the surface with a wet spoon. Cover with plastic film or foil and store in the refrigerator: taramasalata will keep well for 2-3 days. To serve as a pâté, garnish the taramasalata with a few black olives and quartered lemons just before serving, and accompany it with unleavened bread or brown (whole wheat) toast. To serve as a dip for strips of raw vegetables, thin the pâté by beating in a few spoonfuls of soured cream just before serving.

Serves 4-6

Baked lobster

F resh lobster is undoubtedly one of the greatest treats in the world – and one of the most expensive. Its flavour is so fine that it seems a pity and quite unnecessary to dress it up with a wine sauce or other elaborate garnishes. It is hard to improve on plain grilled or baked lobster, garnished with lemon wedges, but it is a nice idea to serve a sauce in a separate bowl, so that everyone can dip into it if they wish.

Metric/Imperial	American
3 lobsters, each weighing 700-900g(1½-2lb)	*3 × 1½-2lb lobsters*
the juice of 1 lemon	*juice of 1 lemon*
salt and freshly ground black pepper	*salt and freshly-ground black pepper*
175g(6oz) unsalted butter, at room temperature	*¾ cup unsalted butter, at room temperature*
30ml(2 tablespoons) toasted breadcrumbs	*2 tablespoons toasted bread crumbs*
15ml(1 tablespoon) grated Parmesan cheese	*1 tablespoon grated Parmesan cheese*
wedges of lemon	*wedges of lemon*
OR Hollandaise sauce (page 143, steps 3-5)	*OR Hollandaise sauce (page 143, steps 3-5)*
OR butter sauce (page 161, step 5)	*OR butter sauce (page 161, step 5)*

1. Lobster that has been killed by boiling is unsuitable for grilling or baking: it would in effect be cooked twice, which would cause the flesh to toughen and to lose flavour. Buy live lobsters direct from a fisherman if you can, but otherwise from a reputable fishmonger or fishmarket known to receive regular supplies – and always cook and eat lobster on the day you buy it. Look for lobsters which stretch their claws, arch their backs and flap their tails noisily when picked up; choose those which feel heavy in proportion to their size. Avoid any that are lethargic or covered with barnacles – the latter is usually a sign of old age!

2. If you cannot bring yourself to kill live lobster, ask the fishmonger (dealer) to do it for you when you collect the lobsters. He will drive a knife through the brain then split the lobster in half. To kill a lobster yourself, follow this easier, method. Lay it on its stomach on a heavy chopping board, cover the jointed tail shell with a cloth and hold it down firmly with one hand. Take a heavy knife with a sharp point in the other hand. Quickly and firmly plunge the blade tip deep into the flesh at the point where the lobster body and tail sections are joined together. This blow will sever the spinal cord killing the lobster instantly (muscle spasms may continue for a while).

3. Split the top end of the lobster in half through the length of the head and body by bringing down the knife blade hard. Then make a second cut through the tail section to split the lobster completely in two. Remove the stomach sac, which lies in the head, and the black thread of intestine. Leave the creamy, green-black liver which lies in the body cavity, also the roe which is found in hen lobsters (this is greenish-black when raw: like the shell of a lobster it only turns coral coloured when cooked). Drain and reserve the lobster juices. Remove and discard any chips of shell. Crack the claws with a sharp blow of a hammer or with nutcrackers.

4. Lobster should be served immediately after being cooked. Since most grill pans are not large enough to take 3 lobsters together, I find it more practical to bake lobster in the oven, where there is enough room to cook several simultaneously. Using the oven also has another advantage: because heat circulates all round there is no need to turn the lobsters during cooking. Preheat the oven to 180°C (350°F) gas mark 4, placing one baking tray on the shelf just above the middle, and a second baking tray on the shelf just below the centre.

5. Butter two gratin dishes and lightly rub the lobster shells all over with buttered paper until they gleam. Divide the halved lobsters between the two dishes, laying them cut side up and supporting them against each other. Season the flesh with a little salt, a generous grind of black pepper, and a good squeeze of lemon juice. Then cover the flesh completely with flecks of softened, unsalted butter. Place one dish on each hot baking tray and cook for 15 minutes. Then baste the lobsters with the buttery juices in the gratin dishes, adding the reserved lobster juices and any remaining lemon juice. Return the dishes to the oven, reversing their positions, and cook for 15 minutes more. Meanwhile preheat the grill (broiler).

6. Remove both dishes from the oven, and increase oven temperature to 220°C (425°F) gas mark 7. Baste the lobsters with the buttery juices once again, mix the toasted breadcrumbs and cheese and sprinkle over the lobsters. Return one dish to the top shelf of the oven, place the other under the grill (broiler). In both cases cook for 3-5 minutes more, then serve immediately. *Serves 6*

Salmon trout in aspic

Salmon trout is often said to combine the finest qualities of trout and salmon and to be better than either, so this name seems more appropriate than sea trout, sewin or peel as it is also variously called in Britain. The flavour is delicate, the flesh sweet, firm and prettily coloured. In America brown or river trout is sometimes known as salmon trout. Simple cooking is, as always, best for showing off such excellence, and fresh salmon trout gently poached, jellied and accompanied by a lemon-flavoured mayonnaise is a treat one is not liable to forget.

Metric/Imperial	American
1 fine fresh salmon trout weighing 1.8kg(4lb)	*1 4lb river trout*
a few slices of cucumber	*a few cucumber slices*

For the mayonnaise:

4 large (no. 2) egg yolks	*4 large egg yolks*
575ml(1pt) olive oil	*2½ cups olive oil*
45-60ml(3-4 tablespoons) lemon juice	*3-4 tablespoons lemon juice*
salt and freshly-ground white pepper	*salt and freshly-ground white pepper*

For the aspic jelly:

fish stock, (page 10, steps 1-4)	*fish stock (page 10, steps 1-4)*
450g(1lb) cheap white fish fillets	*1lb white fish fillets*
1 egg white and shell	*1 egg white and shell*
50-75ml(2-3fl oz) dry sherry	*3-4 tablespoons dry sherry*

1. The salmon trout should be bought and cooked on the morning of the day you plan to eat it, but it is wise to order in advance. It is however practical to make the fish stock a day ahead. Ask the fishmonger to let you have turbot and/or sole bones and heads for the stock as these are rich in gelatine which will give the stock good texture: when reduced, it will naturally set to a soft jelly making the addition of commercial gelatine unnecessary. After straining the stock, return the liquid to the cleaned-out pan. Add the fish fillets and simmer, uncovered, until the fish has yielded all its flavour and the liquid is reduced to about 700ml (1¼pt) or 3 cups of very well flavoured stock. Strain the stock through a cheesecloth-lined sieve and season to taste. Cool the stock as quickly as possible, cover it and refrigerate it overnight. This is important as fish stock can sour quite quickly.

2. The mayonnaise can also be made a day ahead. This is one of the best sauces in the world but one that many people – even very experienced cooks – seem to dread making. I have found that mayonnaise always emulsifies properly if eggs, oil and mixing bowl are placed at room temperature at least 1 hour before starting to make the mayonnaise. A trick to ensure that you add the oil drop by drop, is to put the oil in a bottle stoppered with a cork with a V-shaped notch up the side – so that the oil just drips through.

3. Put the yolks into the bowl. Beat them with a balloon whisk for a minute: this will make them sticky and more receptive to the oil. Add some salt, pepper and one-quarter of the lemon juice and beat for half a minute more. Then start adding the oil, drop by drop, beating the mixture slowly, steadily and without stopping. Change hands and/or the direction of beating whenever you wish but keep beating and make sure that one drop of oil is absorbed by the egg yolks before adding the next.

4. When the mayonnaise is very thick and about a third of the oil has been absorbed, the remaining oil can be added in a slow trickle. However, it is wise to stop pouring every few seconds to check that the oil is being properly incorporated into the mayonnaise. The mixture will gradually become too stiff to beat easily, so thin and flavour it with small quantities of the remaining lemon juice at intervals. When all the oil has been added, beat in any left-over lemon juice and adjust seasoning to taste. Finally beat in 45ml (3 tablespoons) boiling water, a spoonful at a time: this should prevent a skin from forming and help stabilize the mixture. Turn the mayonnaise into a small bowl, cover it and chill until required.

5. The simplest and best way of poaching salmon trout (and indeed salmon) is the Scottish method, which avoids any possibility of overcooking the fish. Lay the fish on the perforated plate of a fish kettle or on a rack in a similar large pan, and lower it into the kettle. Pour on enough cold water to cover the fish by 2.5cm (1in) or so. Add salt, allowing 40g (1½oz) or 3 tablespoons for every 4½L (8pt) or 1US-gal of water, and let it come slowly to boiling point. As soon as the water reaches a fast boil, remove the pan from the heat, skim off any scum, cover the pan with a well-fitting lid and set it aside in a cool place – not the refrigerator – until almost cold. The fish will continue to cook as the liquid cools and, being immersed in liquid, the flesh will remain beautifully moist and succulent. The beauty of this method is both that it uses little fuel and that it can be used for any size of fish; the larger the fish the more water will be required and the longer this will take to cool.

6. Turn the cold, softly-jellied fish stock into a pan. Place over low heat until just melted. Add the egg white and crushed shell and clarify the stock (as described on *page 18, step 7*). Stir in the sherry and cool the aspic, standing it in a bowl of ice cubes.

127

7. Lift the salmon trout out of its liquid. Drain it and slide it gently onto a double sheet of damp, greaseproof or waxed paper as long as the fish and twice its width. Using a small sharp knife, cut through the skin around the head of the fish, across the tail, and along the length of back and belly of the fish. Carefully peel away the skin from the upper surface, holding the knife against the flesh as you ease the skin away. Gently scrape away any brown-coloured flesh to reveal the beautiful pink thick fillets of fish. Fold the paper around the fish and gently roll it over, then skin the second side in the same way.

8. Working from the head to tail, carefully insert the knife blade between the top fillet and backbone and gently ease and loosen the fillet from the bone. Using two fish slices, lift the complete top fillet up off the fish. Use scissors to snip through the backbone at head and tail end, and carefully peel the bone away from the lower fillet. Replace the upper fillet, and carefully transfer the whole prepared fish onto a serving dish or platter. This whole operation is a delicate one, so allow yourself plenty of time and do not panic. Any small slips of the knife can be masked by the aspic and cucumber garnish – and no amount of breaks in the flesh will impair the magnificent flavour of the fish!

9. When the aspic is cold and approaching setting point (that is when its texture is thickened to a syrup) spoon a thin film of it all over the upper fillet of the fish. Let it set. Arrange a simple garnish of half a dozen or so paper-thin slices of cucumber over the glaze. Coat the fish with a second thin layer of aspic, coating the garnish too, and place in the refrigerator to set. Pour the rest of the aspic into a shallow dish and chill until set.

10. Just before serving, turn the aspic out onto a sheet of wet greaseproof or waxed paper. Chop it with the full length of a knife blade dipped in cold water, and arrange the chopped jelly round the fish. Serve with the prepared mayonnaise, a cucumber salad and plenty of fresh, really good brown bread. *Serves 8*

Salmon coulibiac

Coulibiac, or Kulibiaka as it is sometimes called, is the best fish pie I have ever eaten. It is, like many Russian dishes, rather substantial – but not heavy: the richness of the salmon and butter are tempered by the fresh flavours of dill and lemon, and by the lovely chilled sour cream sauce which accompanies the dish. Puff pastry or brioche dough can be used to encase the pie filling: brioche dough takes time to make, and I would always use a defrosted packet of frozen puff pastry (in the US, 2 cans of quick dinner roll pastry) when in a hurry. As well as containing fish, mushrooms and eggs – ingredients which are used in fish pies the world over – coulibiac also includes cereal. This can be kasha (roasted buckwheat), or buckwheat pancakes cut into ribbons, or rice. I think brown rice makes the best choice because it adds attractive nutty flavour and texture to the pie.

Metric/Imperial	American
For the brioche pastry:	**For the brioche pastry:**
225g(½lb) strong plain flour	*½lb all-purpose flour*
7g(¼oz) dried yeast	*¼oz package active dry yeast*
45ml(3 tablespoons) warm milk	*3 tablespoons warm milk*
2·5ml(½ teaspoon) caster sugar	*½ teaspoon superfine sugar*
5ml(1 teaspoon) salt	*1 teaspoon salt*
3 medium-sized (no. 3) eggs	*3 eggs*
125g(¼lb) unsalted butter, at room temperature	*½ cup unsalted butter, at room temperature*
30ml(2 tablespoons) clarified butter (p 91, st 4)	*2 tablespoons clarified butter (page 91, step 4)*
30ml(2 tablespoons) fine dry breadcrumbs	*2 tablespoons fine dry breadcrumbs*
OR 375g(13oz) packet puff pastry	*OR 2 cans refrigerated quick dinner roll pastry*
For the filling:	**For the filling:**
700g(1½lb) filleted salmon	*1½lb piece salmon*
175g(6oz) mushrooms, sliced	*about ¼-½lb mushrooms, sliced*
3 hard-boiled eggs	*3 hard-cooked eggs*
125g(¼lb) brown rice	*½ cup brown rice*
250ml(9fl oz) fish stock (page 10, steps 1-4)	*generous 1 cup fish stock (page 10, steps 1-4)*
1 doz spring onions, green and white chopped	*1doz scallions, green and white finely chopped*
1 lemon	*1 lemon*
75g(3oz) unsalted butter	*6 tablespoons unsalted butter*
a small bunch of parsley	*a small bunch of parsley*
a few sprigs of fresh dill	*a few sprigs of fresh dill*
OR 10ml(2 teaspoons) dried dill weed	*OR 2 teaspoons dried dill*
freshly-grated nutmeg	*freshly-grated nutmeg*
30ml(2 tablespoons) melted butter	*2 tablespoons melted butter*
salt and freshly-ground black pepper	*salt and freshly-ground black pepper*
For the sauce:	**For the sauce:**
275ml(½pt) soured cream	*1¼ cups sour cream*
15ml(1 tablespoon) lemon juice	*1 tablespoon lemon juice*
15ml(1 tablespoon) fresh dill	*1 tablespoon fresh dill*
OR 5ml(1 teaspoon) dried dill weed	*OR 1 teaspoon dried dill*
freshly-ground black pepper	*freshly-ground black pepper*

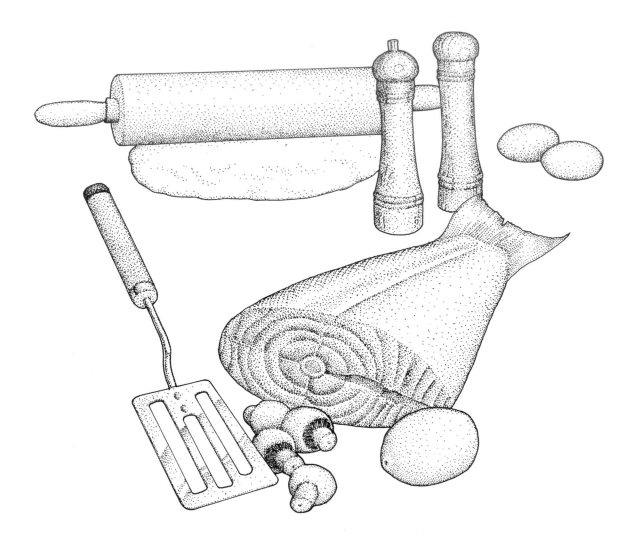

1. Start about 14 hours ahead if you are going to make the brioche pastry (which is not the easiest of doughs). First dissolve the sugar in the warm milk, sprinkle on the yeast and set aside for 10-15 minutes until the yeast is reactivated and frothy. Cream the unsalted butter until softened. Scald a mixing bowl with boiling water to warm it, empty and dry it. Sift the flour and salt into the bowl. Make a hollow in the middle and break the eggs into it. Add the frothed-up yeast and stir with a wooden spoon to make a paste. Then work in the creamed butter with one hand, slapping the very sticky mixture against the side of the bowl until the ingredients are well blended and the dough is smooth and shiny.

2. With a plastic spatula scoop the dough into a ball. Sprinkle it with a little flour, cover the bowl with a sheet of lightly-oiled plastic film and set it aside in a warm place until the dough has at least doubled in bulk and is light and spongy looking – this will take about 2 hours.

3. Punch and knead the risen dough, slapping it on a work surface with one hand. Using the plastic spatula, form the dough into a ball. Put it back into a clean, floured bowl, Cover it with oiled plastic film and refrigerate for about 8 hours. At the end of this time it will be a relief to find that the dough has firmed to a more manageable consistency.

4. About 3 hours before serving salmon coulibiac, take the brioche dough out of the refrigerator and bring it slowly back to life for 2 hours in the warm kitchen. Or if using frozen puff pastry, allow 2 hours for defrosting (follow the dinner roll label).

5. Meanwhile prepare the filling. Measure the fish stock into a saucepan. Salt it and bring it to boiling point. Pour in the rice, stir once, cover and simmer very gently for 40 minutes. Skin the salmon and cut the flesh into thin slices. Melt 50g (2oz) or 4 tablespoons butter in a frying-pan. Add the fish and cook it just long enough to firm the flesh – about 2-3 minutes. Lift the salmon out with a fish slice, drain it and cool it. Gently cook the chopped spring onions (scallions) in 25g (1oz) or 2 tablespoons butter until slightly softened. Stir in the mushrooms, 45ml (3 tablespoons) lemon juice and a good seasoning of salt and pepper. Cover and continue cooking over gentle heat for 5 minutes, stirring or shaking the pan occasionally. Then remove the lid, increase heat slightly and cook for a few minutes more until most of the moisture is driven off.

6. When the rice is tender and has absorbed all the cooking liquid, stir it into the mushroom mixture away from the heat. Add a grating of nutmeg, about 45ml (3 tablespoons) chopped fresh parsley, 15ml (1 tablespoon) chopped fresh dill or 5ml (1 teaspoon) dried dillweed, and salt and pepper to taste. Spread the mushroom and rice mixture out on a plate and let it cool slightly. Slice the hard eggs on a separate plate. Season them with 45ml (3 tablespoons) chopped fresh parsley, a little dill, a squeeze of lemon juice and some salt and pepper.

7. Whichever dough you are using, divide it in two and roll out each piece to a rectangle about 35 × 20cm (14 × 8in). Lay one rectangle on a floured baking sheet. Spread half the rice and mushroom mixture over it, taking care to leave a clear 2.5cm (1in) border. Arrange the slices of egg on top, then the salmon, then the rest of the rice and mushroom mixture. Brush the pastry edges with cold water.

8. Drape the second piece of pastry over a rolling pin and place it carefully over the filling. Press and pinch the pastry edges firmly together to seal the parcel securely. Use any pastry trimmings to make decorations for the top of the pie, fixing them into position with a little cold water. Make two large holes in the top of the coulibiac and half insert a piece of thin rolled-up cardboard in each. This is to allow steam to escape during baking and to make it easy to pour in melted butter just before serving. Set the coulibiac aside while you preheat the oven to 220 °C (425 °F) gas mark 7: this rest will allow the pastry to recover from handling.

9. When the oven is hot, glaze the pastry with melted clarified butter and, if you wish to be traditional, sprinkle it with fine dry breadcrumbs. Bake the pie for 25-30 minutes until golden. While it cooks, prepare the sauce. Turn the chilled sour cream into a bowl. Beat it until smooth. Season it with lemon juice, dill and generous grinds of black pepper. Slide the cooked coulibiac onto a warmed serving dish. Pour 15ml (1 tablespoon) melted butter into each hole in the top of the pastry. Remove the rolled-up cardboard funnels and serve.

Serves 6

Trout with almonds

Beautifully speckled river or brook trout cooked and eaten within an hour or two of being caught are, as every trout fisherman will agree, one of the finest foods in the world. Lemon, butter, salt and pepper are the natural allies of trout, but the addition of nut-brown almonds seems to me to complement the fish's flavour and texture to perfection.

Metric/Imperial	**American**
4 trout, each weighing 175-225g(6-8oz)	*4 × ½lb brook or river trout*
100g(¼lb) clarified butter (page 62, step 3)	*½ cup clarified butter (page 62,step 3)*
50g(2oz) flaked almonds	*½ cup flaked almonds*
a little plain flour	*a little plain flour*
1 lemon, cut into quarters	*1 lemon, quartered*
15ml(1 tablespoon) lemon juice	*1 tablespoon lemon juice*
salt and freshly-ground black pepper	*salt and freshly-ground black pepper*

1. Lay the cleaned and dried fresh, whole trout on a work surface and rub the skins gently with a generous grind of black pepper: this gives delicious piquancy to the rich skin which, when crisply fried in butter, is almost the best part of the fish. Then dust them all over with a little sifted flour seasoned with salt.

2. Warm a serving dish and some dinner plates, and quarter the lemon for garnishing the fish. Do this before beginning to fry the trout for they cook very quickly and should be served instantly they have

been fried,while the butter is still a bubbling golden foam.

3. If you have a heavy-bottomed frying-pan large enough to cook all the fish (with their heads on of course) at once, so much the better. If not, you will have to cook them two at a time and keep the first pair warm while you cook the others. Start cooking 20 minutes before eating in the latter case. Place the pan over medium heat. Add half the butter if cooking two fish at a time, or three-quarters if cooking all the trout together. When the butter is

foaming, add the fish, side by side, taking care that the underside of each fish is lying very flat so that all the skin will fry to a rich, crisp brown. After 4 minutes steady cooking in the bubbling butter, check that the underside of the fish is crisp and golden brown. If not, cook for a minute or so more. Turn the fish carefully, using a fish slice and palette knife (spatula) to avoid piercing the trout skin, and cook at the same steady heat for 4-5 minutes more. Then lift the trout out of the pan onto the warmed serving dish.

4. When all four trout are cooked, wipe out the pan with paper towels. Return the clean pan to the heat. Add the remaining 25g (1 oz) or 2 tablespoons of butter and the almonds. Cook, stirring occasionally, until the almonds are fried to a pale gold on both sides. Let the butter bubble up for a moment longer so that the colour becomes a shade richer. Meanwhile stir a light seasoning of salt and pepper into the lcmon juice then quickly add this to the butter. Stir once as it bubbles up, pour it over the trout and serve immediately. *Serves 4*

Stuffed clams or mussels

Mussels or clams, stuffed with a garlic, parsley and lemon-flavoured butter, make a deliciously appetizing beginning to a meal, and the smell that wafts from the oven while they are baking is marvellously inviting. In fact the butter is so good that I often use it in other ways; it is the perfect accompaniment to grilled fish and is delicious as a stuffing for baked potatoes.

Metric/Imperial	American
3kg(3qt) mussels	*3-4qt hard-shell clams*
OR 36-42 clams (quantity depends on size)	*OR 3-4qt mussels*
175g(6oz) butter, at room temperature	*1¼ sticks butter, at room temperature*
3 small garlic cloves, finely chopped	*3 small garlic cloves, finely chopped*
45ml(3 tablespoons) fresh chopped parsley	*3 tablespoons fresh chopped parsley*
7-10ml(1½-2 teaspoons) lemon juice	*1½-2 teaspoons lemon juice*
crustless white bread crumbed and dried	*dry white breadcrumbs from 3 slices bread*
salt and freshly-ground black pepper	*salt and freshly-ground black pepper*

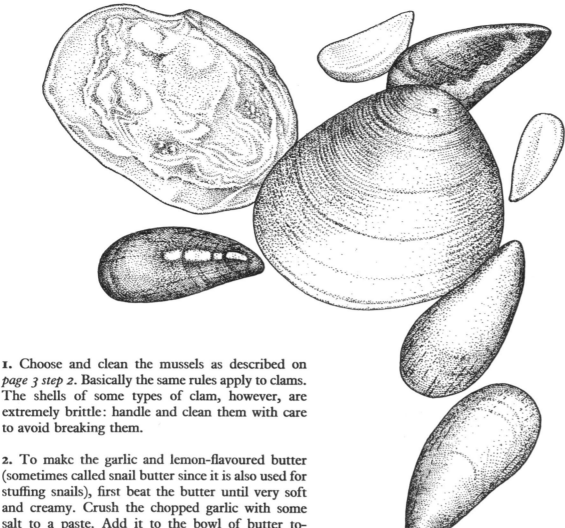

1. Choose and clean the mussels as described on *page 3 step 2*. Basically the same rules apply to clams. The shells of some types of clam, however, are extremely brittle: handle and clean them with care to avoid breaking them.

2. To make the garlic and lemon-flavoured butter (sometimes called snail butter since it is also used for stuffing snails), first beat the butter until very soft and creamy. Crush the chopped garlic with some salt to a paste. Add it to the bowl of butter together with the parsley, lemon juice and a generous seasoning of salt and pepper. Mash and stir until the mixture is well-blended, then set aside in a cool place.

3. Put a baking sheet in the oven: preheat to 230°C (450 °F) gas mark 8. Choose a heavy-bottomed pan large enough to hold all the shells. Put enough water into it to cover the base by 1.2cm ($\frac{1}{2}$in). Place the pan over high heat and bring to a rolling boil. Add the shellfish to the pan, cover with a well-fitting lid and cook over high heat for about 5 minutes until the shells are forced open by the steam (very large clams may need slighly longer). Shake or stir the pan gently every now and then to ensure the steam circulates to all parts of the pan. Remove the pan from the heat, take out all the shells and discard any that have not opened. Remove the empty half shells of half those that have opened, completely shell the rest. Divide the shellfish between 6 individual dishes, placing two clams or mussels in each half shell. Put a nugget of the snail butter on top of each, and cover with a sprinkling of the toasted breadcrumbs.

4. Standing the dishes on the preheated baking sheet, bake for 7-10 minutes until piping hot, golden and bubbling. Serve immediately with plenty of hot crusty bread to mop up the butter. *Serves 6*

†Mussel and clam shells sometimes topple over during baking with the result that the butter runs out of the shells and the flesh dries out. A simple way to solve this problem is to bake them in lined dishes and thus prevent slipping. Butter each dish generously. Lay in it a slice of thick, crustless, lightly-buttered bread. Make small hollows here and there in the bread and lay a shell in each one. The bread will crisp and 'fry' deliciously during baking.

Jugged kippers

I t never ceases to amaze me that the process of kippering herrings was only introduced in the middle of the nineteenth century. Kippers, or kippered herrings as they are more correctly called, seem synonymous with the institution called 'a proper British breakfast', and I always imagine they must have been enjoyed for centuries. Jugging is the simplest and cleanest way to prepare kippers – and ideal if, like me, you enjoy eating breakfast but do not relish the idea of cooking first thing in the morning! It is of course important to buy fish that have been kippered without additives (they are recognizable by their pale smoky colour), not the imitations that are dyed to a shade of mahogany.

Metric/Imperial
2 plump freshly cured kippers
50g(2oz) unsalted butter
freshly-ground black pepper

American
2 whole plump kippers
4 tablespoons unsalted butter
freshly-ground black pepper

1. Choose a large earthenware or china jug, tall and wide enough to stand a pair of kippers in so that only their tails appear above the rim. Fill it with freshly-boiled water and let it stand for 5 minutes or so to heat it thoroughly. If you can stand it over the central-heating boiler, on the side of the hob or stove or on any other warm surface, so much the better.

2. Boil a second kettle of fresh water. As soon as it reaches boiling point, empty the jug, stand the kippers in it and pour on boiling water to cover them, right up to the rim. Cover the jug with a dome of foil and leave for 5-10 minutes – kippers do not really need cooking, just heating through. Lift the fish out by their tails, blot them quickly on paper towels, and lay them on very hot plates. Top each with pats of butter, preferably stamped into thin rounds. Grind pepper over them and serve immediately. *Serves 2*

VEGETABLES
&
SALADS

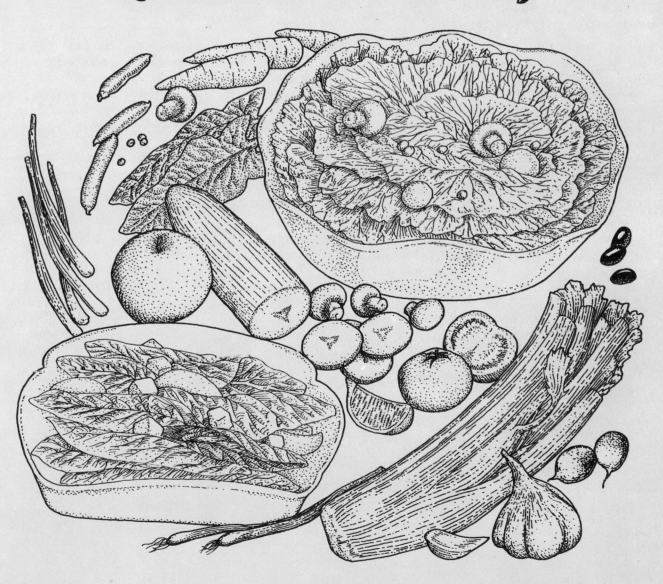

Potato salad

A really good potato salad is an excellent dish, and it is so easy to improvise, ringing the changes with different flavourings. Sometimes I add a scattering of tiny black olives, sometimes a handful of chopped watercress, sometimes feathery fronds of fennel. The only problem, and it is a major one in Britain, is getting hold of the small waxy varieties of potato that I feel are essential for this salad. The streak of Irish blood in me insists we grow these potatoes, for summer would not be summer without potato salad.

Metric/Imperial	American
900g(2lb) firm-fleshed, small, new potatoes	*2lb small new potatoes*
150ml(¼pt) rather acid vinaigrette dressing	*¾ cup rather acid vinaigrette dressing*
a good-sized bunch of young spring onions	*a good-sized bunch of scallions*
OR half a Spanish onion	*OR half a Bermuda or sweet onion*
150ml(¼pt) mayonnaise (page 127, step 2-4)	*⅔ cup mayonnaise (page 127, step 2-4)*
30ml(2 tablespoons) fresh chopped parsley	*2 tablespoons fresh chopped parsley*
30ml(2 tablespoons) fresh chopped mint	*2 tablespoons fresh chopped mint*
30ml(2 tablespoons) fresh chopped chives	*2 tablespoons fresh chopped chives*
coarse salt	*coarse salt*
freshly-ground black pepper	*freshly-ground black pepper*

1. Start making potato salad about 1¼ hours before serving it. Wash the potatoes gently but do not peel them or scrub away their skins. Select, in so far as is possible, those of an even size so that they will all complete cooking at the same time. Steam the potatoes until tender. How long they will take to cook is difficult to say, since much depends on size and also on the variety of potato you are using. But it is wise to check progress – stabbing a potato with a skewer – at regular intervals, for few things are less appetizing than overcooked potato salad.

2. As soon as the cooked potatoes are cool enough to handle, strip away the skins: they will peel away neatly and easily. Chop the potatoes roughly, so that they are in nice large chunks, and put them into a mixing bowl. Add some coarse salt and a generous grind of black pepper. Make the vinaigrette dressing with rather more vinegar than you normally use and pour it over the salad. Trim and chop the onions. Don't make the pieces too tiny, potato salad isn't a dainty dish and good bites of onion flavour are an essential part of it. Add the onions to the bowl, and turn the potatoes gently in the mixture from time to time as they cool. Adding the vinaigrette and seasonings while the potatoes are still hot is one of the clues to making a successful potato salad, for the potatoes absorb the flavours as they cool.

3. Just as important is draining off excess vinaigrette dressing just before serving – and the potatoes should be served just as soon as they have cooled. Turn the potatoes into a large strainer placed over a second bowl to let the surplus dressing drip away, then return the potatoes to the first bowl. Thin the mayonnaise to a cream with a spoonful or so of warm water and stir it into the potatoes, a little at a time, as you may need all of it. It should coat the potatoes thinly but evenly.

4. Finally, turn the potatoes into a serving dish or salad bowl. Mix the fresh chopped herbs together and scatter them over the potatoes to make a deliciously scented and colourful garnish. *Serves 6*

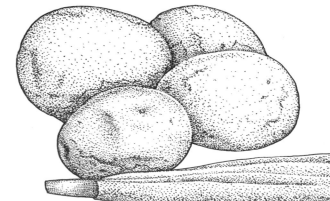

Imam Bayaldi

The first time I saw aubergines (eggplants) was in a Turkish market – lustrous purple skins gleaming royally in a dusty wicker basket. I was told that this vegetable was believed by the locals to be endowed with magical properties, and that it was known as 'poor man's meat' in some Arab countries. I can understand why. The Middle East abounds with aubergine (eggplant) recipes, and Imam Bayaldi is one of the very best. It is rich and well flavoured and tempted me (at least on a temporary basis) to become a vegetarian. The name means 'the high priest swooned' in Turkish. Legends vary as to the reason why: some say he swooned from sheer gastronomic delight, others that he fainted when he calculated the cost of the olive oil needed to make the dish. This version certainly delights my palate but the amount of olive oil it uses is relatively modest.

Metric/Imperial	American
3 large aubergines	3 eggplants
350g(¾lb) onions	¾lb onions
350g(¾lb) tomatoes	¾lb ripe tomatoes
2 garlic cloves, finely chopped	2 cloves garlic, finely chopped
40g(1½oz) pinenuts	1½oz(¼ cup) Indian nuts
50g(2oz) raisins	2oz(⅓ cup) raisins
1 large lemon	1 large lemon
150ml(¼pt) olive oil	5 tablespoons olive oil
5ml(1 teaspoon) caster sugar	1 teaspoon superfine sugar
a few parsley sprigs	a few parsley sprigs
2.5ml(½ teaspoon) cumin seeds	½ teaspoon cumin seeds
2.5ml(½ teaspoon) ground cinnamon	½ teaspoon ground cinnamon
salt and freshly-ground black pepper	salt and freshly-ground black pepper

1. Cut each aubergine (eggplant) in half lengthways and wipe the skins clean. Carefully scoop out the pulp with a small spoon, taking care not to pierce the skins. Put the pulp into a colander, sprinkling generous quantities of coarse salt between layers. Put a small plate on top, weigh it down and set aside (on the draining board by the sink is best). Leave for half an hour to draw out some of the bitter juices. Sprinkle the insides of the empty shells with salt and set them aside too.

2. Meanwhile prepare the stuffing ingredients. Chop the onions quite finely. Crush the garlic. Dip the tomatoes in boiling water, drain, peel away skins and chop the flesh. Chop the parsley. Squeeze the lemon juice. Crush the cumin seeds in a mortar with a pestle or using the back of a wooden spoon.

3. Rinse the aubergine (eggplant) shells and pulp under cold running water to wash away the salt. Dry them thoroughly with plenty of paper towels.

4. This delicious cooked vegetable dish is served cold, so you should prepare it several hours or a day before serving. Warm half the olive oil in a saucepan. Add the cumin, the onions, garlic, and aubergine (eggplant) pulp (but not the shells). Fry gently for 10 minutes or until the onions are softened and slightly coloured. Stir the pan from time to time. Then increase heat a little, add the tomatoes and continue cooking for another 10 minutes or so until the tomatoes have pulped down and most of their moisture has evaporated. Stir the pan frequently during this time to prevent the vegetables from sticking. Remove from the heat, then stir in the dried fruit and nuts, the cinnamon, 30ml (2 tablespoons) chopped fresh parsley and salt and pepper to taste. Sharpen with a squeeze of lemon juice if you like.

5. Stuff the shells with the vegetable mixture, and place them side by side in a sauté pan or a not too deep flameproof dish with a lid. Just touching each other is best, as they will then support each other during cooking. Carefully pour the lemon juice and remaining olive oil round the stuffed shells but not into them. Add the sugar and enough hot water to come at least halfway up the sides of the stuffed shells.

6. Place the pan over medium heat and bring to simmering point. Immediately reduce heat to the gentlest possible simmer, cover the pan with a lid, and cook for 1 hour – by which time the vegetables should be perfectly tender. Use an asbestos mat if necessary to keep the heat really low, or alternatively bake the dish in an oven preheated to 160°C (325°F) gas mark 3.

7. Remove the pan from the heat but leave the vegetables in the cooking liquor until quite cold. If the pan is pretty enough to use for serving, then drain off the cooking liquor with a bulb baster. Alternatively lift the stuffed shells carefully out of the pan onto a pretty serving dish, using a fish slice or wide spatula and slotted spoon. Cover the vegetables with a dome of foil and refrigerate until shortly before serving. Remove the dish from the refrigerator about 30 minutes before serving and garnish each halved aubergine (eggplant) with fresh chopped parsley. *Serves 6*

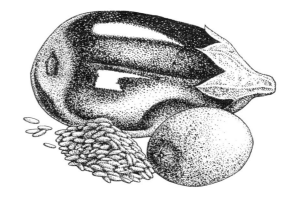

Asparagus Hollandaise

Samuel Pepys, the famous English diarist, was a noted pleasure-seeker and his writings are peppered with descriptions of the meals he enjoyed. In a typical entry in the spring of 1667 he records 'had 100 stalks of best asparagus with salmon for dinner'. Asparagus fresh from the garden is perhaps the greatest of all vegetable treats – the difference between home-grown and bought asparagus being more marked than is the case with any other vegetable. Today we have neither the appetites nor the finances to consume 100 stalks, but a modest bunch of asparagus served with a classic Hollandaise sauce is a treat I hope to enjoy at least once each year.

Metric/Imperial	American
900g(2lb) fresh asparagus	*2lb fresh asparagus*
salt	*salt*
half a lemon, sliced	*half a lemon, sliced*
For the Hollandaise sauce:	**For the Hollandaise sauce:**
225-275g(8-10 oz) unsalted butter	*1-1¼ cups unsalted butter*
4 large (no. 2) egg yolks	*4 large egg yolks*
22ml(1½ tablespoons) dry white wine or water	*1½ tablespoons dry white wine or water*
15ml(1 tablespoon) lemon juice	*1 tablespoon lemon juice*
salt and freshly-ground white pepper	*salt and white pepper*
extra lemon juice to taste	*extra lemon juice to taste*

1. Choose asparagus stalks of about the same thickness so that they will all take the same time to cook. The heads or tips should be firm and closed. The stalks should have a good amount of green without long woody bases. Wash the stalks carefully to remove any sand or grit. Trim off the woody bases to make the stalks all the same length, and scrape the stems with a knife to remove scaly leaf points. Set aside one stem, which will be used to test cooking time, divide the rest into four bunches. Tie each bunch with soft string in two places.

2. Fill a tall saucepan, such as the bottom of a doubleboiler, with enough water to come two-thirds of the way up the asparagus stems. Salt the water lightly, add the slices of lemon and bring to the boil. Stand the four bunches of asparagus and the single stem in the pan and cover it with a dome of foil high enough not to touch the asparagus tips. Like this, the tougher stems will cook in the water while the tender tips cook in the steam. Steam cooking takes longer and is gentler than agitated water, so the whole vegetable will be done at the same time. When the water comes back to boiling, reduce heat to a gentle simmer. How long the asparagus will take to cook depends on its age and size, but 10-15 minutes is usual. Test the loose stem after 10 minutes by piercing the thickest part with a knife.

3. Make the Hollandaise sauce while the asparagus is cooking – or, if you prefer, you can make the sauce beforehand. It can be kept warm in a covered bowl placed over a pan of hot water for up to an hour. Fill the bottom part of a doubleboiler with a little water and bring to a bare simmer. Cut two pieces, each piece about 15g (½oz) or 1 tablespoon, from the block of chilled butter. Dice the rest of the butter into small pieces. Put them into a saucepan over low heat. Remove the pan from the heat as soon as the butter is melted – do not let it get oily. Set aside.

4. Away from the heat, beat the egg yolks in the top part of the doubleboiler with a balloon whisk for 2 minutes. Add a good pinch of salt, the wine or water and lemon juice and beat for another 30 seconds. Add one of the pieces of chilled butter and place the pan over the barely simmering water. Stir the mixture steadily with the whisk. The butter will melt and amalgamate with the eggs; it will become creamy and begin to thicken. Within 2-3 minutes it will cling to the wires of the whisk and you will see the base of the pan between strokes. Remove the pan from the heat.

5. Immediately add the remaining piece of chilled butter and whisk until it has been absorbed by the eggs; adding the chilled butter at this stage prevents the eggs from continuing to cook. Now start whisking in the hot melted butter, drop by drop at first and then, when the mixture begins to get really thick, more rapidly. When all the butter has been absorbed and the sauce is smooth and thick, season it to taste with salt, pepper and extra lemon juice.

6. When the asparagus is cooked, lift it carefully out of the pan. Drain it well, cut the string, and arrange each bunch on a hot plate. Put a small bowl of the sauce on each plate and serve immediately.

Serves 4

Salade Niçoise

I associate this salad with long, lazy, informal lunches eaten outdoors in fine summer weather. Even if the sunshine is not brilliant, the colours and flavours of the dish can make me believe I am in the south of France! One of the joys about salade Niçoise is the fact that most of the ingredients used are staple items and, if you can supplement these with fresh garden vegetables, it is a dish which can be conjured up at short notice for unexpected guests. There is no need to stick rigidly to the vegetables listed here. This recipe is my preferred version but authoritative sources suggest using artichoke bottoms (hearts), young broad (lima) beans, diced cucumber and new potatoes as additions or alternatives, and the salad is often served on a bed of crisp lettuce hearts.

Metric/Imperial	American
700g(1½lb) young, stringless French beans	1½lb fresh green beans, French cut
1 large crushed garlic clove	1 large crushed clove garlic
vinaigrette dressing	vinaigrette dressing
900g(2lb)small, firm tomatoes	2lb medium-sized firm tomatoes
7 hard-boiled eggs, halved	7 hard-cooked eggs, halved
290g(10½oz) canned, best tuna fish	14oz canned, best tuna fish
3 × 50g(1¾oz) cans anchovy fillets	3 × 2oz cans anchovies
1 very large or 2 smallish red peppers	1 large or 2 small sweet red peppers
3 dozen small black olives	3 dozen black olives

1. Top and tail the beans (remove tips); steam until just tender. Refresh the beans under cold running water and drain very thoroughly. Cut into half lengths if long and place in a mixing bowl. Stir the crushed garlic into a good quantity of vinaigrette dressing and immediately pour this over the beans. Set aside until cold.

2. Meanwhile, pour boiling water over the tomatoes. Leave for 1 minute, drain them and peel away skins. Cut each tomato into quarters, scoop out and discard the seeds. Cut the red pepper(s) into quarters, lengthways, remove seeds and pith (white fibre) and flatten the flesh as much as possible. Cook, skin side up, under a hot grill (broiler) until the papery-thin skins blacken and blister. As soon as the peppers are cool enough to handle, peel away the skins and cut the flesh up into strips. Drain the tuna and break the fish into large chunks. Put it into a large mixing bowl and add the prepared tomatoes and peppers.

3. By this time the beans should be cold. Lift them out of the vinaigrette dressing with a slotted spoon and lay them over the base of a salad bowl. Pour the vinaigrette over the tuna, tomatoes and peppers. Toss lightly until well mixed and lightly coated with the dressing. Lift them out of the vinaigrette, again using a slotted spoon, and arrange them on top of the beans in the salad bowl. Re-use the vinaigrette a third time, this time dribbling a coffee (demi-tasse) spoonful of the dressing over each halved egg yolk to moisten it nicely. Add the eggs to the salad bowl and scatter the olives among them. Finally, drain the anchovy fillets from the oil in which they are canned,

and arrange them in a lattice pattern across the top of the salad. Serve immediately, preferably accompanied by some hot garlic bread.   *Serves 6*

† To make hot garlic bread, cut a French or Vienna loaf into slices without cutting through the base. Fan out the slices and spread one side of each generously with garlic butter (made as described on *page 135, step 2*). Press the loaf together again, wrap it in foil and bake in a hot oven for 15-20 minutes, unwrapping the upper part of the foil for the last five minutes to crisp the crust.

Spicy red cabbage

Spicy red cabbage makes a substantial and warming vegetable dish which I love to serve on cold winter days, and it is a particularly good accompaniment for the rich meats such as pork and goose which make such admirable cold-weather eating. This delicious inexpensive dish is very practical too. The casserole of vegetables can be prepared in advance and you can set an automatic oven timer to switch itself on in your absence so that the steaming red cabbage is ready to welcome your return (in this case allow a total of 3 hours cooking time).

Metric/Imperial	American
700g(1½lb) red cabbage	*1½lb red cabbage*
225g(½lb) onions	*½lb onions*
1 cooking apple or crisp eating apple	*1 tart apple or a dessert apple*
175g(6oz) prunes	*about 1 cup prunes*
1 garlic clove	*1 clove garlic*
5cm(2in) cinnamon stick	*2in stick cinnamon*
2 cloves	*2 cloves*
5ml(1 teaspoon) cumin seeds	*1 teaspoon cumin seeds*
5ml(1 teaspoon) coriander seeds	*1 teaspoon coriander seeds*
30ml(2 tablespoons) red wine vinegar	*2 tablespoons red wine vinegar*
30ml(2 tablespoons) redcurrant jelly	*2 tablespoons redcurrant jelly*
25g(1 oz) butter	*2 tablespoons butter*
salt and freshly-ground black pepper	*salt and freshly-ground black pepper*
freshly-grated nutmeg	*freshly-grated nutmeg*

1. Pull away and discard any damaged outer cabbage leaves. Quarter the cabbage and cut out the tough stalk (core). Shred the cabbage finely, grating it against a mandolin or slicing it with a sharp knife. Put the cabbage into a large casserole (Dutch oven) which has been greased with butter. Preheat the oven to 150°C (300°F) gas mark 2.

2. Peel and finely chop the onions. Crush the garlic clove with plenty of salt, and add to the pot together with the onions. Peel, quarter and core the apple. Dice it and add to the pot. Add the prunes too – the large Californian variety are best, preferably already-pitted. Whatever variety you use, there is no need to soak them in advance: they will become tender during the long cooking, being plumped up by the juices exuded by the cabbage, apples and onions, yet not so over-cooked that they will disintegrate.

3. Crush the cumin and coriander seeds lightly with the back of a spoon. Add them to the casserole together with a grating of nutmeg and a generous grind of black pepper. Pour on the wine vinegar and mix all the ingredients together very thoroughly. Using your hands is a bit messy but most effective. Tie the cloves and the piece of cinnamon in a piece

of cheesecloth and bury the spice bag among the vegetables. Add the redcurrant jelly. Press the mixture well down into the pot, then cover the surface with the butter cut into flakes. Lay a circle of buttered greaseproof or waxed paper immediately on top and put on the lid.

4. Cook the cabbage dish for 2¾ hours, stirring the mixture occasionally if you are in the kitchen while it cooks. Remove the lid and the buttered paper, taste the cabbage and adjust seasoning to taste. Remove the spice bag, squeezing the juices back into the dish. Stir everything once or twice and, since the ingredients will have reduced during cooking, transfer them to a smaller warmed casserole or vegetable dish for serving. *Serves 6*

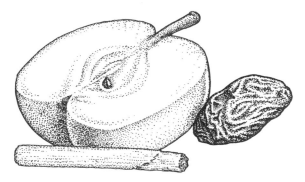

Ratatouille

One of the things I like so much about this excellent French vegetable dish is the fact that it is equally good eaten hot or cold. All the best vegetables of late summer are combined to make a rich, well-flavoured stew: each ingredient is distinct yet blends deliciously with the others.

Metric/Imperial	American
225g(½lb) aubergines	½lb eggplant
225g(½lb) courgettes	½lb baby zucchini
225g(½lb) onions	½lb onions
2 red peppers	2 sweet red peppers
1 green pepper	1 green pepper
2 garlic cloves	2 cloves garlic
350g(¾lb) tomatoes	¾lb tomatoes
3 dozen coriander seeds	3doz coriander seeds
5ml(1 teaspoon) lemon juice	1 teaspoon lemon juice
5ml(1 teaspoon) caster sugar	1 teaspoon superfine sugar
90ml(6 tablespoons) olive oil	6 tablespoons olive oil
60ml(4 tablespoons) fresh chopped basil	4 tablespoons freshly-chopped basil
coarse salt	coarse or sea salt
freshly-ground black pepper	freshly-ground black pepper

1. Firm young fresh vegetables are essential for a really good ratatouille. The vegetables must not be chopped too small and they must not be cooked for too long – or the resulting dish will be a disintegrated mush instead of a richly-flavoured stew in which each ingredient is tender and blends with the rest yet retains its own individuality.

2. The first important step is to salt the aubergines (eggplants) and courgettes (zucchini) to rid them of excess moisture. Cut the unpeeled aubergines (eggplants) into cubes about 2cm (¾in) square. Place them in a colander, sprinkling coarse salt between layers, press a saucer on top and weigh it down. Slice the unpeeled courgettes (zucchini) into rings about 1cm (⅓in) thick. Put them into a separate colander or strainer, again sprinkling salt between layers, pressing a saucer and weights on top. Set both vegetables aside to drain for 1 hour.

3. While the two vegetables are draining, prepare the remaining ones. Slice the onions (which should ideally be fairly small ones) quite thinly. Cut away stalk, seeds and all the white pith or membrane from the red and green peppers, and then chop the flesh into fairly large chunks. Peel the garlic cloves and chop them very finely indeed. Put the tomatoes into a bowl. Pour on enough boiling water to cover and leave for 1 minute to loosen the skins. Drain and refresh under cold water. Drain again. Slip off the skins. Quarter the tomatoes, or if large divide into one-eighths. Remove central cores if tough and spoon out the juice and seeds. Removing the pulp is important as it is watery and would make the ratatouille too liquid if included in the dish. Crush the coriander seeds in a mortar with a pestle, add a good seasoning of salt and pepper, the sugar and lemon juice. (If the tomatoes used are home-grown and have a particularly good flavour, the quantities of lemon juice and sugar can be reduced by half.)

4. When the aubergines (eggplants) and courgettes (zucchini) are ready, rinse them under cold running water and turn them onto a double thickness of paper towels. Gather the paper towels up round the vegetables and squeeze gently but firmly with your hands to extract moisture and to dry the vegetables.

5. Warm the olive oil in a large heavy-bottomed saucepan. Add the onions and garlic and cook over low heat for 10 minutes until softened but not coloured. Stir in the cubes of prepared aubergine (eggplant) and the red and green peppers. When they are coated all over with oil, cover the pan with a lid and leave to simmer over very low heat for 20 minutes, just shaking or gently stirring the pan from time to time. Then add the courgettes (zucchini) to the pan together with the coriander and other seasonings. Stir them gently, cover the pan and cook for 5 minutes more. Now add the tomatoes

to the pan: do not stir them into the pan but just tip them in on top of the other vegetables. Cover the pan again and cook for 5 minutes more. Finally, remove the lid from the pan, sprinkle on the basil and stir it and the tomatoes into the vegetable stew. Let the mixture simmer uncovered for 5 minutes to ensure the tomatoes are heated through and to allow a little moisture to evaporate. Check seasoning and adjust to taste. Turn the ratatouille onto a serving dish and serve immediately. Alternatively, cook ahead, allow to become cold (but do not chill) and serve cold.

Serves 4

Dolmades

The Greeks are almost as fond of wild vegetables as they are of cultivated varieties, and sensibly make use of wild artichokes, young dandelion leaves and other fresh wild vegetables and herbs as and when they come into season each year. Using vine leaves to make tasty and pretty-looking packaging for savoury rice is typical of the thrifty and ingenious approach to cookery among Greek mountain people. In other countries we may have to buy cans, rather than pluck the leaves freely from the vine. Dolmades nonetheless make economic (and I think particularly delectable) mouthfuls to nibble with wine or ouzo before a meal or to serve as part of a mixed hors d'oeuvres.

Metric/Imperial	American
about 300g(11oz) fresh vine leaves	about ¾lb fresh vine leaves
OR 425g(15oz) can of vine leaves in brine	OR 1lb can vine leaves
115g(¼lb) long grain rice	⅔ cup long grain rice
115g(¼lb) finely chopped onion	⅔ cup finely chopped onion
1 large garlic clove	1 large clove garlic
15g(½oz) pinenuts	1 tablespoon Indian nuts or pignolias
225g(½lb) can Italian tomatoes	10 oz can whole Italian tomatoes
45ml(3 tablespoons) chopped fresh mint	3 tablespoons chopped fresh mint leaves
1 juicy lemon	juice of 1 lemon
575ml(1pt) chicken stock	2¼ cups chicken stock or bouillon
90ml(6 tablespoons) olive oil	6 tablespoons olive oil
15ml(1 tablespoon) tomato purée	1 tablespoon tomato purée
5ml(1 teaspoon) caster sugar	1 teaspoon superfine sugar
salt and freshly-ground black pepper	salt and freshly-ground black pepper

1. All sorts of ingredients can be used to stuff vine leaves, but this meatless stuffing is particularly good. Always make dolmades a day before serving. First prepare the stuffing. Warm the olive oil in a heavy-bottomed pan over low heat. Add the finely chopped onion and cook for 4-5 minutes. Chop the garlic very finely, and add it to the pan together with the rice. Cook over the lowest possible heat, stirring frequently, for about 15 minutes. Meanwhile chop the mint and roughly chop the canned tomatoes. Add the tomatoes and their juice to the pan. Add the mint, the sugar and 5ml (1 teaspoon) lemon juice. Stir these ingredients into the rice, then cover the pan and simmer over very gentle heat for 15-20 minutes until the liquid is nearly all absorbed. If there is any liquid left at the end of this time, drain it off and reserve. Turn the rice mixture onto a plate and set aside until cold.

2. If fresh vine leaves are used, they will need brief cooking before they are used to wrap the rice stuffing. Canned vine leaves need to be drained and blanched: this will make them more pliable and easier to separate. Bring a large, wide saucepan of water to boiling point. Add the stack of vine leaves, and a generous quantity of salt if fresh vine leaves are used. Simmer for 1 minute if fresh vine leaves are used, for 5 minutes if canned vine leaves are used. In either case, flip the stack of vine leaves over with a metal spatula halfway through blanching time. Turn the contents of the pan into a colander and drain well, then rinse the leaves under cold running water and drain again. Carefully separate the leaves, pulling them gently away from the stack one at a time. This is the most difficult part of the operation and great care is needed to avoid tearing the leaves. Pat the leaves dry with paper towels. Lay the largest, best-shaped and blemish free leaves in a single layer on a large work surface, arranging them vein side up. Set any torn leaves and the smaller whole leaves aside.

3. Season the cold rice mixture to taste with salt, freshly-ground pepper and a little extra mint if wished. Stir in the pinenuts (Indian nuts). Spoon a small quantity of the mixture onto a large leaf, near the stalk end. Fold the stalk end of the leaf over the stuffing, fold the sides of the leaf inwards, then roll up neatly and tightly so that the stuffing is contained in the vine leaf and looks like a miniature cigar-shaped parcel about 2.5 × 5cm (1 × 2in). Use the rest of the stuffing to fill the other large vine leaves in the same way. If any is left over, use smaller quantities as appropriate to stuff the reserved whole small vine leaves.

4. Preheat the oven to 150°C (300°F) gas mark 2. Choose a large gratin or shallow baking dish just large enough to take the dolmades in a single layer. Put the stuffed vine leaves into the dish in a single layer (use two dishes if necessary), arranging them with the seams underneath and wedged fairly close together to prevent unrolling. Measure the stock into a small saucepan, add any leftover rice cooking liquid, the juice of half a lemon, the tomato purée and a good seasoning of salt and pepper. Stir the ingredients together until well blended, then bring to the boil. Pour as much of this liquid over the dolmades as is necessary to cover them. Arrange any leftover or broken vine leaves on top, and cover the dish with foil. Cook for 1½ hours.

5. Leave the cooked dolmades in the gratin or baking dish until quite cold. Then, if the dish is pretty enough for serving, remove the covering of leaves and drain off any liquid remaining in the dish using a bulb baster. Alternatively, remove the covering of leaves, then carefully lift the dolmades onto a cake rack to drain. Then transfer them to a pretty serving dish. In either case, cover the dolmades with fresh foil and store in a cool place (preferably not the refrigerator) for 12-24 hours before serving.

Serves 4-6

Hummus bi tahini

The earthy flavour of chick-peas (garbanzos) combined with nutty sesame seed paste (called tahini) makes this famous Arab dish my favourite vegetable pâté. It is delicious with pre-dinner drinks or to start a meal. It also makes an excellent dip for strips of raw vegetables such as carrots, celery, cucumber and spring onions (scallions) when diluted to thinner consistency.

Metric/Imperial	American
115g(¼lb) chick-peas	¼lb garbanzos
150ml(¼pt) tahini paste	about ¾ cup tahini paste
2 large garlic cloves, finely chopped	2 large cloves garlic, finely chopped
2 large juicy lemons	2 large juicy lemons
10ml(2 teaspoons) olive oil	2 teaspoons olive oil
salt	salt
fresh chopped parsley	fresh chopped parsley
a pinch of paprika	a pinch of paprika
OR roasted, ground cumin seed for garnishing	OR roasted, ground cumin seed for garnishing

1. Starting at least 24 hours before you intend to eat the hummus, put the dried chick-peas into a large bowl. Pour on cold fresh water – about three times the volume of the chick peas. Leave them to soak overnight in a cool place.

2. Next day, strain the liquid from the chick-peas, and rinse them very thoroughly under cold running water. Put the rinsed and drained peas into a large saucepan and cover generously with fresh cold water. Do not add any salt: it toughens the chick-pea skins and prevents the peas from softening properly. Bring slowly to boiling point. Reduce heat, cover the pan with a lid and simmer gently until the chick-peas are so tender that they can easily be crushed between finger and thumb. How long this will take depends on the freshness of the peas. (Very old ones will never soften adequately, even if you cook them for days so it is wise to buy from a shop which has good turnover.) Two hours cooking time is a good average in my experience.

3. Drain the cooked peas, reserving about 275ml (½pt) or ¼ cup of the cooking liquid. Crush the garlic cloves with plenty of salt. Put them into the goblet of a blender. Squeeze the lemons and add 60ml (4 tablespoons) of their juice to the goblet. Add an equal quantity of the cooking liquid, and all the chick-peas. Reduce the mixture to a smooth purée.

4. Scrape the purée out into a mixing bowl. Using a fork, gradually beat in the tahini paste. When the mixture is smoothly blended, thin it to a very thick cream and adjust seasoning to taste. I find that about 120ml (8 tablespoons) of extra liquid are needed to get the right consistency: this can be cooking liquid or lemon juice, or a mixture of both. It is best to add the liquid just a spoonful at a time: check consistency and taste for seasoning after each spoonful has been absorbed by the mixture, adding salt and/or more garlic if necessary.

5. When the consistency seems right, turn the hummus bi tahini into a shallow dish. Cover it with plastic film or foil and refrigerate until serving. It will keep well for 5 days.

6. Just before serving, drizzle the olive oil over the surface of the hummus. Garnish the middle with a little chopped fresh parsley, and sprinkle a ring of either paprika or toasted and ground cumin seeds around the edge. Serve with a small dish of black olives, and warmed pitta bread which can be broken into pieces and dipped into this delicious vegetable pâté.

Serves 6-8

Braised chestnuts

The Italians are professionals at drying chestnuts and the French are clever at canning them but, for a vegetable dish, fresh chestnuts are a must. Fresh chestnuts are admittedly a bit of a nuisance to peel but effort is amply rewarded by the results – tender, sweet, floury chestnuts bathed in a rich savoury sauce. Served with gamebirds, venison or hare, braised chestnuts make a superb and unusual alternative to potatoes. Served with sausages, they lift a modest family dish into the luxury class – memorably good if you also serve a dish of fried bread croûtons and baby Brussels sprouts that have been steamed and tossed in melted butter.

Metric/Imperial	American
700g(1½lb) fresh Spanish chestnuts	1½lb chestnuts
1 onion	1 onion
1 celery stalk	1 stalk celery
75g(3oz) butter	6 tablespoons butter
575ml(1pt) strong brown beef stock	2¼ cups beef stock or broth
90ml(6 tablespoons) Marsala or dry white wine	6 tablespoons Marsala or dry white wine
20ml(1 slightly heaped tablespoon) arrowroot	1 slightly heaped tablespoon arrowroot
salt	salt
freshly-ground black pepper	freshly-ground black pepper
a handful of fresh chopped parsley	¼ cup fresh chopped parsley

1. When peeling chestnuts it is important to remove not only the shells but also the papery-thin bitter skin that sticks firmly to the kernels. The easiest way to peel chestnuts is as follows. Discard any mouldy or damaged chestnuts. Using a sharp knife score the rest around the 'waists'. Bring a pan of water to the boil, add the scored chestnuts and bring back to boiling point. Reduce heat to simmering, cover the pan with a lid and cook for 5-10 minutes.

2. When the chestnuts are half-cooked, turn out the nuts into a colander and drain them well, then wrap all but one in a thick cloth (this is because the warmer the chestnuts are the easier it is to remove shell and skin). Insert the point of a knife into the scored shell and lift off both shell and skin, the two should slip off together quite easily. Peel the rest of the chestnuts in the same way, discarding any that do not look completely wholesome.

3. Chop the onion and celery quite finely. Melt half the butter in a flameproof casserole (Dutch oven). Add the onion and celery, stirring them into the butter until coated all over. Cover the pot and cook over gentle heat for 8-10 minutes until the vegetables are transparent and slightly softened.

4. Preheat the oven to 150°C (300°F) gas mark 2. Sift the arrowroot into a cup. Blend it to a paste with a little of the wine, then stir in the rest of the wine.

When the onion and celery are softened, scatter the peeled chestnuts on top of them. Add a seasoning of salt and freshly-ground black pepper.

5. Pour on the stock and the wine mixture. Check that the chestnuts are covered by about 1.25cm (½in): if necessary add some water to increase the level of the liquid. Bring to simmering point, stirring continuously.

6. Cover the pot with a lid and transfer it to the centre of the oven. Cook until the chestnuts are tender and floury, taking care not to let them overcook or to disintegrate. This usually takes 40 minutes but can be quicker or longer. Test after 25 minutes by piercing a chestnut with the point of a sharp knife. If they are not ready, check at 5-10 minute intervals until cooked.

7. By the time the chestnuts are cooked, they will probably have absorbed most of the liquid, leaving a small quantity of rich, syrupy sauce. If the chestnuts are tender before the sauce is sufficiently reduced, strain off the liqiud and reduce it by fast boiling. If the sauce is very syrupy and the chestnuts are still not tender enough, add a little more boiling stock or water to the pot. In either case, check seasoning just before serving. Stir in the remaining butter and, when it has melted, sprinkle on the fresh chopped parsley.

Serves 4-6

Courgettes à la Grecque

Vegetables served à la grècque are vegetables cooked with lemon, wine, olive oil, herbs and seasonings, then left to cool before serving. They make a dish which is attractive to look at, and the taste is fresh and aromatic. I like to serve them as a light first course. They also make an excellent and unusual side salad to serve with plain roasts and chops or steak, and can be served as part of a cold buffet. Courgettes as they are called in France and Britain, or zucchini as they are called in Italy and America, have a delicate flavour when they are young and tender – choose those which are no more than 10cm (4in) long after trimming – they are, I think, particularly well suited to this cooking method.

Metric/Imperial	American
450g(1lb) small courgettes	*1lb small zucchini*
1 large onion	*1 large onion*
1 large garlic clove	*1 large clove garlic*
1 lemon	*1 lemon*
1 small bunch of parsley	*1 small bunch parsley*
5ml(1 teaspoon) coriander seeds	*1 teaspoon coriander seeds*
2 bay leaves	*2 bay leaves*
a sprig of thyme, preferably lemon thyme	*1 sprig thyme, preferably lemon thyme*
OR a pinch of dried thyme	*OR a pinch of dried thyme*
60ml(4 tablespoons) olive oil	*4 tablespoons olive oil*
90ml(6 tablespoons) fairly dry white wine	*6 tablespoons fairly dry white wine*
salt and freshly-ground black pepper	*salt and freshly-ground black pepper*

1. Trim the courgettes (zucchini) and wipe the skins clean. Slice each one into four long pieces, then cut each piece across to make sticks about 5cm (2in) long. Chop the onion and garlic very finely. Measure the wine into a jug or cup, add an equal quantity of cold water and about 22ml (1½ tablespoons) freshly-squeezed lemon juice.

2. Warm the olive oil in a sauté pan. Add the chopped onion and garlic and stir to coat them all over with the oil. Cover the pan and sweat the vegetables over low heat for 10 minutes, shaking the pan occasionally during this time. Crush the coriander seeds with the back of a spoon, and lightly crush the stalks of some parsley (reserve the leaves). Add both seeds and stalks to the pan and cook stirring for 1 minute. Pour on the liquids and add the bay leaves and thyme. Bring the mixture to boiling point, and let it bubble and simmer un-covered for 3-4 minutes.

3. Add the prepared courgettes (zucchini) to the pan. Bring back to simmering point, cover the pan and cook gently for 7 minutes, stirring or shaking the pan from time to time to help the vegetables to cook evenly. Shaking the pan is, on the whole, preferable as it is less likely to bruise the delicate vegetables. Add some salt and a generous grind of black pepper to the pan, and continue cooking the vegetables quite gently for 5-7 minutes more (this time without the lid) until the vegetables are quite tender.

4. Turn the vegetables and juices onto a serving dish and set aside until cold. Just before serving, remove the parsley stalks, bay leaves and sprig of thyme. Squeeze them gently so that the juices drip back onto the dish. Check and adjust seasoning to taste, and sprinkle on a garnish of bright green, freshly-chopped parsley leaves. Serve with plenty of hot crusty bread.

Serves 4

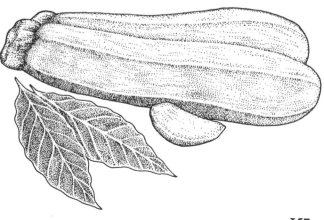

Stuffed tomatoes

Firm, ripe, richly-flavoured tomatoes, as big as clenched fists, are perfect for stuffing – especially if home-grown and freshly-picked. In fact these big Mediterranean-style, or beef-steak tomatoes as they are called in America, are the only sort worth stuffing. Varieties such as Moneymaker, favoured by commercial growers chiefly for their uniform size are too small, insipid tasting and watery in texture. A robust Provençal-style stuffing, as given here, complements fine tomatoes beautifully; and if the tomatoes are served on crisp rounds of thick bread fried in olive oil, so very much the better.

Metric/Imperial	American
6 fine tomatoes each about 200g(7oz)	6 tomatoes, each about ½lb in weight
175g(6oz) onions, peeled weight	1 medium-sized onion
125g(¼lb) mushrooms	¼lb mushrooms
3 fat garlic cloves	3 fat cloves garlic
25g(1 oz) black olives, stoned weight	1-2 tablespoons pitted black olives
40g(1½oz) long-grain rice	¼ cup long-grain rice
50g(1¾oz) can anchovy fillets	2oz can anchovy fillets
60ml(4 tablespoons) fresh chopped parsley	4 tablespoons fresh chopped parsley
30ml(2 tablespoons) grated Parmesan cheese	2 tablespoons grated Parmesan cheese
6 thick slices of white bread	6 slices thick white bread
olive oil for frying	olive oil for frying
salt	salt
a little caster sugar	a little superfine sugar
freshly-ground black pepper	freshly-ground black pepper

1. Cut a thin slice off the top of each tomato. Using a teaspoon carefully scoop out the pulp and seeds. Be careful not to pierce the sides of the tomatoes. Sprinkle the inside of each tomato shell with a little salt, sugar and a grind of black pepper. Turn the shells upside down and leave to drain for half an hour. Chop the tomato pulp and put it into a sieve. Leave for a few minutes to drain off some of the liquid.

2. Meanwhile chop the onions and garlic very finely. Warm some olive oil in a saucepan. Add the onion and garlic and cook over low heat for 5-6 minutes until slightly softened. Chop the mushrooms into quite small pieces. Add them to the saucepan and cook, stirring, for 2-3 minutes. Stir in the drained tomato pulp. When it is hot, stir in the rice. Season with a little salt and a generous amount of black pepper. Cover the pan with a tight-fitting lid and reduce heat as low as possible. Cook gently for 20 minutes until the rice is swollen with the liquids from the vegetables and cooked to perfect tenderness. Away from the heat, stir in the chopped parsley. Drain the anchovies (reserving their oil) and snip them into the saucepan. Also chop the stoned (pitted) olives and mix them into the rice. Turn the mixture out onto a shallow dish and leave it for 5-10 minutes until slightly cooled.

3. While the rice mixture is cooling, preheat the oven to 180°C (350°F) gas mark 4. Brush a gratin dish with a little of the oil from the anchovy can. Cut the bread into rounds, each one large enough to stand a tomato on. Fry the rounds of bread in olive oil until golden on both sides. Drain them well on kitchen paper towels and keep hot.

4. When the oven has reached the correct temperature, check the rice mixture for seasoning and add salt and pepper to taste. Spoon the stuffing into the tomato shells, packing it in quite firmly. Stand the tomatoes side by side in a gratin dish and bake until they are hot and tender but not disintegrating – this will take from 20-30 minutes depending on the variety of tomato used. Arrange the fried bread on a hot serving dish. Carefully lift a stuffed tomato onto each slice. Sprinkle a little Parmesan cheese over each and serve immediately. *Serves 6*

Artichokes & butter sauce

A globe artichoke is the edible flower of a type of thistle. It is the most beautiful-looking of all vegetables, and makes very fine eating indeed. Artichokes can be served cold – with mayonnaise or vinaigrette dressing – or stuffed with shellfish bound with a little mayonnaise. In my opinion they should be only just cold: if cooked and cooled in the morning for serving at dinner, their delicate flavour becomes stale – and this is why the cold artichokes one eats in restaurants are so often disappointing. Artichokes are best, I think, served still warm from the cooking pot, when a simple hot butter sauce makes the ideal accompaniment.

Metric/Imperial	American
4 globe artichokes	4 globe artichokes
1 lemon	1 lemon
175g(6oz) clarified butter(page 62, step 3)	¾ cup clarified butter(page 62, step 3)
30ml(2 tablespoons) fresh chopped parsley	2 tablespoons fresh chopped parsley
30ml(2 tablespoons) fresh chopped chives	2 tablespoons fresh chopped chives
salt and freshly-ground black pepper	salt and freshly-ground black pepper

1. Choose firm, fresh green heads with fleshy, closely-packed leaves. Avoid heads with loosely-packed leaves, and any that have leaves that are purplish and split as this is the sign of an ageing and tough artichoke. Always cook and serve artichokes on the day of picking or buying them.

2. Rinse the artichokes very thoroughly under cold running water to remove any dirt that may be trapped between the leaves. Shake dry and leave upside down to drain for a few minutes. Grate the lemon zest (rind) very finely and reserve it for the sauce, together with 22ml (1½ tablespoons) of the juice. Trim the artichokes by cutting off the stalks as close as possible to the heads. Pull off and discard the circle of leaves closest to the base. Rub the cut surface of each artichoke with a slice of lemon to prevent discoloration. It is fashionable in some restaurants to trim the tips of the artichoke leaves but this spoils the looks of this beautiful vegetable and encourages flavour to leak out during cooking.

3. Put the remaining lemon into a very large saucepan together with some salt and plenty of water. Bring to a fast boil. Plunge the artichokes into the boiling water. As soon as the water returns to boiling, reduce heat to simmering, cover the pan with a lid and cook until the artichokes are tender. This will take between 20 and 40 minutes depending on size. To test whether an artichoke is cooked, pull away one of the base leaves: it should come away easily and the flesh at the base of the leaf should feel tender when nibbled. Drain the cooked artichokes upside down in a colander.

4. The artichokes can be served whole just as they are, but everyone will appreciate it if you remove the inedible choke for them. To do this, stand the artichokes the right way up as soon as they have drained. Gently pull apart the thick scaly leaves in the top centre of the artichoke. Hold them open with an inverted egg cup or small glass for a minute or two so that they lose enough heat to prevent burning your fingers. Then prise the leaves open still further and you will find an inner cap of tender young leaves. Lift the whole cap out and reserve it. Underneath you will see the hairy, inedible bristles of the choke which are rooted in the fleshy artichoke bottom. The latter is the best part of the artichoke, so scrape the choke out carefully with a teaspoon, leaving the bottom of the artichoke intact. Replace the cap of tender leaves and fold the scaly outer leaves back over the cap. Without a helper, it is not practical to prepare more than four artichokes in this way or they will be nearly cold by the time you have finished. Set each artichoke on a warm plate and keep warm while you prepare the sauce.

5. To make the butter sauce, simply heat the butter, lemon juice and zest (rind) in a small saucepan until very hot. Season it with salt and pepper and, away from the heat, stir in the fresh chopped herbs if you are including them – I think they add extra colour and piquancy to the sauce. Pour the sauce into four small ramekins, put one on each plate and serve immediately. Since this dish is eaten in the fingers, give everyone a large napkin and a bowl of warm water for washing his or her fingers. Also provide a dish for discarding leaves after the flesh has been nibbled from the base. *Serves 4*

Leeks provençale

Leeks are a favourite vegetable in my family, and we look forward each year to the day when the first slender ivory and green stems are ready to pull up from the garden. Of all the ways we eat leeks, I think this is the very best: the warm tomato sauce and the freshness of the leeks make a beautiful combination of flavours and colours. Serve this dish as a first course, hot or cold, but always with plenty of good, crusty, bread.

Metric/Imperial	American
12 small young leeks	*12 small young leeks*
30ml(2 tablespoons) olive oil	*2 tablespoons olive oil*
4 large tomatoes	*4 large tomatoes*
2 garlic cloves, finely chopped	*2 cloves garlic, finely chopped*
a pinch of caster sugar	*a pinch of fine sugar*
a squeeze of lemon juice	*a squeeze of lemon juice*
30ml(2 tablespoons) fresh chopped parsley	*2 tablespoons fresh chopped parsley*
salt and freshly-ground black pepper	*salt and freshly-ground black pepper*

1. Early season leeks that are really young, tender and slim are ideal for this delicious and appetizing salad. Cut off the roots and remove the green tops to within about 10cm (4in) of the white stems, and trim them all to the same length. Discard any tough outer leaves. Wash the leeks very thoroughly indeed: split them with a sharp knife to within 7.5cm (3in) of the base, fan the leaves open and hold under cold running water to wash away the grit and earth that collects between the layers of tightly-packed leaves. As an extra precaution, stand the leeks, root end up, in a pitcher of cold water for 5-10 minutes to help draw out any stubborn gritty remains. Drain the leeks and shake them thoroughly to get rid of the water.

2. Lay the prepared leeks in a steamer basket and place over a pan of salted simmering water. Cover and cook until the leeks are tender but retain slight crispness. If the leeks are really young and tender this should not take more than 8 minutes, but check

by piercing the thick base with a skewer or the point of a knife. The leeks can be boiled instead, but steaming is preferable since it tenderizes the vegetables without danger of their becoming waterlogged or mushy. Drain the leeks for 5 minutes while you prepare the sauce, then lay them in rows in a shallow serving dish.

3. To make the sauce, first pour boiling water over the tomatoes and slip off their skins. Chop the tomato flesh and crush the garlic with a little salt. Use olive oil from Provence for authentic flavour if you can and warm it in a small heavy-bottomed saucepan. Add the tomato flesh, the garlic and parsley and cook over fairly high heat for 2-3 minutes, stirring all the time. Remove the pan from the heat. Stir in the sugar and lemon juice (if the tomatoes are really sweet and full of flavour, sugar and lemon juice may be unnecessary). Season to taste with salt and freshly-ground black pepper. Pour the tomato mixture over the leeks. Serve while warm or when cold.

Serves 4

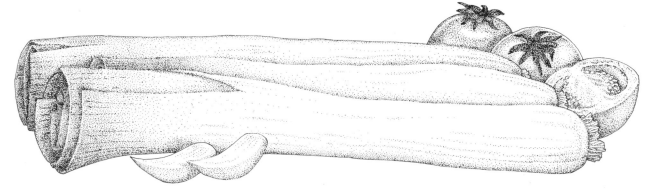

Cucumber raita

I n India chilled yoghurt salads are made using a variety of fruit and vegetables. Very simple and deliciously refreshing, they make an ideal side dish to serve with curry and other spicy foods. The Turkish yoghurt salad called cacik, which is popular throughout the Middle East, is clearly related to raita but it is usually more heavily flavoured, containing quite a lot of garlic and dried mint. I think cucumber raita with a little bit of green pepper is the best of all yoghurt salads. When I am Calorie counting I frequently eat it as a first course alternative to the inevitable grapefruit.

Metric/Imperial	American
half a cucumber	*half a cucumber*
half a small green pepper	*half a small green bell pepper*
half a small onion	*half a small onion*
425ml(¾pt) yoghurt	*2 cups plain yogurt*
7.5ml(¾ teaspoon) cumin seeds	*¾ teaspoon cumin seeds*
a pinch of chilli powder	*a pinch of chili powder*
plenty of salt	*plenty of salt*
fresh chopped coriander or parsley leaves	*fresh chopped coriander or parsley leaves*

1. Warm the cumin seeds in a frying-pan over low heat for a few minutes to bring out their aroma, then crush them with the back of a spoon. Chop the onion quite finely. Turn the yoghurt into a bowl and beat it until very smooth and creamy. Fresh home-made yoghurt gives the best results. Add the onion and cumin to the bowl together with a little chilli (chili) powder and a good seasoning of salt. Mix together,

cover and leave in a cool place for 30 minutes.

2. Sponge the cucumber skin clean and dry it, then dice the cucumber. Remove stalk, pith (white fiber) and seeds from the pepper, and dice the flesh. Just before serving, stir the vegetables into the flavoured yoghurt, and garnish the dish with chopped fresh herbs. *Serves 4*

DESSERTS

Profiteroles

Choux pastry never ceases to delight me. It is so quick and easy to make – no rubbing in, no chilling, no rolling out – and it seems magic that such tiny quantities of ingredients can swell to produce so many featherlight golden bubbles of pastry. Filled with whipped cream when cold, piled into a pyramid and coated with chocolate sauce, profiteroles make a handsome party piece. I like a mixture of fresh and sour cream for the filling. This, plus my mother's bitter chocolate sauce, makes a more sophisticated dish than the sometimes sickly, over-rich versions I have eaten in restaurants.

Metric/Imperial

For the choux pastry:
65g(2½oz) plain flour
50g(2oz) unsalted butter
a pinch of salt
2.5ml(½ teaspoon) caster sugar
2 medium-sized (no. 3) eggs

For the cream filling:
150ml(¼pt) double cream
45ml(3 tablespoons) single or soured cream

For the bitter chocolate sauce:
30ml(2 tablespoons) butter
30ml(2 tablespoons) golden syrup
45ml(3 tablespoons) cocoa powder
15ml(1 tablespoon) caster sugar
5ml(1 teaspoon) instant coffee powder

American

For the choux pastry:
½ cup plus 2 tablespoons all-purpose flour
4 tablespoons unsalted butter
a pinch of salt
½ teaspoon superfine sugar
2 medium-sized eggs

For the cream filling:
⅝ cup double cream
3 tablespoons light or sour cream

For the bitter chocolate sauce:
2 tablespoons butter
2 tablespoons corn syrup
3 tablespoons cocoa powder
1 tablespoon fine sugar
1 teaspoon instant coffee powder

1. Always make profiteroles on the day you serve them and preferably serve them as soon as possible after baking. Before you begin, preheat the oven to 220°C (425°F) gas mark 7, for the pastry must be baked as soon as made and the oven must be really hot. Grease a baking sheet with buttered paper. Measure and sift the flour onto a sheet of greaseproof or waxed paper. Measure 140ml (¼pt) or ⅝ cup water into a small saucepan. Add the butter, cut into small pieces, the sugar and the salt. Set the pan over low heat, let the butter and sugar melt, then bring slowly to a rapid boil. Immediately remove the pan from the heat, quickly shoot the flour into the pan, and beat with a wooden spoon until the dough is smooth and leaves the sides of the pan clean. Turn the ball of dough into a mixing bowl and let it cool slightly while you prepare the eggs.

2. Break the white of one egg into a bowl by itself. Put the yolk and the other whole egg into a second bowl and whisk lightly with a fork. Beat the egg white with a balloon whisk only long enough to make a very soft snowy foam. The dough will now be sufficiently cooled. With a wooden spoon, beat the egg yolk mixture into the dough, a large spoonful at a time. Then beat in as much of the egg white as is needed to make a very smooth, glossy dough (with some brands of flour you may not need every drop of egg white). Beat thoroughly but fairly swiftly, aerating the mixture as much as possible. Using two teaspoons, shape the dough into 30 fat blobs, spacing them at intervals on the baking sheet.

3. Quickly put the tray into the oven, on the shelf just above the middle, and bake for 15 minutes. Reduce temperature to 190°C (375°F) gas mark 5 and bake for 15 minutes more. Do not open the oven door until the full time is up, even though the choux buns will smell heavenly and might appear to be ready. They will magically puff up into golden bubbles quite quickly but must continue to bake uninterrupted, until crisp and set. If you peek or remove them from the oven too soon they will quickly collapse and become flabby.

4. When the time is up, remove the tray from the oven and turn off the heat. Quickly make a slit halfway around the 'waist' of each bun and return the tray to the cooling oven for 5 minutes: this is to allow the steam trapped inside each bun to be released, and the centre of the pastry to dry out. If the centres are still slightly damp after this time, scoop out any damp dough with a teaspoon handle and discard it. Cool the profiteroles on a wire rack.

5. Never fill the profiterole until shortly before serving. Put the sauce ingredients into a small pan in the order given. Stir over very low heat until everything is well blended, smooth and hot – but do not let the mixture boil. Set the pan aside and sprinkle 10ml (2 teaspoons) cold water over the surface of the sauce. Whip the creams until stiff, using a mixture of fresh and sour cream if you want a fresh-tasting richness, and stuff some into each profiterole through the slit. Pile the profiteroles into a pyramid on a serving dish. Stir the water into the chocolate sauce to cool it and make it glossy, pour it over the profiteroles and serve. *Serves 4-6*

French apple tart

Butter, lemon, cinnamon and sugar combine deliciously with apples in this classic fruit tart, which is a good example of the sort of French cooking I most admire. The ingredients used are commonplace and inexpensive, yet the resulting dish looks extremely handsome and tastes just that little bit special. I find it most practical to cook the purée in advance, usually a day ahead to be sure that it is both stiff and cold when used. Use one of those pretty fluted china flan dishes (a quiche pan) if you like but, if you do, be sure to stand the dish on a baking sheet while it cooks (and to preheat the baking sheet with the oven) or the pastry will not cook through and become as crisp as it should.

Metric/Imperial	American
For the sweet rich shortcrust pastry:	**For the sweet rich shortcrust pastry:**
225g(½lb) plain flour	2 cups all-purpose flour
a pinch of salt	a pinch of salt
10ml(2 teaspoons) caster sugar	2 teaspoons superfine sugar
140g(5oz) unsalted butter, at room temperature	⅝ cup unsalted butter at room temperature
1 medium-sized (no. 3) egg, separated	1 medium-sized egg, separated
For the filling and glaze:	**For the filling and glaze:**
1.4kg(3lb) Cox's or crisp dessert apples	3lb red dessert apples
50g(2oz) caster sugar	¼ cup superfine sugar
75g(3oz) unsalted butter	6 tablespoons unsalted butter
5ml(1 teaspoon) ground cinnamon	1 teaspoon ground cinnamon
the juice and zest of 1 large lemon	the juice and rind of 1 large lemon
90ml(6 tablespoons) apricot jam, sieved	6 tablespoons apricot jam

1. Reserve one-third of the apples for the topping. Peel, core and chop the rest. Put them into a large heavy-based pan without any liquid or sweetener. Cover with a lid and cook over very low heat until the fruit is perfectly tender. Stir or shake the pan frequently at first to prevent the fruit from sticking to the pan base. Turn the contents of the pan into a sieve placed over a bowl and leave for 7-10 minutes to drain off the juices. Reserve the juices and return the apples to the pan. Add the sugar, butter, cinnamon and finely grated lemon zest (rind) plus half the lemon juice. Beat the mixture with a balloon whisk to make a fluffy purée. Return the pan to low heat and cook, stirring frequently, until the purée is reduced to a fairly thick aromatic paste or *marmelade* as the French call it. Set aside, uncovered, until completely cold.

2. To make the pastry, sift the flour, salt and sugar into a mixing bowl. Cut the butter into the flour with a palette knife or spatula until reduced to pea-sized pieces, then rub in lightly with your fingers until the mixture resembles fine breadcrumbs. Mix the egg yolk with 15ml (1 tablespoon) very cold water. Pour it into a hollow in the middle of the flour.

Using the palette knife gradually draw the dry ingredients into the liquid to make a ball of dough. If the dough seems very stiff add a few drops more of icy-cold water. Turn out and knead the dough lightly, then wrap and chill it for at least 45 minutes – the high fat content means that this dough needs chilling for a longer time than a plain shortcrust pastry.

3. Preheat the oven to 200°C (400°F) gas mark 6, placing a baking sheet on an upper shelf. Roll out the chilled pastry and use to line a 25cm (10in) fluted French flan tin with removable base (or a quiche pan). Prick the pastry base all over with a fork, line with a large circle of greaseproof or waxed paper, weight it with dry beans and chill for 10 minutes more. Partially bake blind for 10 minutes. Then remove beans and paper, brush the pastry base with egg white (this will seal the pastry and prevent the apple filling leaking into it) and bake for 8 minutes more.

4. While the pastry is blind baking, peel, core and thinly slice the remaining apples. Toss them in the remaining lemon juice to prevent discoloration.

Reduce oven temperature to 190°C (375°F) gas mark 5. Spread the cold apple purée over the base of the pastry case. Cover with the drained apple slices, arranging them decoratively in concentric circles, working from the pastry rim to the middle. Sprinkle 5ml (1 teaspoon) caster (superfine) sugar over the apples and bake the tart for 25-30 minutes until the apple slices are tender and just beginning to brown at the edges.

5. While the tart is cooking, heat together in a small pan the sieved apricot jam and 45ml (3 tablespoons) juices reserved from the apple purée, to make a syrupy glaze. When the tart is cooked, brush the warm glaze over the apple slices and leave in a cool place until set. Serve the tart while still slightly warm from the oven, or when cold. A bowl of lightly-whipped cream makes a delicious smooth accompaniment.

Serves 8

Steamed orange pudding

When it comes to making puddings, whether boiled, steamed or baked, no one can beat the British. King George I was so partial to them that he was nicknamed 'Georgie Porgie pudding and pie'. Even the French acknowledge British superiority in this field of cooking: 'Blessed be he that invented pudding, for it is manna', wrote a seventeenth century Frenchman, François Misson 'Ah what an excellent thing is an English pudding'. I have chosen a marmalade pudding – indeed an excellent thing and particularly English – and I offer a choice of accompanying sauces, one warm, foamy and light, the other firm, icy and heady with brandy.

Metric/Imperial	American
75g(3oz) self-raising flour	¾ cup self-rising flour
75g(3oz) fresh brown breadcrumbs	1¼ cups fresh brown bread crumbs
75g(3oz) soft brown sugar	⅔ cup soft brown sugar
75g(3oz) shredded suet	¾ cup shredded suet
105ml(7 tablespoons) rich cut marmalade	7 tablespoons orange marmalade with peel
the zest of 2 lemons	rind of 2 lemons
60ml(4 tablespoons) lemon juice	4 tablespoons lemon juice
1 medium-sized egg plus 1 yolk	1 medium-sized egg plus 1 yolk

For the mousseline sauce:	For the mousseline sauce:
1 large (no. 2) egg plus 2 yolks	1 large egg plus 2 yolks
65g(2½oz) caster sugar	⅓-½ cup superfine sugar
30ml(2 tablespoons) orange juice	2 tablespoons orange juice
15ml(1 tablespoon) lemon juice	1 tablespoon lemon juice
30ml(2 tablespoons) double cream	2 tablespoons heavy cream

For the brandy butter:	For the brandy butter:
125g(¼lb) unsalted butter, softened	½ cup unsalted butter, softened
75g(3oz) icing sugar, sifted	¾ cup sifted confectioners' sugar
the zest of a small orange	rind of a small orange
15-30ml(1-2 tablespoons) brandy	1-2 tablespoons brandy
a little freshly-grated nutmeg	little freshly-grated nutmeg

1. About 2½ hours before serving the pudding, stand a trivet in a large pan. Half-fill it with water and bring to the boil over low heat. Choose a 700ml (1½pt) or 4 cup heatproof bowl and butter it generously. Line the bottom of the bowl with a circle of greaseproof or waxed paper and butter it. Cut a circle of foil about 7.5cm (3in) larger in diameter than the top of the bowl. Butter it and make a 1.25cm (½in) pleat in the middle.

2. Sift the flour into a mixing bowl. Add breadcrumbs (the magic ingredient for light-textured puddings), sugar, suet and lemon zest (rind). Mix well. Chop the marmalade peel into very small pieces and stir in with the lemon juice. Beat the eggs lightly, add them and stir the contents of the mixing bowl vigorously until everything is thoroughly blended. Scrape the mixture into the prepared

pudding bowl and cover with the greased and pleated foil. Tie securely with string, and make two loops of string to use as handles. Carefully lower the pudding onto the trivet in the pan of boiling water.

Cover the pan with a lid and steam for 2 hours, adding extra boiling water to the pan when necessary.

3. A mousseline sauce is very quickly made and best cooked just before serving. It will however save time if you measure out the ingredients in advance: put the eggs and sugar into the top of a doubleboiler, mix the fruit juices together in a cup, and put the cream in a separate cup. Warm a jug or sauceboat.

4. When the pudding is ready, remove it from the pan. Let it stand for a couple of minutes so that it shrinks slightly from the sides of the bowl and is easier to turn out.

5. To complete the mousseline sauce, partially fill the bottom of a doubleboiler with water and bring to barely simmering. Add the fruit juices to the eggs and sugar. Put the top of the doubleboiler in place and whisk the ingredients steadily until thickened, hot and frothy – about 5 minutes. Away from the heat whisk in the cream, a spoonful at a time, then pour the sauce into the warmed jug or sauceboat. Uncover the pudding, run a palette knife between bowl and sponge, then invert the pudding onto a warmed serving plate and peel away the paper. Serve immediately with the sauce of your choice. *Serves 6*

†If serving brandy butter, prepare it ahead. First beat the softened butter with an electric whisk or wooden spoon until pale and creamy. Sift on the icing (confectioners') sugar. Add the zest (rind) and nutmeg and beat again until the mixture is well-blended, light and fluffy, then beat in the brandy. When it is absorbed, turn the butter into a small serving bowl, cover and chill until required.

Zabaglione

Zabaglione is probably the most famous of all Italian desserts – a delectable foam very simple and very sophisticated. Providing you always keep eggs and a bottle of Marsala in the house, it is an instant treat which is a boon on emergency occasions: zabaglione takes little more than 5 minutes to cook and is a joy to eat.

Metric/Imperial	**American**
4 large (no. 2) egg yolks	*4 large egg yolks*
50g(2oz) caster sugar	*2 tablespoons superfine sugar*
90ml(6 tablespoons) Marsala	*6 tablespoons Marsala wine*
5ml(1 teaspoon) grated lemon zest (optional)	*1 teaspoon finely-grated lemon rind (optional)*

1. Fill four small wine glasses with hot water. Leave to stand for 5 minutes to warm thoroughly, then empty and dry. Meanwhile heat a little water to barely simmering in the bottom part of a double-boiler. Away from the heat, break the egg yolks into the top part of the double-boiler. Add the sugar.

2. Place the egg and sugar mixture over the pan of barely simmering water. Whisk with a rotary or electric whisk (beater) for about 2 minutes until the mixture begins to thicken. Add the Marsala and lemon zest (rind) if used (it helps cut the richness of the dish) and continue whisking until the mixture is the consistency of very softly whipped cream and has almost doubled in bulk – about 3-5 minutes. Pour the zabaglione into the warmed glasses and serve immediately, with sponge (lady) fingers if available. *Serves 4*

Chocolate mousse

Every man I know loves chocolate and this rich mousse, flavoured with a hint of orange, never fails to please. It looks and tastes so ritzy that it somehow creates the impression that hours have been spent on its preparation. It is a good choice for a party I think: it has to be prepared in advance but takes only minutes to make, leaving you free to concentrate on other dishes.

Metric/Imperial	American
3 large eggs	*3 large eggs*
175g(6oz) plain dark dessert chocolate	*6oz(1 package) semi-sweet chocolate pieces*
the finely grated zest of an orange	*the finely grated rind of 1 orange*
15ml(1 tablespoon) water	*1 tablespoon water*
65ml(2½fl oz) double cream	*5 tablespoons double cream*

1. Break the chocolate into small pieces. Put it into a bowl (or the top pan of a doubleboiler) together with the water. Stand the bowl on a trivet in a pan of barely-simmering water. Place over very gentle heat, stirring continuously until the chocolate is melted. Remove from the heat and set aside while you separate the eggs. Beat the egg yolks, one at a time, into the melted chocolate, then stir in the orange zest (rind). Scrape the mixture into a mixing bowl to cool it slightly.

2. In a separate bowl, whisk the egg whites until they stand in peaks. Fold them into the chocolate mixture, then spoon the mousse into 6 pots-de-chocolat or demitasse cups or tiny ramekins. Chill for at least 3 hours, preferably overnight, before serving. Whip the cream until stiff and top each mousse with a good dollop just before serving. Add decorations, such as coffee beans or curls of caraque chocolate (see *page 201, step 5*), on top if you like.

Serves 6

Raspberry cheesecake

Cheesecake that is lightened with whisked egg whites and set with gelatine has a lovely frothy, mousse-like texture which makes it delicious and not too rich to eat on a fine summer's day. Raspberries make a delicate fruity finishing touch – but it is wise not to garnish the cheesecake heavily, or it will prove difficult to slice and serve neatly. Far better, I think, to use the majority of the berries to make an accompanying Melba sauce.

Metric/Imperial	American
For the biscuit-crumb base	**For the crumb crust:**
175g(6oz) digestive biscuits	2 cups graham crackers
85g(3oz) unsalted butter, melted	½ cup butter, melted
8ml(1 heaped teaspoon) ground cinnamon	1 heaped teaspoon ground cinnamon
For the filling:	**For the filling:**
450g(1lb) cream cheese	2 × 8oz packages cream cheese
150ml(¼pt) soured cream	⅝ cup sour cream
3 medium-sized eggs, separated	3 medium-sized eggs, separated
1 orange	1 orange
1 lemon	1 lemon
75ml(5 tablespoons) caster sugar	5 tablespoons superfine sugar
22ml(1½ tablespoons) gelatine powder	1½ tablespoons powdered gelatine
For the topping and sauce:	**For the topping and sauce:**
900g(2lb) raspberries	2pt fresh raspberries
90ml(6 tablespoons) icing sugar	6 tablespoons confectioners' sugar

1. Break the biscuits (crackers) into large pieces. Put them into a heavy-duty plastic bag, secure tightly, excluding all air, and beat with a rolling pin to reduce to crumbs. Stir the crumbs into the melted butter and flavour with the cinnamon. Lightly oil an 18-20cm (7-8in) round cake tin with removable base and spring clip sides (a 9in spring-form pan) and press the mixture firmly and evenly over its base. Refrigerate while preparing the filling.

2. Grate the citrus zests (rind) into a mixing bowl. Squeeze the citrus juices into a small pan, sprinkle on the gelatine, soak for 5 minutes, then dissolve over low heat and set aside to cool slightly. Add the egg yolks and sugar to the mixed citrus zests (rind), and cream together until fluffy and light. Press the cheese through a sieve onto the yolk mixture and beat with a wooden spoon until very smooth and thick. Gradually beat in the sour cream, and then the cooling gelatine. Whisk the egg whites until they stand in peaks; fold them into the mixture. Pour the cheesecake filling onto the crumb base, smoothing the surface with a palette knife or spatula. Cover the top of the cheesecake with a dome of foil and refrigerate for 4 hours or until firmly set.

3. Reserve 225g (½lb) whole hulled berries to garnish the cheesecake. Use the rest to make an accompanying Melba sauce. Either rub the berries through a fine nylon sieve or pass them through the fine blade of a vegetable mill to extract seeds and reduce the flesh to a purée. Sweeten the sauce with the sifted icing (confectioners') sugar, turn it into a pretty bowl or sauceboat. Cover and chill until ready to serve.

4. Unhinge the spring clip sides of the cake tin (pan). Place the cheesecake (still on the metal base) on a serving plate, garnish with the reserved whole berries, and serve with the accompanying raspberry sauce.

Serves 8-10

Fresh fruit salads

At the end of a rich meal, the clean light taste of fresh fruit is marvellously welcome. A handsome bowl of raw fruit is lovely, but it is even more delightful to have the fruit peeled, prepared and presented ready to eat in the form of a fresh fruit salad (US compote). Not for me fruit salads that are laced with liqueurs or swimming in a heavy sugar syrup; the joy of it lies in its pure, fresh fruitiness. All sorts of fruit can be used depending on season and budget. The illustration shows a mixture of many fruits served in the shell of one of them. Here are two simple combinations that I think taste and look particularly refreshing and delicious.

Metric/Imperial	American
For a green and cream fruit salad:	**For a green and cream fruit salad:**
2 small ripe ogen melons	*1 honeydew melon*
225g(½lb) white grapes	*½lb seedless muscat or green grapes*
2 small firm bananas	*2 small firm bananas*
1 kiwi fruit (chinese gooseberry)	*1 kiwi fruit*
1 large juicy lemon	*1 large lemon*
30-45ml(2-3 tablespoons) caster sugar	*2-3 tablespoons superfine sugar*
generous 15ml(1 tablespoon) fresh mint	*generous tablespoon chopped fresh mint leaves*
For a red fruit salad:	**For a red fruit salad:**
225g(½lb) redcurrants	*½lb red currants*
120g(¼lb) dark red dessert cherries	*¼lb dark red dessert cherries*
120g(¼lb) large strawberries	*½pt strawberries*
120g(¼lb) raspberries	*½pt raspberries*
45-60ml(3-4 tablespoons) caster sugar	*3-4 tablespoons superfine sugar*
a small pinch of ground cinnamon	*small pinch ground cinnamon*
the juice and zest of 1 orange	*juice and zest 1 orange*
15ml(1 tablespoon) lemon juice	*1 tablespoon lemon juice*

1. For the green and cream fruit salad, halve the melons and scoop out seeds. Remove the flesh with a melon ball cutter to shape it into small balls. Take care not to pierce the melon skins, which will make pretty serving dishes. Put the melon balls into a bowl. Skin the grapes and remove all the seeds – a chore but doing little things like this makes all the difference between good and distinguished results. If the skins do not peel away easily, loosen them by dipping the grapes into boiling water – a few at a time and for a few seconds only. Cool the grapes under cold running water, drain and peel. Use a sterilized hairpin or a cocktail stick (pick) to extract the seeds. Add the grapes to the bowl of melon balls. Sprinkle on the sugar and half the lemon juice. Cover and leave in a cool place for 1-1½ hours. The sugar will dissolve in the lemon juice and help to draw out some of the melon and grape juices to make a delicious, light and very fruity syrup.

2. Shortly before serving, bring the fruit bowl to room temperature. Add to it any juices that have collected in the bottom of the melon shells. Slice the bananas, sprinkle them with remaining lemon juice to prevent discoloration. Add bananas and juice to the bowl together with the mint. Toss lightly and divide between the melon shells. Peel the

kiwi fruit. Cut the brilliant green flesh into slices, and tuck a few slices into each portion.

3. To make the red salad, first remove the stalks from the currants and stone (pit) the cherries. Put the currants into a pan. Sprinkle with the sugar, cinnamon and orange zest (rind). Add 30ml (2 tablespoons) orange juice. Cover the pan and shake it vigorously to distribute the flavourings. Set the covered pan over low heat and cook gently for 5-7 minutes until the sugar has melted and the currant juices have begun to flow. Add the cherries to the pan, cover it again, turn off the heat, but leave the pan on the stove. The cherries do not need cooking in the normal sense of the word but the residue heat will encourage them to yield up their juices, and the redcurrants will continue to soften slightly but without disintegration.

4. When the contents of the pan are barely tepid, cut the strawberries in half. Add them to the pan together with the raspberries and remaining citrus juice. Mix everything lightly together then turn the mixture into a pretty bowl. Cover and leave to macerate for a minimum of 4 hours in a cool place. During this time the juices of all the fruits will mingle to flavour the fruit and to make an ambrosial fruity red syrup. *Each fruit salad serves 4*

Crème brulée

As the name suggests, this pudding is a cream topped with sugar that is burnished to a sheet of brittle gold. It is very rich indeed and is best accompanied by a bowl of fresh berries – unsugared and unadorned in any way. In the eighteenth century, rose or orange flower water was sometimes used to scent the cream.

Metric/Imperial	American
5 medium-sized (no. 3) egg yolks	*5 medium-sized egg yolks*
575ml(1pt) double cream	*2½ cups heavy cream*
caster sugar	*superfine sugar*
1 vanilla pod	*1 vanilla bean*
OR 2.5ml(½ teaspoon) orange flower water	*OR ½ teaspoon orange flower water*

1. Scald the cream, with the vanilla if using. Cover and set aside to infuse for 20 minutes, then scald the cream again and remove the vanilla.

2. Put a little water into the bottom of a double-boiler and bring to a bare simmer over low heat. Away from the heat, whisk the egg yolks and 20ml (1 slightly heaped tablespoon) caster (superfine) sugar in the top part of the doubleboiler. Pour on the hot cream in a thin stream, whisking all the time. Place the pan over barely simmering water and cook gently, stirring continuously, until thickened to a custard – about 2-5 minutes. Remove from the heat (and stir in the scented water if using). Pour

the cream into one large shallow dish or several small dishes. Chill, uncovered, for 8 hours or more.

3. Two hours before serving, preheat the grill (broiler) to very fierce heat. Sprinkle the top of the chilled cream with sugar, making an even layer at least 3mm (⅛in) thick and taking care to cover the entire surface of the cream. Place the dish under the heat and cook just long enough to melt and cara-melize the sugar. Turn the dish as necessary to get an even effect. Return the dish to a cold place: as the caramelized sugar cools it will become brittle. Serve very cold, alone or with fresh berries.

Serves 6

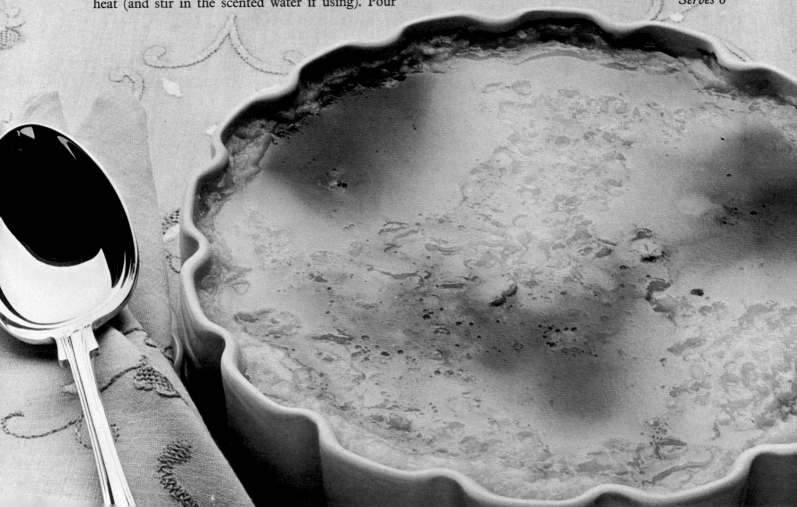

Granita di caffe

I become addicted to this every summer – it is very stimulating and superbly refreshing. Sometimes I vary the brew by adding cinnamon sticks to the coffee while it infuses, but it must always be served the true Italian way: icy cold, very strong with plenty of thick whipped cream.

Metric/Imperial	American
125-150g(4-5oz) finely ground continental coffee	*10 tablespoons finely ground continental coffee*
75g(3oz) caster sugar	*⅓ cup superfine sugar*
225-275ml(8-10fl oz) double cream	*1-1¼ cups heavy cream*

1. Set the refrigerator or freezer to its coldest setting. Scald a large jug with boiling water, then empty it. Measure the sugar and the freshly-roasted, finely ground continental coffee into the jug. Pour on 1.1L (2pt) or 5 cups freshly-boiled water and stir for half a minute. Cover with a lid or foil wrap the pot in a tea cosy or a towel to keep it hot while the coffee infuses. After 20 minutes strain twice through a cheesecloth-lined sieve, and cool the coffee as quickly as possible, standing the bowl of coffee in a larger bowl packed with ice.

2. Pour the cold coffee into a chilled loaf tin (bread pan). Cover and freeze for about 1½ hours, stirring the mixture every half hour, until the mixture is a granular slush. As soon as the granita reaches this consistency, turn it into tall chilled glasses. Whip the cream – until stiff if you want to serve it piped or in dollops on top of the granita. Or, as I prefer, whip it only to the soft peak stage, so that it can be swirled on top of the granita but will quickly dribble and mingle deliciously with the iced coffee mixture. *Serves 4*

Norwegian creams

Crème caramel is the most famous of all baked custard puddings but this lesser known and delicately flavoured custard is even more delicious I think – and it is easier to make because it is served in the dish in which it is baked. Use one large dish or, for a pretty party look, small individual dishes: a small soufflé or gratin dish or ovenproof ramekins are the ideal choice. Vary the decorations according to mood and taste; use a scattering of caraque chocolate, or crushed praline, or sugared violets rather than flaked and toasted almonds if you prefer.

Metric/Imperial	American
570ml(1pt) creamy milk	2½ cups creamy milk
1 cinnamon stick	1 stick cinnamon
75ml(5 tablespoons) best apricot preserve	5 tablespoons best apricot preserve
the finely grated zest of half an orange	the finely grated rind of half an orange
ground cinnamon	ground cinnamon
4 large (no. 2) eggs	4 large eggs
30ml(2 tablespoons) caster sugar	2 tablespoons caster sugar
220ml(7½fl oz) double cream	scant 1 cup thick cream
40g(1½oz) flaked and toasted almonds (optional)	¼ cup flaked and toasted almonds (optional)
caraque chocolate (page 201, step 5 – optional)	caraque chocolate (page 201, step 5 – optional)

1. This soothing and excellent baked custard is served cold, so it must be made several hours in advance of serving and can be made a day, or even two days, ahead.

2. Break the cinnamon stick into short lengths and crush lightly with your fingers to bruise and release the aromatic oils. Tie it up in a piece of cheesecloth and place in a saucepan. Pour on the milk and bring slowly to scalding point – that is cook until the milk bubbles round the edges of the pan. Cover the pan with a lid and set it aside to infuse for 20 minutes.

3. Meanwhile heat the oven to 160°C (325°F) gas mark 3, and select a soufflé dish of approximately 1L (1¾pt) or 1 US qt capacity, or 6-8 individual soufflé dishes. Cut out foil circle(s) large enough to make lid(s) for the dish(es). Measure the apricot jam into a small bowl. Add the orange zest (rind) and 2.5ml (¼ teaspoon) ground cinnamon. Beat with a spoon until slightly softened and well mixed, then spread the mixture over the base of the soufflé dish(es). Stand the dish(es) in a roasting pan.

4. Break the yolk of one egg into a mixing bowl. Reserve the white in a cup to use for topping the custard after baking and chilling. Add the three remaining whole eggs to the yolk, and whisk lightly together with a balloon whisk.

5. Remove the lid from the milk pan. Place the pan over low heat and bring the liquid back to scalding point. Remove from the heat and lift out the bag of cinnamon. Squeeze it so that the flavoured milk drips back into the pan. Stir in the sugar. When it has dissolved, pour the hot milk onto the eggs. Do this gradually, gripping the milkpan in one hand and holding it well above the bowl so that the liquid falls in a slow trickle. Whisk the contents of the bowl continuously as you pour. Strain the custard mixture through a fine sieve to extract the gelatinous threads that hold the egg yolks in the centre of the whites, and carefully pour it into the prepared dish(es). Cover each with foil lid(s), and pour enough boiling water into the roasting pan to come halfway up the sides of the dish(es). Place the pan in the oven and bake for about 50 minutes to set the custard.

6. Remove the cooked custard(s) from the hot water bath, uncover and allow to become cold. Then cover again and refrigerate for a minimum of 2 hours.

7. One or two hours before serving, whip the cream. Whisk the reserved egg white with a pinch of ground cinnamon and fold it into the whipped cream. Spread the cream over the custard(s) and scatter the flaked and toasted almonds or caraque chocolate over the top.   *Serves 6-8*

Silk-thread fruit

These delicious Chinese fruit fritters are so-called because as soon as fried they are dipped into a molten toffee syrup and then quickly plunged into iced water so that the caramel sets in brittle threads. It is an attractive and unusual pudding to serve at home. Peaches and pears can also be cooked by this method.

Metric/Imperial	American
2 dessert apples	2 red apples
2 firm bananas	2 firm bananas
juice of half a lemon	juice of half a lemon
peanut oil for frying	peanut oil for frying
15ml(1 tablespoon) sesame seeds (optional)	1 tablespoon sesame seeds (optional)

For the batter:	For the batter:
115g(¼lb) plain flour	1 cup all-purpose flour
good pinch salt	good pinch of salt
2.5ml(½ teaspoon) ground cinnamon	½ teaspoon ground cinnamon
the finely grated zest of half a lemon	finely grated rind of ½ a lemon
scant 150ml(¼pt) tepid water	½ cup lukewarm water
2 medium-sized egg whites	2 medium-sized egg whites

For the syrup:	For the syrup:
175g(6oz) granulated sugar	¾ cup granulated sugar
10ml(2 teaspoons) peanut oil	2 teaspoons peanut oil
125ml(4fl oz) water	½ cup water

1. First make the batter. Sift the flour, salt and cinnamon into a bowl. Stir in the lemon zest (rind). Make a hollow in the middle, pour in the water and gradually stir the dry ingredients into it to make a smooth creamy batter. Set aside.

2. Peel the bananas and slice them into chunks. Put them into a bowl, add the lemon juice and a few drops of water and toss lightly. Peel, quarter and core the apples. Cut each quarter across to make about 3 good-sized chunks. Add the pieces of apple to the bowl. Toss lightly in the acidulated water to prevent discoloration, cover and set aside.

3. To make the syrup, simply place the ingredients into a pan in the order given. Place over low heat and stir occasionally until the sugar is melted. Then let the syrup simmer gently, uncovered, over low heat until it is pale gold – about 15 minutes. Meanwhile prepare a small bowl of iced water, oil a pair of spoons and warm the frying-oil in a deep-fat pan. Attach a thermometer to the side of the pan, pour in the oil and heat it to 180-190°C (350-375°F). Drain the fruit, and pat it dry with paper towels. Whisk the egg whites and fold them into the batter.

4. When the syrup is pale gold, switch off heat but leave the pan where it is to keep warm. Dip the fruit into the prepared batter. Check that the oil has reached the correct temperature, then deep fry the fruit in batches so that they do not touch each other. They will take about 2 minutes to puff up and become golden. Remove each batch from the pan carefully with a slotted spoon; drain on paper towels, and keep hot. When the last batch of fruit is frying gently reheat the syrup.

5. Some people consider silk-thread fruit even more delicious if sesame seeds are added. Stir them into the syrup after reheating it. If you enjoy table-top cookery, complete the dish at table.

6. Away from the heat and using oiled spoons, dip each golden fritter in turn first into the syrup to coat it with the stickly toffee and then into the bowl of iced water – the cold water will set the toffee to a brittle caramel. Dip the fruit as quickly as possible. Put each as and when ready onto a serving plate lined with kitchen paper to absorb the cold water that drains off. Remove the paper quickly and serve the fritters immediately. *Serves 4*

Kaffecreme

Bavarian custard is a classic. Rich with egg yolks and cream, and lightened by the final inclusion of egg whites, its texture is velvety smooth. When flavoured with coffee, as here, it makes a memorably good pudding – elegant, sophisticated yet pure and simple. It seems to me gilding the lily to decorate kaffecreme with whipped cream or to serve a jug of thin cream with it. But a simple decoration of roasted coffee beans or a few curls of caraque chocolate looks pretty.

Metric/Imperial	American
425ml(¾pt) fresh creamy milk	2 cups whole (creamy) milk
35-40ml(2 generous tablespoons) instant coffee	2 rounded tablespoons instant coffee
6 large (no. 2) egg yolks	6 large egg yolks
125g(¼lb) caster sugar	½ cup superfine sugar
10-15ml(2-3 teaspoons) gelatine powder	2-3 teaspoons powdered gelatin (see method)
150ml(¼pt) double cream	⅝ cup heavy cream
3 large (no. 2) egg whites	3 large egg whites
a little caraque chocolate (page 201, step 5)	chocolate curls (page 201, step 5)
plus 2.5ml(½ teaspoon) icing sugar	plus ½ teaspoon confectioners' sugar
OR a few roasted coffee beans	OR a few roasted coffee beans

1. This delectable pudding can be made in and served from a pretty glass dish. Or it can be set in a decorative mould and unmoulded before serving. The former not only involves less work for the cook (and it looks just as pretty in my opinion) but it has the advantage of needing less gelatine: this means the texture is more delicate, in keeping with the fine flavour of the pudding. You will need a dish or mould of 1.4L (2½pt) or 6 cups capacity. If the pudding is to be unmoulded for serving, brush the mould with a little flavourless oil and invert onto a paper towel to drain the excess.

2. Measure the milk into a pan and bring slowly to scalding point. Meanwhile bring a small quantity of water to a bare simmer in the base of a doubleboiler. Away from the heat, put the egg yolks into the top of the doubleboiler. Gradually add the sugar, whisking all the while. After 2-3 minutes, the mixture will be pale and creamy, and thick enough to fall in ribbons when the whisk is lifted. Stir the coffee powder or granules into the scalded milk. When dissolved, add it to the egg yolk mixture – still away from the heat. Pour the milk in a thin stream, holding the milk pan high and whisking the eggs all the time as you pour. Set the pan over the barely simmering water. Cook gently, stirring continuously, until the custard thickens – this can take

10-15 minutes.

3. Turn the rich coffee custard into a bowl and let it cool. Meanwhile soak then dissolve the gelatine in 30ml (2 tablespoons) water. Use the smaller quantity of gelatine powder if the pudding is to be served in the dish in which it sets, the larger quantity if the pudding is to be unmoulded. Stir the melted gelatine gently but thoroughly into the custard, then stir in the cream. Refrigerate the mixture until it is cold and approaching setting point. This process can be speeded up by standing the bowl of creamy custard in a dish containing iced water or ice cubes. How long it will take depends on the temperature of your refrigerator. It is wise to check progress and to stir the mixture gently every 5-10 minutes.

4. When the custard cream is almost but not quite set, whisk the egg whites. Fold them delicately but thoroughly into the custard cream and pour it into your chosen dish. Cover and chill until set firm.

5. To serve, unmould the pudding, if appropriate, then decorate it. Either sprinkle caraque chocolate (or chocolate curls) over the top then dust it with the merest whisper of sifted icing (confectioners') sugar. Or simply stud the pudding with a few freshly-roasted coffee beans. *Serves 8*

Crêpes Suzette

Watching a dish being cooked beside my restaurant table is something I hate. I dislike it partly out of jealousy (it is done with a conjurer's brilliance which I know I cannot match) but mostly because one of the pleasures of dining out, as I'm sure every cook will agree, is to be completely free of anything to do with the kitchen. My antipathy was so strong that I never ate crêpes Suzette until a year or so ago in a friend's house. Mercifully cooked in the kitchen, they came to the dining table quietly licked by brandy flames – mouthwateringly tender little pancakes bathed in a rich orange sauce. I was converted. This dish is irresistibly good and I now make it often – but always out of the sight of my guests.

Metric/Imperial	American
For the crêpe batter:	**For the crêpe batter:**
115g(¼lb) plain flour	*1 cup all-purpose flour*
a pinch of salt	*a pinch of salt*
5ml(1 teaspoon) caster sugar	*1 teaspoon superfine sugar*
2.5ml(½ teaspoon) orange zest	*½ teaspoon grated orange rind*
2 medium-sized eggs	*2 medium-sized eggs*
15ml(1 tablespoon) Cointreau	*1 tablespoon Cointreau*
125ml(4½fl oz) milk	*generous ½ cup milk*
125ml(4½fl oz) water	*generous ½ cup water*
30ml(2 tablespoons) melted butter	*2 tablespoons melted butter*
For the sauce and for flaming:	**For the sauce and for flaming:**
6 large sugar lumps, or 25g(1 oz) caster sugar	*6 large lumps or 1½ tablespoons superfine sugar*
2 oranges	*2 Florida oranges*
75g(3oz) unsalted butter	*6 tablespoons unsalted butter*
15ml(1 tablespoon) Cointreau	*1 tablespoon Cointreau*
extra Cointreau or brandy	*extra Cointreau or brandy*

1. Sift the flour, salt and sugar into a bowl. Make a hollow in the middle and put in the remaining batter ingredients (excepting the butter). Mix them together with a balloon whisk, then gradually whisk the liquids into the dry ingredients. Continue whisking until you have a creamy, perfectly smooth batter. Just before cooking the crêpes, stir in the cool melted butter: this will enrich them and prevent sticking during cooking.

2. Rub a 15cm (6in) omelette pan lightly with butter and thoroughly warm it over medium-low heat. Draw the pan to one side. Hold it in one hand and a spoon in the other hand. Add about 22ml (1½ tablespoons) of batter to the pan and shake and tilt it until the entire base is thinly coated with batter. Place the pan back on the heat and cook for 45-60 seconds until the bottom of the crêpe has dried out to a pale golden brown. Shake the pan to check that the crêpe is not sticking. If necessary loosen the edge of the crêpe with a palette knife or spatula. Then turn the crêpe over. Toss it if you

wish. I find it easier to lift one edge of the crêpe with my fingers and to flip it over gently. Cook on the second side for less than 30 seconds, then slide the crêpe out of the pan onto a warm plate.

3. Cook the rest of the batter in the same way, making a total of 16-18 very thin and very tender crêpes. Stir the batter every now and then to check that the orange zest (rind) is evenly distributed. It may be necessary to rub the base and sides of the pan with butter once in a while. Use only as much butter as is necessary to barely coat the pan: the aim is to prevent sticking, on no account should the crêpes be fried in fat or they will become crisp and tough. Keep the cooked crêpes warm in a low oven, arranging them, slightly overlapping, in a circle on a warm plate so that they can be easily separated for finishing off in the sauce.

4. To make the rich orange-flavoured sauce which makes this famous dish so special, first rub the sugar cubes over the orange skins so that they absorb the aromatic oils. If, like me, you do not normally have sugar cubes in the house, there is no need to buy them specially for this dish. Instead measure some caster (superfine) sugar into a saucer and finely grate the orange zest (rind) onto it. Squeeze the juice.

5. Put the butter into a 25-30cm (10-12in) frying-pan. Add the orange-flavoured sugar, 125ml (4½floz) or a generous ½ cup of the orange juice and 15ml (1 tablespoon) Cointreau. Set over very low heat indeed and crush the sugar. As soon as the butter and sugar are melted, add the first crêpe to the pan. Turn it to moisten both sides with the sauce, then fold it in half and in half again. (Waiters do this with a flourish of spoon and fork but using fingers is quicker and easier for mere mortals.) Slide the folded crêpe to the edge of the pan farthest away from you. Soak and fold the remaining crêpes and arrange them, slightly overlapping at the back of the pan. Tilt the pan occasionally so that

the sauce runs to the front to moisten each crêpe very thoroughly as you fold it.

6. When all the crêpes are folded, increase heat very slightly. Let them slip and slide gently round the pan until they are very hot and the sauce is bubbling in a delicious and aromatic way. Sprinkle the crêpes with a little sugar and turn off the heat. Quickly warm about 60ml (3 tablespoons) brandy or Cointreau, or a mixture of both, in a small pan, then pour it over the crêpes, set alight and carry the dish to the table.   *Serves 4-6*

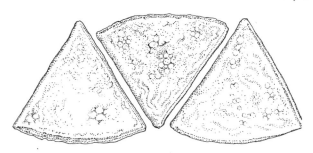

Blackberry bombe

Blackberries rate high on my list of favourite fruits, and it pleases me that they can be gathered for free from the hedgerows and byeways near my Wiltshire country home. These wild brambles make a beautiful and somewhat unusual ice-cream, which becomes a stunning party piece if moulded around a lemon-flavoured bombe mixture – the pale-coloured centre is only revealed when the ice is cut into slices for serving.

Metric/Imperial

For the blackberry ice-cream:
450g(1lb) fresh blackberries
150g(5oz) caster sugar
6 sweet geranium leaves
OR 3 curls of thinly-pared lemon rind
5ml(1 teaspoon) lemon juice
200ml(7fl oz) double cream

For the bombe mixture:
40g(1½oz) caster sugar
2 large (no. 2) egg yolks
10ml(2 teaspoons) lemon juice
the finely grated zest of half a lemon
30ml(2 tablespoons) whipped cream
1 large (no 2) egg white

American

For the blackberry ice-cream:
1lb fresh blackberries
generous cup superfine sugar
6 sweet (rose) geranium leaves
OR 3 curls thinly-pared lemon rind
1 teaspoon lemon juice
⅞ cup heavy cream

For the bombe mixture:
3 tablespoons superfine sugar
2 large egg yolks
2 teaspoons lemon juice
the finely grated rind of half a lemon
2 tablespoons whipping cream
1 large egg white

1. To make the ice-cream first dissolve the sugar in 150ml (¼pt) or ½ cup water. Add the geranium leaves or lemon rind to the pan and boil, uncovered, for 7 minutes to make a rich syrup. Cover, cool, then chill it. Put the blackberries through the fine blade of a vegetable mill to extract seeds and to reduce flesh and juices to a purée. Measure and chill 425ml (¾pt) or 1½ cups. Stir the lemon juice into the blackberry purée. Strain the syrup through a sieve into the purée to extract the flavourings – press them with a wooden spoon to extract the juices – then stir in. Whip the cream very softly, so that it barely holds its shape. Gently and gradually stir the blackberry mixture into the cream: it is important to add only a little blackberry at a time or the acidity of the fruit might curdle the cream. Turn the mixture into a chilled loaf tin (bread pan), cover with foil and freeze for a minimum of 4 hours in total – but during the first 1½ hours you should take it out of the freezer every 45 minutes and beat it vigorously with an electric whisk or wooden spoon. This is to break up ice crystals as they form, so that the ice-cream will have a good smooth texture. While the ice-cream is freezing, chill a mould or bowl of 850ml (1½pt) 4 cups capacity – it should be at least 10cm (4in) deep.

2. Next day, turn four-fifths of the frozen ice-cream out into a bowl and beat it with a whisk or wooden spoon until slightly softened: it should not be runny but of a workable consistency. Use this ice-cream to line the bottom and sides of the chilled mould: the fact that the mould is icy cold will help the ice-cream to stick. Use a spoon to smooth the ice-cream and pack it tightly to make an even, but not too thick layer. Take care to see that the sides of the mould are as well covered as the base. Cover with foil and freeze until solid – about 1½-2 hours.

3. Meanwhile make the bombe mixture. Dissolve the sugar in 150ml (¼pt) or ½ cup water then boil until the syrup reaches 102°C (217°F). Then plunge the base of the pan into a bowl of iced water to cool the syrup. Put a little water into the base of a doubleboiler and bring to a bare simmer. Break the egg yolks into the top part of the doubleboiler, place it over the simmering water and beat with an electric whisk (beater) until pale and slightly thickened. Away from the heat gradually whisk the cooling syrup into the yolks, making sure that each addition is well blended. Replace the pan over the simmering water and cook, whisking continuously, until the mixture has doubled in bulk – about 8 minutes with an electric whisk. Remove the pan from the heat, plunge its base into the bowl of iced water (you may have to add extra ice cubes at this stage) and continue whisking until it is cold.

4. When the ice-cream in the bombe mould is thoroughly frozen and the bombe mixture is completely cold, gently stir the lemon juice and zest (rind) into the bombe mixture. Then fold in the whipped cream, followed by the stiffly whisked egg white. Spoon the mixture into the cavity in the mould, cover with foil and freeze for a further 1½-2 hours until it is solid. Then beat the reserved ice-cream until workable and spread it over the top of the mould so that the frozen bombe mixture is completely encased and hidden by ice-cream. Level the top, cover the mould and freeze again for a minimum of 2½ hours.

5. Dip the mould into hand-hot water to loosen the ice-cream – about 15 seconds for a metal mould, about 45 seconds for a china bowl – then invert the bombe onto a chilled serving plate. Heat a palette knife or spatula in boiling water, dry it, then stroke it over the surface of the ice-cream to give it a professional 'polish'. Return the bombe, uncovered, to the freezer for a few minutes to firm the surface. Decorate the bombe by surrounding it with fresh whole raw blackberries, and serve. *Serves 6-8*

Nègresse en chemise

This traditional Viennese speciality is perhaps my favourite of all chocolate puddings. It is easy to make, impressive to look at, and very rich and delicious to eat. The name means 'negress in a night shirt' – the idea being a contrast of the black, exquisite steamed and chilled thick chocolate soufflé mixture, with the white whipped cream which masks the pudding completely just before serving. Replace some of the coffee with extra rum if you wish; or omit rum, increase the coffee and flavour it with a little ground cinnamon if you prefer.

Metric/Imperial	American
190g(6½oz) plain chocolate (dessert or cooking)	6½oz unsweetened or semi-sweet chocolate
15ml(1 tablespoon) instant coffee powder	1 tablespoon instant coffee
30ml(2 tablespoons) boiling water	2 tablespoons water
15ml(1 tablespoon) rum	1 tablespoon rum
175g(6oz) unsalted butter, at room temperature	¾ cup unsalted butter, at room temperature
175g(6oz) caster sugar	¾ cup superfine sugar
6 large (no. 2) eggs, separated	6 large eggs, separated
225ml(8fl oz) double cream	1 cup heavy cream
50ml(2fl oz) soured cream	¼ cup sour cream

1. Grease a 2L (3½pt) or 2 US qt heatproof bowl (a deep one makes for the most impressive looking results) with a little butter or flavourless oil. Also grease a large sheet of foil and make a big pleat across the middle: this will cover the pudding during cooking and allow room for expansion. Put a trivet in a large pan, half fill with water and bring to the boil.

2. Reserve 15g (½oz) chocolate for decorating the finished dish. Break the rest into pieces and put them into a small bowl. Add the coffee dissolved in the boiling water and stand the bowl in a pan of

water over low heat until the chocolate has melted. Stir in the rum and turn the mixture into a very large, clean, cold mixing bowl.

3. Beat the butter with a wooden spoon or whisk until pale and creamy. Add the sugar and beat again until the mixture is pale and fluffy, almost doubled in bulk. Then beat in the egg yolks, one at a time. Gradually beat the mixture into the cooling chocolate and blend well.

4. Whisk the egg whites until stiff and fold them gently but thoroughly into the bowl of chocolate and egg yolks. Turn the mixture into the prepared pudding bowl, cover with the pleated, greased foil and tie securely with string under the rim of the bowl. Trim away excess foil. Carefully lower the pudding bowl onto the trivet in the pan of boiling water. Cover the pan with a lid and steam for about 45 minutes until risen and set.

5. Lift the basin out of the pan and set aside in a draught-free place until the pudding is quite cold – it will sink a little as it cools.

6. Shortly before serving, remove the foil, run a palette knife around the sides of the pudding to loosen, then unmould the pudding onto a plate. Whip the creams together and use to mask the cold chocolate soufflé completely. Grate the reserved chocolate (or make caraque curls, *page 201, step 5*) and sprinkle on top of the pudding. *Serves 8-10*

190

Iced lemon soufflé

I love the fresh, clean taste of lemons. Their tangy flavour comes through clearly in this iced soufflé, which makes a fine dish to serve at the end of a rich meal. Although the texture of the soufflé is creamy, it contains no cream: this makes this pudding an acceptable treat for slimmers.

Metric/Imperial	American
2 large lemons	2 large lemons
3 large (no. 2) eggs, separated	3 large eggs, separated
125g(¼lb) caster sugar	½ cup superfine sugar
75ml(3fl oz) cold water	6 tablespoons cold water
10ml(2 teaspoons) gelatine powder	2 teaspoons powdered gelatin
25g(1 oz) flaked almonds	2 tablespoons flaked almonds

1. This deliciously refreshing soufflé looks most dramatic if served so that it appears to have risen above the dish, but it tastes every bit as good, and is less trouble for the cook, if served in a larger dish so that the surface of the soufflé is level with the rim of the dish. To achieve the risen effect, you will need a very small soufflé dish – just over 575ml (1pt) about 2½ cups capacity. Make a collar for the dish using a double thickness of greaseproof or waxed paper, deep enough to overlap the dish and to stand a good 4cm (1½in) above it. Clip it with a paper clip and secure the paper around the rim with a rubber band. Brush the inside of the collar with flavourless oil. For an unrisen effect, use a 850ml (1½pt) or 4 cup soufflé dish or bowl: it does not need to be oiled.

2. Measure the water into a small pan. Sprinkle on the gelatine powder and soak for 5 minutes. Then dissolve over low heat and set aside to cool. While the gelatine is soaking, fill the base of a doubleboiler half full of water, set it over low heat and bring to a bare simmer. Away from the heat, finely grate the lemon zest (rind) into the top of the doubleboiler, and add the lemon juice and sugar. Add the egg yolks to the lemon and sugar. Whisk the mixture for 1 minute, then place it over the pan of barely simmering water. Cook very gently, beating the mixture with a rotary whisk (beater) all the while, until the sugar is dissolved, the egg yolks warmed and thickened with the fruit juice about 5-6 minutes. Remove the top of the boiler from the heat, set it over a bowl of cold water and continue whisking until the mixture is very pale, billowy and thick – another 5-6 minutes. Then blend in the cooling gelatine, whisking the ingredients together

thoroughly. Turn the mixture into a bowl and chill until approaching setting point. It will reach this stage very quickly: check progress, stirring gently every few minutes.

4. When the mixture is nearly set, whisk the egg whites until they stand in peaks. Fold them delicately but thoroughly into the lemon and yolk mixture, using a metal spoon and figure-of-eight movements. Turn the mixture into the soufflé dish, cover and refrigerate until set firm. Meanwhile toast the almonds, if using, under a grill (broiler) or in a low oven, and allow them to become cold.

5. To serve, gently remove the paper clip and rubber band from the paper collar. Insert a palette knife or spatula between the soufflé and the paper. Slowly move the knife around the soufflé, pressing lightly against it and easing away the paper as you go. Scatter the cold toasted almonds over the surface of the soufflé, or top the soufflé with whipped cream if you prefer. Serve alone or with a jug of thin pouring cream

Serves 4-6

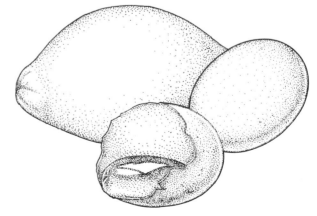

Strawberry angelcake

I have chosen this famous American cake because it is far and away the best recipe I know for using up a large number of egg whites – and in summer months, when I make lots of custard-based ice-creams, mayonnaise and Hollandaise type sauces, my refrigerator often seems filled with leftover egg whites! Some versions of angel-food cake seem to me over-sweet: the inclusion of lemon juice, orange zest (rind) and cinnamon give this one just the right balance I think. It is not a difficult recipe but quick, light handling is essential for perfect results so prepare the ingredients in the order given.

Metric/Imperial	American
75g(3oz) plain flour	¾ cup all-purpose flour
25g(1 oz) cornflour	1 tablespoon cornstarch
a good pinch of salt	generous pinch of salt
2.5ml(½ teaspoon) ground cinnamon	½ teaspoon ground cinnamon
225g(½lb) caster sugar	1 cup superfine sugar
10 medium-sized egg whites	10 medium-sized egg whites
15ml(1 tablespoon) lemon juice	1 tablespoon lemon juice
15ml(1 tablespoon) hot water	1 tablespoon hot water
5 ml (1 teaspoon) cream of tartar	1 teaspoon cream of tartar
2 oranges	2 oranges
225-900g(½-2lb) strawberries	½-2pt strawberries
icing sugar	confectioners' sugar
extra lemon juice	extra lemon juice

1. Bring the eggs to room temperature at least 1 hour before starting to make the cake. Thoroughly wash and dry an angel cake pan or a mould about 21.5cm (8½in) in diameter and 10cm (4in) deep with a central funnel and removable base. Heat the oven to 180°C (350°F) gas mark 4. Sift the flour and cornflour (cornstarch) into a bowl. Sift the salt, cinnamon and about one-third of the sugar into the same bowl. Then sift the combined ingredients twice more, lifting the sifter well above the bowl to aerate the mixture thoroughly. Grate the orange zest (rind) finely onto a saucer.

2. Divide the egg whites, lemon juice and water between two very large mixing bowls. It is best to use a balloon whisk or manual rotary whisk, although it is somewhat tiring on the wrists, because either will produce greater volume than will an electric beater. Whisk the contents of one bowl until foamy, add half the cream of tartar and whisk again until the egg whites stand in stiff peaks. Whisk the contents of the second bowl in the same

way, incorporating the remaining cream of tartar, then tip the mixture into the first bowl. Sift and whisk in the remaining sugar, 15ml (1 tablespoon) at a time. Add the orange zest (rind) with the last spoonful of sugar. Sift and gently fold the flour mixture into the egg whites. Add only a few spoonfuls at a time and use light, figure-of-eight movements when folding to ensure thorough but delicate blending.

4. Turn the mixture into the ungreased cake tin (pan). Draw a knife through the mixture to release any large air pockets and level the surface. Bake just below the centre of the oven for 45 minutes or until the surface of the cake feels firm and springs back when lightly pressed. Invert the cake tin (pan) on to a cooling rack but do not attempt to lift the tin away from the cake until it is cold, about 1½ hours.

5. Just before serving, dust the top of the cake with a whisper of icing (confectioners') sugar and fill the centre with whole hulled strawberries – about 225g (½lb) will be needed. If you wish to serve an accompanying sauce, sieve or crush the extra berries, heighten flavour with sugar and fresh orange and lemon juice to taste, and pour into a sauceboat.

Serves 8-10

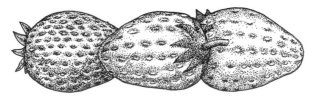

Rhubarb pie with custard

I look forward each year to the arrival of those first, brilliant pink sticks of early forced rhubarb – a welcome splash of colour and delicious fresh flavour to enliven sunless late winter months. A buttery, crisp shortcrust pastry makes an excellent foil for tender, slightly tart fruit, and a true custard sauce (or crème anglaise as the French call it) makes the perfect accompaniment. What better way to end a family Sunday lunch?

Metric/Imperial
For the filling:
700-800g(1½-1¾lb) early rhubarb
the finely grated zest of 1 orange
15ml(1 tablespoon) sifted cornflour
125g(¼lb) caster sugar
5ml(1 teaspoon) ground cinnamon
OR 30ml(2 tablespoons) chopped stem ginger

For the shortcrust pastry:
175g(6oz) plain flour
85g(3oz) unsalted butter
about 30ml(2 tablespoons) water

For the custard sauce:
425ml(¾pt) single cream
a vanilla pod
4 medium-sized (no. 3) egg yolks
20ml(1½ tablespoons) vanilla sugar (page 201, st 3)
5ml(1 teaspoon) cornflour

American
For the filling:
1½-1¾lb young rhubarb
the finely grated rind of 1 orange
1 tablespoon sifted cornstarch
½ cup superfine sugar
1 teaspoon ground cinnamon
OR 2 tablespoons chopped candied ginger

For the shortcrust pastry:
1½ cups all purpose flour
6 tablespoons unsalted butter
2 tablespoons water

For the custard sauce:
1½ cups light cream
1 vanilla bean
4 egg yolks
1½ tablespoons vanilla sugar (page 201, step 3)
1 teaspoon cornstarch

1. First make the custard. Put the cream into a small pan with the vanilla pod (bean), and bring slowly to scalding point (that is when bubbles appear on the surface of the cream). Meanwhile, bring a little water to a bare simmer in the base of a doubleboiler. Away from the heat, beat the egg yolks in the top part of the doubleboiler together with the cornflour (cornstarch) and sugar. Pour on the hot cream in a thin stream, whisking all the time. Remove the vanilla pod (bean). Place the top part over the pan of barely-simmering water and cook, stirring, until thickened to a smooth cream. Turn the custard into a pretty sauce bowl (boat), cover and chill until ready to serve.

2. About 1½ hours before you intend to serve the pie, make the shortcrust pastry (as described on *page 206, step 1*), wrap and chill it for 20 minutes. Meanwhile heat the oven to 200°C (400°F) gas mark 6 and prepare the pie filling. Wipe the fruit, trim away papery 'wings' from the base and remove the leaves; cut into oblique slices. Pack the fruit into a pie dish (pan), mounding it high in the middle and sprinkling orange zest (rind), cornflour (corn-

starch), sugar and cinnamon (or ginger) between layers.

3. Roll out the pastry to rather larger than the pie dish. Cut away the outer strip of pastry, lay it on the dampened rim of the dish and brush it with water. Lay the pastry lid on top, trim, flute into scallops with a vertical knife and raise the rim by cutting into it horizontally. Make a small slit in the pastry top to allow steam to escape during cooking, and brush all over with milk.

4. Place the dish on a baking sheet and bake for 10 minutes. Reduce heat to 190°C (375°F) gas mark 5 and bake for a half hour more. Sprinkle the pie with a little sugar and allow it to cool slightly before serving.

Serves 6

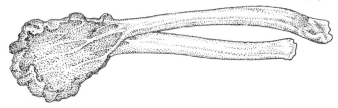

Raspberry charlotte

Some iced charlottes are made with gelatine, others with chantilly cream, but those made with almond butter cream are the most delicious of all – and this version, which does not include the usual liqueurs, is a particular favourite of mine, very fragrant and subtle in flavour.

Metric/Imperial	American
450g(1lb) firm, top quality fresh raspberries	*1pt fresh raspberries*
175g(6oz) unsalted butter, at room temperature	*¾ cup unsalted butter, at room temperature*
120g(¼lb) caster sugar, preferably vanilla sugar	*½ cup superfine sugar, preferably vanilla sugar*
120g(¼lb) almond kernels	*½ cup whole almonds*
2 large oranges	*2 large oranges*
half a large lemon	*half a large lemon*
275ml(½pt) double cream	*1¼ cups heavy cream*
about 22 crisp sponge finger biscuits	*2 doz lady fingers*

1. Select a charlotte mould of 1.1L (2pt) or 5 cups capacity. Cut a circle of greaseproof or waxed paper to fit inside the base and a second larger circle of paper to fit the top of the mould. If you do not own a charlotte mould, use a soufflé dish instead or any other straight sided mould of the same capacity, bearing in mind that a mould 9-10cm (3½-4in) deep will show off this pudding to best advantage.

2. Put the almonds into a small bowl. Pour on enough boiling water to cover and leave for 1 minute to loosen the skins. Drain, refresh under cold running water and drain again. Slip off and discard brown skins, put the nuts into an electric blender or grinder and reduce to a finely ground consistency. Using fresh nuts and grinding them yourself just before use means that the almonds retain all their oils and flavour, whereas packaged ready-ground nuts are often rather dusty and dull in flavour. Finely grate the zest (rind) of both oranges onto a saucer and set aside. Squeeze the juice from both oranges and the half lemon into a small measuring jug (cup).

3. Put the butter into a mixing bowl and beat it with a wooden spoon until pale and creamy. Add the sugar (for vanilla sugar see *page 201, step 3*) and beat again until the mixture is light and fluffy. Add the ground almonds and grated orange zest (rind) to the mixing bowl together with 75ml (3fl oz) or 6 tablespoons of the mixed orange and lemon juice. Stir and beat the ingredients until thoroughly blended together. Whip the cream, then fold the mixture into it.

4. Spoon one-third of the orange and almond butter cream into the prepared mould, spreading it evenly over the base. Reserving about one-quarter of the raspberries to decorate the pudding, lay half the remainder in the mould on top of the cream. Press

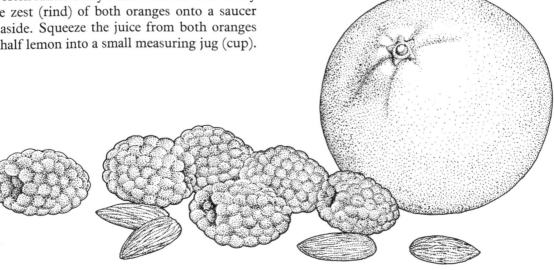

the fruit very lightly so it just begins to sink into the cream. Repeat the butter cream and raspberry layers again, then finish with the remaining butter cream. Lay the large circle of greaseproof or waxed paper on top, cover with a plate, add some weights and refrigerate for at least 8 hours. This is important as the orange and almond butter cream must have time to solidify and set firmly with the fruit embedded in it.

5. Unmould and decorate the pudding just before serving, because the butter cream filling will soften if left at warm room temperature for too long. Peel away paper, run a wet palette knife or spatula round the inside of the dish, then turn the pudding out onto a plate. Dip the unsugared backs of the sponge (lady) fingers, one at a time, into the reserved fruit juice to moisten. Shake off excess then stick onto the sides of the pudding. This method of adding the fingers after unmoulding gives results that look and taste best: if used to line the mould before adding the raspberry filling, they may break up when the pudding is unmoulded. Decorate the top of the pudding with the reserved berries. *Serves 8-10*

Turinois

W hen I am so busy coping with the turkey, wrapping presents and decorating the Christmas tree that there seems little time for cooking, I turn to this recipe for chestnut pudding with a sigh of relief. It is luxurious and very Christmassy – yet, if made with canned chestnut purée, it takes no more than ten minutes to make.

Metric/Imperial
900g(2lb) fresh Spanish chesnuts in their shells
OR 440g(15½oz) canned non-sweet chestnut purée
175g(6oz) unsalted butter, at room temperature
125g(¼lb) caster sugar
225g(½lb) best plain dark dessert chocolate
30ml(2 tablespoons) brandy
a few pieces of marrons glacés for decorating
OR a few extra squares of chocolate

American
2lb chestnuts in their shells
OR about 2 cups puréed canned chestnuts
¾ cup unsalted butter, at room temperature
¼lb superfine sugar
½lb unsweetened chocolate
2 tablespoons brandy
few pieces of marrons glacés for decorating
OR extra chocolate for decorating

1. Make the pudding a day ahead. The weight of fresh chestnuts given is generous enough to allow for discarding any bad ones which may be included. Score and skin all the sound ones as described on *page 154, step 1*. Once peeled put them into a saucepan, add water to cover and bring slowly to boiling point. Cover the pan with a lid and simmer gently for about 30 minutes or until the chestnuts feel quite tender when pierced with the tip of a knife blade.

2. Drain the chestnuts well and reduce to a purée by passing them through the finest blade of a vegetable mill or by blending. (A spoonful or so of the cooking liquid may be needed if using a blender.) Measure out 440g (15½oz) or 2 cups of the purée to use for this pudding. (Reserve any extra leftover purée to use in a stuffing for meat.) Break the chocolate into small pieces. Melt in a bowl placed over hot water, stirring occasionally.

3. Put the butter into a mixing bowl and beat with a wooden spoon or electric whisk until pale and creamy. Use sugar that has been stored in a jar with a vanilla pod (bean) if possible. Add the sugar and beat again until the mixture is fluffy and light. Add the cold puréed chestnuts to the mixing bowl (if using canned purée, use straight from the can – but do check that it is unsweetened). Beat the purée into the mixture. When thoroughly blended and quite smooth, add the cooling melted chocolate, the brandy and 15ml (1 tablespoon) water. Beat again.

4. Brush the base and sides of a small loaf tin (3 cup bread pan) with flavourless oil. Stand it upside down on a paper towel for a minute or so to drain off excess oil, then spoon the Turinois mixture into it, packing it well into the corners and levelling the top with a palette knife or spatula. Cover with a bit of grease-proof or waxed paper, lightly oiled, then with a foil 'lid' and refrigerate for 8 hours or more until thoroughly chilled and set firm.

5. To make caraque chocolate to decorate the pudding, melt a few squares of chocolate in a bowl over hot water. Pour the hot chocolate onto a marble slab or other cold flat surface, spreading it out with a palette knife or spatula. Leave the chocolate to become quite cold and to set very firmly. Then shave off thin layers of chocolate with the blade of a knife: the chocolate will automatically curl as it is shaved.

6. To unmould the Turinois, remove the foil and oiled paper. Run a wet palette knife between the mould and the dessert to loosen it slightly, then invert it onto a chilled serving dish. Decorate with caraque chocolate or slices of marrons glacés. Accompany this rich but rather heavily-textured dish with plenty of chilled pouring (coffee) cream – flavoured with a little brandy if you like. *Serves 8*

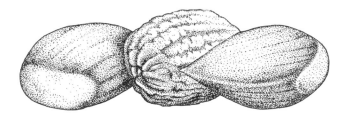

Strawberry shortcake

Scottish cookery is particularly rich in bread, cake and biscuit recipes, so it is hardly surprising that tea is an important meal in Scotland. A traditional, crisp Scottish short-bread, filled with soft fruit and cream, makes a rich and delicious crisp version of short-cake for a summer tea-party. Some cooks include semolina or rice flour when making Scottish shortbread; I prefer a combination of plain flour and cornflour (cornstarch).

Metric/Imperial	American
230g(½lb) unsalted butter, at room temperature	1 cup unsalted butter at room temperature
115g(¼lb) vanilla caster sugar (page 201, step 3)	½ cup superfine vanilla sugar (page 201, step 3)
230g(½lb) plain flour	2 cups all-purpose flour
115g(¼lb) cornflour	⅞ cup cornstarch
700g(1½lb) fresh strawberries	1½pt fresh strawberries
425ml(¾pt) double cream	2 cups heavy cream
15ml(1 tablespoon) orange juice	1 tablespoon orange juice
the finely grated zest of an orange	the finely grated zest of 1 orange

1. Preheat the oven to 160°C (325°F) gas mark 3, and select two fluted flan tins or shallow quiche pans 23cm (9in) in diameter, preferably with removable bases. Assemble ingredients, including vanilla sugar if possible.

2. Heat the butter and sugar together with a wooden spoon or whisk until light and creamy. In a separate bowl, sift the flour and cornflour (cornstarch) together, lifting the sifter well above the

bowl to aerate the mixture very thoroughly. Gradually incorporate the flour mixture into the sugar and butter, using a wooden spoon at first, then your fingers. This should be done as quickly and lightly as possible; the mixture must not be allowed to become warm or oily. If you are inclined to have hot hands, it is a wise precaution to rinse them under cold running water and to dry them before mixing the dough. Then knead the dough lightly and divide into two. Line the base of each flan tin

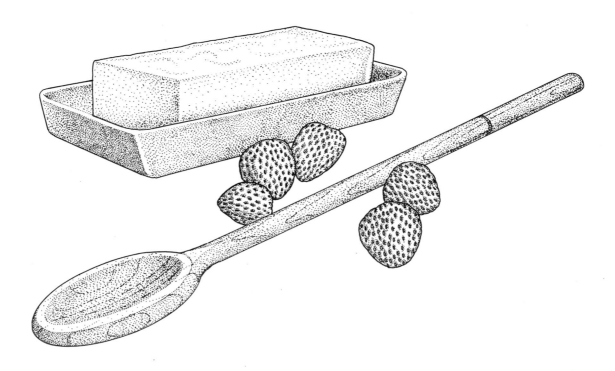

(pan) with one portion. There is no need to roll out the dough. Pressing the dough into place with the back of a metal spoon is just as effective and means that the dough is subjected to less handling. Press it well into the corners, level it smoothly, then prick all over with a fork to prevent rising during baking. Score one circle of dough into ten wedges.

3. Bake the shortbread for 50-60 minutes, until pale gold in colour. Cut the scored circle into wedges and return to the oven for 5 minutes. Turn both circles of shortbread onto a cooling rack and leave until cold. If the shortbread is not for immediate use, store it in an airtight container as soon as cold: it will remain crisp for a few days.

4. If you have a choice, buy wild or Alpine strawberries: their looks, scent and flavour are so good. Not more than 1 hour before serving, hull the strawberries and set a few aside for decorating the shortcake. Slice the rest thickly (if wild or Alpine strawberries are used leave them whole). Stir the orange juice into the cream and whip until stiff, then fold the strawberries and finely grated orange zest (rind) into the cream. Add a spoonful of sifted icing (confectioners') sugar if you wish. Lay the circle of shortbread on a serving plate and spread the strawberry cream on top, piling it up slightly in the middle. Cover with the wedges of shortbread, decorate with the reserved berries, and serve.

Serves 8-10

Apple charlotte

A thick purée of well-flavoured apples encased in golden fried bread, this hot charlotte is very different from a creamy iced charlotte. It is cheap, an excellent way to use cooking apples and, when well made, deserves to be rated as one of the best of traditional British puddings.

Metric/Imperial	American
1.5kg(generous 2¼lb) Bramley apples	2¼-2½ lb tart cooking apples
1 quince (if available)	1 quince (if available)
1 lemon	1 lemon
150g(5oz) unsalted butter	⅓ cup plus 1 tablespoon unsalted butter
125g(¼lb) caster sugar	½ cup superfine sugar
1.5ml(¼ teaspoon) ground cloves or allspice	¼ teaspoon ground cloves or allspice
30ml(2 tablespoons) ground almonds	2 tablespoons ground almonds
6-8 large slices crustless white bread	6-8 large slices white bread, without crusts

1. One of the most important requirements for this traditional English pudding is that the fruit purée be very thick, otherwise there is a danger that the charlotte may collapse when unmoulded for serving. Choose Bramley apples for preference. If unavailable, get the best firm-fleshed and tart flavoured apples you can buy.

2. Heat the oven to 160-180°C. (325-350°F) gas mark 3-4. Peel, core and thinly slice the apples and put them into a flameproof casserole or dutch oven. If a quince is used – I find even a small one adds delicious fragrance to the dish – peel, core and grate it into the casserole. Grate the lemon zest (rind) finely and squeeze the juice. Add both juice and zest (rind) to the casserole. Cover and bake 30 minutes, until tender but not disintegrating. Turn into a sieve (strainer) and drain off the juices. Return the fruit to the casserole and beat it with a balloon whisk to make a fluffy purée. Add 25g (1oz) or 2 tablespoons butter, the sugar and spices. Cook over medium-low heat for a good 15 minutes to drive off as much moisture as possible. Stir the purée frequently during this time to prevent sticking. Remove from the heat and, if you are in any doubt about the purée being stiff enough, stir in the almonds; they will act like blotting paper absorbing surplus moisture – I always play safe and use almonds. Set the purée aside, uncovered, until quite cold.

3. About 1¼ hours before serving, preheat the oven to 220°C (425°F) gas mark 7. Select a heat-proof bowl of 850ml (1½pt) or 4 cups capacity and 10cm (4in) deep. Cut a circle of bread to fit the bottom of the bowl exactly, and a second larger one to fit the top. Fry the small circle of bread in a little of the remaining butter until crisp and pale gold in colour. Cut it into four triangles (this makes it easier to serve the pudding) and place them in the bottom of the bowl. Melt the remaining butter in the frying-pan, and cut the rest of the bread into strips about 3-4cm (1¼-1½in) wide. Dip the strips, one at a time, into the butter to coat on both sides, and use them to line the sides of the bowl. Arrange them so that one strip just overlaps the next; they will mould to the curve of the bowl quite easily. Spoon in the cold apple purée, packing it quite firmly and doming the top slightly. Fold the protruding tips of the strips of bread over the purée. Cover with the remaining large circle of bread, again dipped in melted butter. Dribble any leftover melted butter over the top of the pudding. Cover with greaseproof or waxed paper and a small plate to weight it down. Set aside for 10 minutes: this will ensure the fruit purée settles and is firmly packed.

5. Remove weights, plate and greaseproof or waxed paper. Stand the bowl on a baking sheet, place in the middle of the oven and cook for 30 minutes until the fruit purée is very hot and the bread has 'fried' to a crisp golden finish. Let the pudding cool for 10 minutes before attempting to unmould it; it will become firm and shrink slightly from the sides of the bowl as it cools. Then invert onto a warmed plate and lift the bowl away from the pudding cautiously. If it does not slide away easily or the charlotte does not seem quite firm enough, leave the pudding for another 5 minutes before lifting away the bowl. Serve with plenty of custard sauce (*page 197, step 1*) or fresh cream. *Serves 4*

Lemon meringue pie

I love this favourite American pie for its contrast of flavours and textures – tangy lemon filling, buttery shortcrust pastry and on top marshmallowy soft meringue which is baked to a crisp finish.

Metric/Imperial	American
For the shortcrust pastry:	**For the shortcrust pastry:**
125g(¼lb) plain flour	*1 cup all-purpose flour*
60g(2oz) butter, at room temperature	*¼ cup butter, at room temperature*
For the filling:	**For the filling:**
3 large lemons	*3 large lemons*
115g(¼lb) caster sugar	*½ cup superfine sugar*
25g(1 oz) butter	*2 tablespoons butter*
33g(1¼oz) cornflour	*2 tablespoons plus 1 teaspoon cornstarch*
2 large egg yolks	*2 large egg yolks*
For the meringue:	**For the meringue:**
2 large egg whites	*2 large egg whites*
115g(¼lb) caster sugar	*½ cup superfine sugar*

1. Start by making the shortcrust pastry. Sift the flour into a mixing bowl. Add the butter and cut it up into pea-sized pieces using a metal spatula or palette knife. Then rub the fat into the flour using your fingertips. To make really light pastry you should just lift some of the mixture in your fingers, then, holding your hands well above the bowl, gently run your thumbs along your finger tips allowing the mixture to sift through them and fall back into the bowl. You will quickly find you develop a nice easy rhythm doing this. It may make your wrists ache a bit – but aching wrists are said to be the sign of a good pastry cook! When the mixture is the consistency of fine breadcrumbs, add a little water to the mixing bowl – on average you need 20ml (4 teaspoons) cold water for every 125g (4oz) or 1 cup of flour when making shortcrust pastry. Stir the water in with the palette knife, then use your hands to make the dough into a smooth ball which comes cleanly away from the sides of the bowl. Knead lightly, then put the pastry into a plastic bag and let it 'rest' for 15-20 minutes in the refrigerator.

2. While the pastry 'rests' heat the oven to 200°C (400°F) gas mark 6 and prepare the filling. Measure 275ml (½pt) cold water into a jug. Finely grate the zest (rind) of the lemons into a small saucepan. Add the sugar, sifted cornflour (cornstarch) and enough of the cold water to make a smooth paste, whisking the ingredients together with a balloon or sauce whisk. Gradually whisk in the remaining water then place the pan over medium heat. Cook, stirring continuously, until the mixture thickens and boils, then allow it to continue cooking for 1 minute. Remove the pan from the heat and beat in the butter. Next stir in 75ml (5 tablespoons) freshly-squeezed lemon juice, which will help to cool the mixture slightly, then the egg yolks, one at a time. Set aside until cold.

3. Choose a pie plate with sloping sides and a good rim, measuring about 15cm (6in) across the base and 20cm (8in) across the top. Dampen the rim with a little cold water. Roll out the pastry until about 7.5cm (3in) larger than the top of the pie plate. Cut off the outer edge of the pastry; lay it on the rim of the dish, and brush it with cold water. Lift the remaining circle of pastry onto your rolling pin and lower it into the dish. Press the pastry down firmly against the base and then up the sides of the dish. Press the two pastry rims together to seal them well, then trim away excess pastry with a knife. Decorate the pastry edge by pressing the handle of a teaspoon against the pastry rim all round the dish. Prick the pastry base all over with a fork. This is to make sure no air is trapped under the pastry and to prevent rising or blistering during baking. The tiny holes will close up during baking so do not worry about the filling leaking out. Cover with a circle of greaseproof or waxed paper and weight it down with dried beans. Bake for 15 minutes, then remove the paper and beans and bake for 10 minutes more. This crisping of the pastry beforehand ensures that the filling will not make it soggy.

4. Remove the pastry case from the oven: reduce the temperature to 150°C (300°F) gas mark 2. Put the egg whites into a large, dry, grease-free bowl and whisk them until stiff. A rotary manual whisk (beater) will give far greater volume than an electric whisk (beater) and therefore lighter and better meringue mixture. Make sure the whisk reaches all corners of the bowl and continue whisking until the egg whites stand in stiff peaks. Sift in half the sugar and whisk again. When the sugar is thoroughly blended into the egg whites and the mixture is in stiff peaks, sift in the rest of the sugar and fold it into the mixture with a metal spoon, using light figure-of-eight movements.

5. Spoon the cooled lemon filling evenly over the base of the pastry shell, then cover it with the meringue mixture. Use a palette knife or spatula to spread the meringue mixture, taking it to the very edge of the pastry rim so that it seals the entire top. Bake in the centre of the oven for 45-50 minutes until the top of the meringue is a lovely crisp honey-beige on top and marshmallowy soft underneath. Cool for at least 20 minutes before serving. Serve warm or cold, with cream if liked. *Serves 6*

Coeurs à la crème

Home-made soft cheeses, and commercial varieties such as Demi-Sel and Petite Suisse, are often served for dessert in France. Dusted with a little caster (powdered) sugar to counteract the acidity of the cheese, or sprinkled with soft fresh berries, or veiled with thin cream, they make a simple and delightful dish. Coeurs à la creme is a delectable variation on the theme: a mixture of thick cream and egg white, softer and lighter than cheese. Served with raspberries or strawberries, and perhaps a little thin cream, it makes a classically simple and beautiful dish for summer eating.

Metric/Imperial
425ml(¾pt) double cream
3 large egg whites
450g(1lb) strawberries or raspberries
150ml(¼pt) single cream (optional)

American
2 cups heavy cream
3 egg whites
1pt fresh strawberries or raspberries
⅝ cup light cream (optional)

1. This recipe gets its name from the pretty little heart-shaped moulds in which it is traditionally made. These moulds have perforated bases to allow the mixture to drain, and should be lined with cheesecloth to make unmoulding easy. If you do not possess such moulds, use a strainer, line it with cheesecloth and balance it over a bowl to drain.

2. Whip the cream. Whisk the egg whites until they stand in peaks, then fold them lightly but thoroughly into the cream. Spoon the mixture into the mould(s) and set aside to drain in a cool place for 4-8 hours. Turn out, peel away the cloth and decorate with a few berries. Serve the rest of the berries separately (and the cream in a jug if serving). *Serves 6*

Recipe Index